Remembering the Sixties: A Look at Africa

Godfrey Mwakikagile

Remembering The Sixties: A Look at Africa

First Edition

ISBN 978-9987-16-036-5

New Africa Press
Dar es Salaam, Tanzania

Morocco
Tunisia
Western Sahara
Algeria
Libya
Egypt
Mauritania
Mali
Niger
Chad
Sudan
Eritrea
Djibouti
S
Guinea
B.Faso
Nigeria
L IC Gh B
T
Cent Afr Rep
Ethiopia
Somalia
Sierra Leone
Cameroon
Ug
Kenya
Guinea Bissau
Equatorial Guinea
Gabon
Dem Rep of Congo
Rwanda
Burundi
Gambia
Congo
Tanzania
Angola
Mozambique
Zambia
Madagascar
Zimb
Namibia
Bots
Malawi
Swaziland
South Africa
Lesotho

Introduction

THIS WORK focuses on one of the most critical periods in the history of post-colonial Africa: the euphoric and turbulent sixties when most countries on the continent won independence.

It was a period of high expectations. But it was also a decade of military coups and assassinations, a phenomenon that persisted for decades although there were fewer coups in the 1990s and beyond contrasted with the previous years, especially the sixties and seventies when the largest number of military coups and assassinations of national leaders took place.

One of the most tragic events during the sixties was the assassination of Patrice Lumumba and the ensuing chaos and civil wars which earned the former Belgian Congo the unenviable distinction as the bleeding heart of Africa.

The Congo crisis became a defining moment not only for Congo but for Africa as whole as the newly independent states confronted the harsh realities of nationhood including nation building and consolidating their independence.

Another tragic event was the Nigerian civil war triggered by the secession of Eastern Nigeria which declared independence as the Republic of Biafra, a horrendous tragedy that threatened to destroy the Nigerian federation. It cost up to 2 million lives in the secessionist region before the secessionists capitulated to federal might in January 1970, until then the bloodiest conflict in the history of post-colonial Africa.

Other major events included the Zanzibar revolution in January 1964, and in February 1966, the ouster of Kwame Nkrumah who led Ghana to become the first country in sub-Saharan Africa to win independence.

I have addressed all those subjects and many others in an attempt to provide a comprehensive picture of Africa in the sixties, a defining moment and probably the most critical period in the post-colonial era.

Its complementary volume, *Africa in The Sixties*, addresses similar subjects.

1966

AFRICA witnessed some of the most tragic events in 1966 in her short post-colonial history that had also been marred by other tragedies.

There were two major events. And both took place in the first two months of 1966.

The first one was a military coup in Nigeria on January 15th. It was the bloodiest coup in the continent's history since independence. And it had far-reaching repercussions in Nigeria in the following years. It played a major role in igniting the Nigerian civil war, also the bloodiest in the history of post-colonial Africa during that period.

The coup had a profound impact on the course of events in Nigeria in the following decades when the country came to be dominated by a succession of military rulers.

It also helped to inspire military coups in other parts of Africa. Soldiers in other parts of the continent realised that it was easy to overthrow governments by simply arresting or killing national leaders and by seizing the radio station to announce the government has been overthrown. In those days there was only one radio station in most of the countries across the continent.

The military coup in Nigeria was led by young Igbo army officers. The main leader of the entire operation, at least from the public role he played during and immediately after the coup, was Major Chukwuma Kaduna Nzeogwu.

He was based in Kaduna, Northern Nigeria. It was reported that he personally killed the Northern Premier, Sir Ahmadu Bello, also known as the Sardauna of Sokoto, at the premier's residence. As he stated on Radio Kaduna, 15 January 1966 around noon when he announced the military takeover:

"In the name of the Supreme Council of the Revolution of the Nigerian Armed Forces, I declare martial law over the Northern Provinces of Nigeria.

The Constitution is suspended and the regional government and elected assemblies are hereby dissolved. All political, cultural, tribal and trade union activities, together with all demonstrations and unauthorized gatherings, excluding religious worship, are banned until further notice.

The aim of the Revolutionary Council is to establish a strong united and prosperous nation, free from corruption and internal strife. Our method of achieving this is strictly military but we have no doubt that every Nigerian will give us maximum cooperation by assisting the regime and not disturbing the peace during the slight changes that are taking place.

I am to assure all foreigners living and working in this part of Nigeria that their rights will continue to be respected. All treaty obligations previously entered into with any foreign nation will be respected and we hope that such nations will respect our country's territorial integrity and will avoid taking sides with enemies of the revolution and enemies of the people.

My dear countrymen, you will hear, and probably see a lot being done by certain bodies charged by the Supreme Council with the duties of national integration, supreme justice, general security and property recovery.

As an interim measure all permanent secretaries, corporation chairmen and senior heads of departments are allowed to make decisions until the new organs are functioning, so long as such decisions are not contrary to the aims and wishes of the Supreme Council.

No Minister or Parliamentary Secretary possesses administrative or other forms of control over any Ministry, even if they are not considered too dangerous to be arrested.

This is not a time for long speech-making and so let me acquaint you with ten proclamations in the Extraordinary Orders of the Day which the Supreme Council has promulgated. These will be modified as the situation improves.

You are hereby warned that looting, arson, homosexuality, rape, embezzlement, bribery or corruption, obstruction of the revolution, sabotage, subversion, false alarms and assistance to foreign invaders, are all offences punishable by death sentence.

Demonstrations and unauthorized assembly, non-cooperation with revolutionary troops are punishable in grave manner up to death.

Refusal or neglect to perform normal duties or any task that may of necessity be ordered by local military commanders in support of the change will be punishable by a sentence imposed by the local military commander.

Spying, harmful or injurious publications, and broadcasts of troop movements or actions, will be punished by any suitable sentence deemed fit by the local military commander.

Shouting of slogans, loitering and rowdy behavior will

be rectified by any sentence of incarceration, or any more severe punishment deemed fit by the local military commander.

Doubtful loyalty will be penalized by imprisonment or any more severe sentence.

Illegal possession or carrying of firearms, smuggling or trying to escape with documents, valuables, including money or other assets vital to the running of any establishment will be punished by death sentence.

Wavering or siting on the fence and failing to declare open loyalty with the revolution will be regarded as an act of hostility punishable by any sentence deemed suitable by the local military commander.

Tearing down an order of the day or proclamation or other authorized notices will be penalized by death.

This is the end of the Extraordinary Order of the Day which you will soon begin to see displayed in public.

My dear countrymen, no citizen should have anything to fear, so long as that citizen is law abiding and if that citizen has religiously obeyed the native laws of the country and those set down in every heart and conscience since 1st October, 1960.

Our enemies are the political profiteers, the swindlers, the men in high and low places that seek bribes and demand 10 percent; those that seek to keep the country divided permanently so that they can remain in office as ministers or VIPs at least, the tribalists, the nepotists, those that make the country look big for nothing before international circles, those that have corrupted our society and put the Nigerian political calendar back by their words and deeds.

Like good soldiers we are not promising anything miraculous or spectacular. But what we do promise every law abiding citizen is freedom from fear and all forms of oppression, freedom from general inefficiency and freedom to live and strive in every field of human endeavour, both nationally and internationally. We promise that you will no more be ashamed to say that you are a Nigerian.

I leave you with a message of good wishes and ask for your support at all times, so that our land, watered by the Niger and Benue, between the sandy wastes and Gulf of Guinea, washed in salt by the mighty Atlantic, shall not detract Nigeria from gaining sway in any great aspect of international endeavour.

My dear countrymen, this is the end of this speech. I wish you all goodluck and I hope you will cooperate to the fullest in this job which we have set for ourselves of establishing a prosperous nation and achieving solidarity.

Thank you very much and goodbye for now."

Major Chukwuma Nzeogwu was assisted by Major Timothy C. Onwuatuegwu in leading the coup in the north.

Nzeogwu was born in Kaduna to Igbo immigrants parents in 1937. That's how he got his middle name "Kaduna." He was chief instructor at the Nigerian Military Training College in Kaduna.

He later became a Lieutenant-Colonel in the Biafran army during the civil war. He was killed in combat on 29 July 1967. He was on a night reconnaisance mission against federal troops in the secessionist region.

Another leader of the January 1966 military coup was Major Emmanuel Ifeajuna who led operations in the southern part of Nigeria. He was based in the federal capital, Lagos, in the Western Region.

All three – Nzeogwu, Onwuatuegwu, and Ifeajuna – were Igbos.

There have been reports through the years that the man who was really behind the coup was Ifeajuna. But he fled Nigeria to escape arrest and sought refuge in Ghana after the head of the army, General Ironsi, assumed power on January 17th and started rounding up the coup makers. Nzeogwu then became the spokesman of the conspirators who executed the coup.

Although Nzeogwu led the coup in the north which led to the death of the Northern premier and others, he did not lead only soldiers from the south. There were northern officers and soldiers who participated in the coup and even accompanied him to the residence of the northern premier, Sir Ahmadu Bello. One of them was John Atom Kpera who later became the military governor of Benue State.

In the south also, Major Emmanuel Ifeajuna was accompanied by northern soldiers when he abducted Federal Prime Minister Abubakar Tafawa Balewa from his residence in Lagos. And among the southerners who participated in the coup in the south were Yoruba soldiers and army officers in Lagos and Ibadan.

The Yoruba officers who were in one way or another involved in the January 1966 military coup included Olufemi Olutoye, Adewale Ademoyega, and Oluwole Rotimi. They were all majors. Adewale Ademoyega played a more prominent role than the other Yoruba officers in the coup.

Ifeajuna became a lieutenant-colonel in the Biafran army during the civil war. He was accused of treason and was executed by firing squad on 27 September 1967 together with Brigadier Victor Banjo, Major Phillip Alale and Major Sam Agbamuche.

They were accused of abandoning the Mid-West Region that had been captured by the secessionist forces, thus allowing it to be taken over by federal forces. Yet, the Biafran forces had no chance of holding the region against the federal army.

In spite of what befell him, Ifeajuna will always be remembered as one of the main leaders of the January 1966 military coup, if not the driving force behind it operating from the federal capital itself and as the one who came up with the idea of overthrowing the government.

One of the main causes of the coup was fear of perpetual domination of the Nigerian federation by one ethnic group, the Hausa-Fulani of Northern Nigeria.

The structural imbalance of the federation was a major cause of resentment among many Nigerians, especially southerners, because it favoured northerners.

Not only did it mean that northerners could rule Nigeria indefinitely; it also meant that the allocation of the country's resources would be controlled by northerners who would and did get the largest share of the national pie.

Nothing was done to redress the imbalance or correct the structural flaws of the giant federation, prompting a few young army officers to launch a military coup against the federal government. As Odumegwu Ojukwu, the leader of the secessionist Eastern Region which declared independence in May 1967 as the Republic Biafra, stated in his address to the conference of the Organization of African Unity (OAU) in Addis Ababa, Ethiopia, on 5 August 1968, whose participants tried to end the Nigerian civil war:

"The five years immediately after (independence) were marred by successive crises; notably the Tiv riots of 1960 – 66, the Western Nigeria emergency of 1962, the National census controversy of 1962 – 63, the Federal election crisis of 1964 – 65 and the Western election of 1965 – 66.

By January 1966 it had become clear that, unless the situation was arrested, the successive crises experienced by the country before and since independence would certainly lead to unutterable disaster.

The existing Independence Constitution gave Northern Nigeria a built-in 50 per cent representation in the Federal parliament, an arrangement which assured the region a permanent control of the Federal government.

A great number of the politicians and others in public service were known to be corrupt, ostentatious and selfish. Bribery and nepotism were rife.

There was widespread inordinate ambition for power, an evil mirrored in the prevalence of thuggery, hooliganism and lawlessness....Public men had sown unhealthy rivalry, suspicion and mistrust among the various communities of the country.

Thus the unabashed rigging of the Western election of October 1965 came to be the last straw. The widespread violence which it precipitated took thousands of lives. Law and order broke down in the Western Region.

Since each of the other regions had an interest in the election, it was obvious that the country was on the brink of civil war. And yet the Northern Nigeria-controlled Federal government, the last hope of the people, would not discharge its responsibility.

Indeed many an objective observer interpreted its inaction in the face of the impending national collapse as virtual abdication. These were the circumstances in which some young army officers and men decided to act." – (Odumegwu Ojukwu, *Africa Contemporary Record 1968 – 1969*, p.655).

The Nigerian federation was structurally flawed from the beginning because when the British colonial rulers first formed the federation in 1946, they did not take into account the interests and diversity of the more than 250 ethnic groups which constitute Nigeria to create a political entity that would have been acceptable to all.

Although the coup was led by Igbo army officers, there were officers from other ethnic groups and from different parts of the country including the north who also participated in the coup. As Ojukwu stated:

"They originated from all parts of Nigeria – the North, West, Mid-West and East. It was a revolt against injustice and oppression.

From available information, their aims were threefold: to put an end to the suffering of Nigerian citizens in Tiv land and Western Nigeria, to dethrone the corrupt and dishonest politicians, and to restore public faith at home

14

and retrieve Nigeria's reputation abroad.

They attempted to overthrow the federal and regional governments. In desperation the federal government handed over power to the armed forces under the General Officer Commanding the Army, Major-General J.T.U. Aguiyi-Ironsi, who happened to originate from the then Eastern Nigeria (now the independent Republic of Biafra), and had in no way been connected with the revolution." – (Ibid.).

Among the prominent leaders of the coup from other ethnic groups were the Yoruba of Western Nigeria. One of the Yoruba army officers who played a critical role in the coup was Major Adewale Ademoyega who sent a signal from Lagos, the federal capital, to Major Nzeogwu in Kaduna, Northern Nigeria, indicating that everything was ready in the south and it was time to launch the coup. Major Nzeogwu and his colleagues in the north responded accordingly.

But although army offers from other ethnic groups were involved, Igbo army officers played played the biggest role in the 1966 coup because Igbos in general had legitimate grievances against Northern Nigerians going as far back as 1945 and 1953 when hundreds of their brethren were massacred in the north. Igbos were massacred in Kano in 1945 and in Jos in 1953.

And as late as 1964, just two years before the coup, members of the Northern Nigeria Regional Assembly openly called for the expulsion of all Igbos from Northern Nigeria simply because they were Igbos. As Ibrahim Musa Gashash, minister of land and survey in the regional government of Northern Nigeria, stated in the February-March session of the Northern Regional Assembly:

"I would like to assure members that having heard their demands about Ibos holding land in Northern Nigeria, my ministry will do all it can to see that the demands of members are met. How to do this, when to do it, all this should not be disclosed. In due course, you will see what will happen" (Applause). – (Ibrahim Musa Gashash, in *Africa Contemporary Record*, p. 665).

What happened was the massacre of at least 30,000 Igbos and other Eastern Nigerians, but mostly Igbos, in Northern Nigeria in 1966; a continuation of the genocidal rampage that took place in the 1940s and 1950s when hundreds of Igbos were killed in the north. As Ojukwu stated:

"In May 1953,...Northern Nigerian leaders organized and carried out violent demonstrations during which they slaughtered and wounded hundreds of our people in Kano, Northern Nigeria – acts of genocide which had been perpetrated at Jos in Northern Nigeria earlier in 1945." – (Ojukuwu, *Africa Contemporary Record*, ibid.).

There were also shouts of "Fire the southerners" from the northern representatives in the Northern Regional Assembly in February-March 1964 directed against the Igbos more than anybody else.

Expulsion of Igbos from Northern Nigeria now had official sanction which extended to massacres when Northern Nigerian leaders did nothing to stop the pogroms after the military coup in January 1966. Even the federal government itself, dominated by Northern Nigerians, did nothing.

Thus, even before the coup, there was a general consensus among many Nigerians of all ethnic groups in all parts of the country that there was something seriously wrong with the nation's leadership. And when the government was overthrown, there was a general sense of relief that rotten leaders had been ousted from power.

The people were elated and hoped that it was the dawn of a new era when things would get better. It is an observation that was shared by Federal Nigerian and Biafran leaders, one of the very few things the two sides agreed on. As Chief Anthony Enahoro who led the Nigerian delegation to the OAU conference in Addis Ababa, Ethiopia, on the Nigerian civil war stated in his speech in August 1968:

"Nigeria was plagued with a deep-seated imbalance in its political structure, stemming from the inequality of its component units which placed one of the regions in a dominant position in the federation....

By the end of 1965, five years after independence, (several) factors – agitation in certain areas for self-determination, suspension of the Western Region government and parliament in 1962 by federal action, disputes over the 1962 census, banning of public meetings and the press, the much disputed federal election of December 1964, then another hotly disputed election in the former Western Region (split into two in 1967, one of which became the Mid-West Region) in October 1965 that resulted in widespread rioting, arson and lawlessness – all those factors had combined to produce an explosive situation little short of a breakdown of law and order.

It became increasingly clear that sooner or later there would be a fundamental, and probably violent change. That change came on 15th January, 1966....

In assessing the motives as well as the consequences of the military coup of 15th January, 1966, attention should be drawn to the various interpretations and excuses offered.

Firstly, some people saw in it an attempt to end Northern domination. Secondly, some regarded it as an attempt to remove corruption in government. Thirdly, others hoped that it would introduce an honest and just programme of political and administrative reform to correct the structural imbalance in the federation.

No one quarreled with these aims. Consequently there was an atmosphere of general relief immediately after the coup." – (Anthony Enahoro, *Africa Contemporary Record*, pp. 673, and 674).

Enahoro himself, a prominent Yoruba politician from Western Nigeria, was probably glad the government was overthrown because it was the same government which had imprisoned him earlier.

He went to prison in 1962 and was not released until Colonel Yakubu Gowon came to power after the second military coup at the end of July 1966. Gowon freed him together with another prominent Yoruba politician, Chief Obafemi Awolowo, for the sake of national reconciliation. Otherwise they would have remained in prison.

Enahoro was not only glad to be free; he believed he had been wrongly convicted and even went into hiding until he was caught.

Awolowo was tried for treason and convicted, along with Chief Enahoro, the celebrated fugitive offender who also wrote a book with the same title, *The Fugitive Offender.*

Ojukwu's assessment of the general reaction to the coup across the country was not in any way different from Enahoro's. As the Biafran leader stated:

"The revolution was spontaneously acclaimed in and outside Nigeria. Nigerians basked in the general relief that a corrupt, unpopular and unstable regime had been deposed." – (Ojukwu, *Africa Contemporary Record*, pp. 655 – 656).

And in the words of Margery Perham who knew about Nigeria and its people including the leaders for more than 30 years before the coup, living and working in the country at different times, and who was an official guest of the new federal government at the 1960 independence celebrations:

"A group of Ibo army officers decided than nothing could save Nigeria from a complete northern take-over but political assassination.

So, in a well-organized plot, in the early hours of January 15th, 1966, the northern prime minister Abubakar Tafawa Balewa and the finance minister were abducted in Lagos and murdered.

The same treatment was meted out to Akintola, the western premier in Ibadan, and to the premier of the north, the Sardauna of Sokoto (Sir Ahmadu Bello), at his home in Kaduna. A number of northern army officers were also murdered the same night.

The murders brought constitutional government to an end. The remaining federal ministers handed their powers over to the senior soldier, the Ibo General Ironsi, and a military administration took over the headless federation. Ironsi appointed four military governors, who included Colonel Hassan Katsina, of the royal family, for the Northern Region, and the Oxford graduate soldier, Colonel Ojukwu, for the Eastern Region....

There was at first a general sense of relief at the murders of the two premiers, whose alliance had led to such disorder in the west and which threatened complete northern domination.

The prime minister (Balewa's death), however, was regretted: his honourable character and difficult position in relation to the dominant premier of the north were understood.

There was hope that the corruption and violence of recent years would come to an end." – (Margery Perham, *Africa Contemporary Record*, p. 6; see also *West Africa*, January 1966).

Balewa was not even on the list of the leaders who were targeted for elimination Chukwuma Nzeogwu, the coup leader, had the list.

Balewa's decomposing body was found in a bush on

January 20th, five days after the coup. As Max Siollun states in his book, *Oil, Politics and Violence: Nigeria's Military Coup Culture (1966 – 1976)*:

"Assistant-Superintendent of Police Ibrahim Babankowa visited a clinic to get medication for himself. While he was there he overheard a conversation between two other patients about a mysterious unpleasant smell in their neighborhood.

Babankowa recalled the convoy of army vehicles that had passed his checkpoint on the morning of January 15. Babankowa led his police team on a search of the area the patients came from, and they discovered the decomposing bodies of Balewa and Lt-Colonel Largema in a bush along the Lagos-Abeokuta road. Balewa's body was propped up at the foot of a tree....

The Prime Minister's corpse was identified by the white embroidered gown he was wearing when he was arrested by Major Ifeajuna....The Prime Minister was buried in his family compound in Bauchi....

It appears that, while the arrest of the Prime Minister was part of the plot, his murder may not have been, and Ifeajuna and his co-conspirators may have exceeded their orders by killing him.

In the aftermath of the coup, Nzeogwu rattled off a list of names that were on the Majors' hit list. He mentioned the usual unsurprising suspects such as the Sardauna, Azikiwe, Okpara, Orizu, Okotie-Eboh and Akintola, but Balewa's name was conspicuously absent. Sir Kashim Ibrahim – who was detained and in Nzeogwu's presence at the time – pointedly recalled Nzeogwu's failure to mention Balewa.

Balewa was not killed until it was clear that the coup was doomed to fail. Those who hoped that the Prime Minister was alive all along or that the plotters would use his release as a bargaining chip were disappointed.

Why such violent attacks by the Majors on their

targets? Perhaps to forestall any chance of the former leaders ever returning to power. Major Nzeogwu reasoned that: 'We wanted to get rid of rotten and corrupt ministers, political parties, trade unions and the whole clumsy apparatus of the federal system. We wanted to gun down all the bigwigs on our way. This was the only way. We could not afford to let them live if this was to work.'" – (Max Siollun, *Oil, Politics and Violence: Nigeria's Military Coup Culture (1966 – 1976)*, New York: Algora Publishing, 2009, pp. 67, and 68. See also, Akinjide Osuntokun, *Power Broker: A Biography of Sir Kashin Ibrahim*, Ibadan, Nigeria: Spectrum Books, 1987, pp. 103 – 104; Patrick Chukwuma Kaduna Nzeogwu, in *Daily Telegraph*, Lagos, Nigeria, 22 January 1966).

The circumstances under which Ironsi assumed power were complicated. There was a power vacuum immediately after the coup. The coup makers had not succeeded in seizing power besides assassinating the prime minister and some of the cabinet members as well as the premiers of the Northern and Western regions.

Dr. Nwafor Orizu,who was president of the Nigerian senate, was also the acting president of Nigeria during that time. He became acting president after Dr. Nnamdi Azikiwe, the first president, left the country in October 1965 and was in Britain when the coup took place. Orizu remained in that capacity as acting president during and immediately after the coup and is the one who officially announced on January 16th that the civilian council of ministers – the cabinet that had served under the late Tafawa Balewa – had decided to hand over power to the armed forces with immediate effect.

Ironsi himself, although the highest-ranking army officer, was reluctant to assume power. He did not support the coup and even tried to neutralise it but failed to do so. On January 17th, he formed the Supreme Military Council, effectively assuming control of Nigeria.

There was also a possibility of a counter-coup within hours or days of the first coup if the senior army officers – none of whom participated in the coup – wanted to support the remaining members of the previous civilian administration had they decided to reconstitute the government. The majors who executed the first could have struck again, or other soldiers could have done the same thing: seize power and form their own government.

The fate of the country was therefore in the hands of the military – it was up to the senior military officers to decide what to do next:

"The surviving senior military officers scheduled an emergency meeting at the police headquarters....It took place sometime between Saturday evening/night and early afternoon Sunday (15 January – 16 January 1966). According to Lt-Colonel Njoku the meeting was attended by Major-General Aguiyi-Ironsi, Commodore Wey, Lt-Colonels Banjo, Fajuyi, Gowon, Kurobo and Njoku, and Major Anwunah....Major Nzeogwu remained in control of the Northern Region and was threatening to march south to complete the job....

Aguiyi-Ironsi faced a stark choice. If the status quo under civilian rule was restored, another coup could occur within hours or days. A further coup could come from either within the original circle of conspirators or from the Majors' other sympathizers who were lurking. There were other officers outside the immediate coup circle who shared the Majors' wish to be rid of the government – though they may not have approved of the Majors' violent *modus operandi*. These included Lt-Colonels Fajuyi, Banjo, Ojukwu and Njoku, and Major Madiebo.

Several other junior officers may have also been motivated to emulate the Majors by staging their own coup. In the view of the officers attending the meeting, these circumstances were not conducive to the continuation of civilian rule. Against this backdrop, many officers advocated that the army should take over the government. This, they argued, was the only way to avoid further bloodshed and a violent confrontation with Nzeogwu, as no one could be sure whether the troops would remain loyal to the government.

Lt-Colonel Banjo was one of those in favor of a military take-over....Lt-Colonel Njoku also advocated a military takeover of the government....Commodore Wey gave his views on which officers should be appointed to the military government." – (M. Siollun, ibid., pp. 60, and 61. See also Hilary M. Njoku, *A Tragedy Without Heroes*, Enugu, Nigeria: Fourth Dimension, 1987).

Although many Nigerians rejoiced at the ouster of a corrupt government and an end to northern domination of the federation heralding the dawn of a new era, there was one aspect of the coup no one could have failed to notice only a few days later.

No Igbo federal and regional government ministers and other prominent leaders were killed by the coup makers who were mostly Igbo themselves. Also, no Igbo military officers were killed in the coup except one "junior officer" who, reportedly half-asleep, refused to surrender the key to the armoury in Lagos, the nation's capital.

However, some people have disputed that account. The Igbo officer who was killed was Lieutenant-Colonel Arthur Unegbe. As a lieutenant-colonel, he was not a junior officer.

During the coup, he was the quarter-master general at the army headquarters in Lagos and therefore not directly responsible for handling keys to the armoury.

There was speculation that he was killed because he was a close friend of the highest-ranking army officer of northern origin, Brigadier Zakariya Maimalari, and the coup plotters were afraid that he would alert his friend about the coup if they did not kill him.

General Ironsi was also targeted for elimination, as

coup leader Major Chukwuma Nzeogwu said in an interview after the coup, but the plotters did not get the chance to kill him.

Still, no explanation was given by the coup leaders why Igbo politicians and all the other Igbo army officers were spared, while others – all non-Igbo – weren't, when one of the main purposes of the coup was to get rid of corrupt officials by assassination.

Were Igbos leaders the only ones who were not corrupt? What were they doing working for a corrupt government, as high ranking officials and as decision makers, if they were not corrupt themselves? If they were corrupt like the rest who were killed, why were they spared? Was the purpose of the coup to eliminate only members of particular ethnic groups except Igbos? As Enahoro stated:

"Historians will continue to debate whether what happened in Nigeria on 15th January, 1966, was a rebellion, a coup or a mutiny. Whatever it was, there was a change of government. The civilian administration was removed from office.

In the morning of that date, the prime minister of the federation, Sir Abubakar Tafawa Balewa; the federal minister of finance, Chief Okotie-Eboh; the premier of the Northern Region, Sir Ahmadu Bello; the premier of the Western Region, Chief Samuel Akintola; the second and third ranking officers in the Nigerian army, Brigadier Maimalari and Brigadier Ademulegun; other senior officers – Colonel Sodeinde, Colonel Pam and others – were seized and murdered. All of them had one thing in common – they were not Ibos.

The premier of the Eastern Region, Dr. Michael Okpara; the premier of the Mid-West Region, Chief Dennis Osadebe; the head of the army, Major-General Aguiyi Ironsi; the federal minister of trade, Dr. K.O. Mbadiwe and others in like positions were not killed. They had one thing in common – they were Ibos....

The pattern of killings which emerged revealed that this was a coup organized by young Ibo officers in the army.

Whatever they may claim was their basic plan, its effect was that civilian leaders and senior military officers from other areas and ethnic groups were killed while those from Ibo areas were spared.

All non-Ibo senior military officers above the rank of major who were accessible were killed in the January 15 coup.

There was only one exception to this when a junior officer half-awake through his midnight sleep, was killed in Apapa for refusing to hand over the key of the armoury.

Therefore to most Nigerians, the incidents of 15th January were a clumsily camouflaged attempt to secure Ibo domination of the government of the country." – (Enahoro, ibid., pp. 674 - 675).

Yet, Enahoro's claim that the coup was the work of Igbo army officers is contradicted and refuted by his own admission that officers from his own ethnic group, the Yoruba, also participated in the coup for the same reason he says the Igbos did, tribalism, and inadvertently gives credibility to Ojukwu's contention that it was not just the Igbos who carried out the coup but members of other ethnic groups as well. As Enahoro himself conceded:

"The leaders of the opposition (Enahoro himself, together with Awolowo, and other Yorubas) remained in prison, whereas it was freely said that some Yoruba army officers had participated in the coup expressly for the purpose of securing their release." – (Enahoro, ibd., p. 675).

If Yoruba army officers also participated in the military coup as Enahoro himself conceded, what made the coup "an Ibo Master Plan to dominate the country" as he stated in his speech to the OAU conference in August 1968?

Why would Yoruba army officers who themselves participated in the coup for the benefit of fellow Yorubas allow that to happen or help Igbos achieve such a goal? And why would army officers from other ethnic groups who also participated in the coup do that? Did they participate in the coup to help Igbo army officers overthrow the government in order for them to be dominated by Igbos or did they have other motives shared by the Igbo army officers?

Enahoro also contended that the federal military government formed after the coup was dominated by Igbos because the military head of state, General Ironsi, was an Igbo.

Yet, a look at the composition of the ruling military council, which was the supreme decision-making body – hence the government – for the whole country, clearly shows that the majority of its members were not Igbos or easterners but members of other ethnic groups. There were only two Igbos, Ironsi and Ojukwu, out of nine members of the ruling council.

The Supreme Military Council (SMC) had the following members:

Major-General Johnson Aguiyi Ironsi, supreme commander, Nigerian armed forces and head of state, an Igbo from the East; Brigadier Babafemi Ogundipe, chief of staff, Nigerian armed forces, a Yoruba from the West; Commodore Joseph Edet Akinwale Wey, rear-admiral, commanding officer, Nigerian navy, whose mother was Yoruba from the West, and his father of Ibibio and Efik parantage from the East; Lieutenant-Colonel Yakubu Gowon, chief of staff, army, an Angas (Ngas) from the Middle Belt in the North; Lieutenant-Colonel George Kurubo, commanding officer, Nigerian air force, an Ijaw from the East; Lieutenant-Colonel Chukwuemeka Ojukwu, military governor, Eastern Region, an Igbo from

26

the East; Lieutenant-Colonel Hassan Usman Katsina, military governor, Northern Region, a Fulani from the North; Lieutenant-Colonel David Akpode Ejoor, military governor, the Mid-West Region, an Urhobo from the Mid-West; and Lieutenant-Colonel Francis Adenkule Fajuyi, military governor, Western Region, a Yoruba from the West.

The acting inspector-general of police, Alhaji Kam Selem, later became a member of the Supreme Military Council.

The SMC members came from other regions of Nigeria – North, West, and Mid-West – other than the Eastern Region. Even the three easterners on the ruling military council were not all Igbos; thus, further reducing the number of Igbos among Nigeria's military rulers.

And they all together, not just General Ironsi who was an Igbo and the military head of state, made decisions affecting the country, including approving or rejecting appointments of senior government officials; nor was Ironsi the only author of Decree No. 34, as some of his critics claimed, which abolished Nigeria's three massive regions in favour of a unitary state, triggering a violent reaction from northerners who wanted their region to maintain its numerical preponderance (it claimed to have half the entire population of Nigeria) and supremacy over the rest of the country.

Northern Nigerians had all the levers of power in their hands. And they could manipulate the country at will. Although the military coup succeeded, at least temporarily, in ending such hegemonic control of the country by northerners, it never secured Igbo domination of the federal government. As Ojukwu pointed out:

"The main organs of the central government – the Supreme Military Council and the Federal Executive Council – were representative of all the regions of the country....

27

On May 24, 1966, Major-General Aguiyi-Ironsi promulgated Decree No. 34. That decree was the implementation of a decision of the Federal Military Council in which all the regional military governors were represented.

The Decree was intended to establish a National Executive Council for the whole country with the regional military governors as members to unify the top cadres of the civil service to endure the efficient administration of the country for the duration of the military regime.

Ironically enough, it was this Decree – popularly known as the Unification Decree – that sparked off widespread rioting and violence directed against the lives and property of Eastern Nigerians in Northern Nigeria!

It did not seem to matter to the leaders who planned the riots that Eastern Nigerians were in a terrible minority – 3 out of 9 members – in the Supreme Military Council that took the collective decision.

The death-toll of our people in the massacres of that month stood at 3,000. A high-powered commission was appointed by the Supreme Military Council to investigate the causes and the conduct of the May riots in Northern Nigeria. Northern Nigeria leaders never allowed that commission to meet." – (Ojukwu, ibid., 656).

Much was said about the killing of non-Igbo military officers and people of other ethnic groups especially Hausa-Fulani and other northerners. And there was a lot of evidence to prove that. But the death toll among the Igbos after the January coup, and the subsequent coup in July the same year, was just as appalling, if not more so, in terms of numbers.

And they were targeted for no other reason than that they were Igbo, starting with General Ironsi himself when their enemies started eliminating Igbo leaders. The conflict was clearly defined along ethnic and regional lines.

When General Ironsi announced the abolition of the

regions in his promulgation of Decree No. 34 in his official capacity as the head of the Supreme Military Council, he inadvertently signed his own death warrant.

Not only would a unitary government have ended northern domination of the federation; it also would have seriously affected Northern Nigerians by requiring them to apply for jobs on competitive basis in a streamlined and unified civil service along with the more educated southerners – Igbos and Yorubas.

The only way they could have avoided that was by doing two things: force General Ironsi to rescind the order (Decree No. 34) and return the country to the status quo ante – the good old days when Nigeria was a federation dominated by northerners; and massacre the Igbo who had "swamped" the north, "taking jobs away" from the northerners, or expel them from the region.

Thus, one of the tragedies of the January 1966 military was that Igbos were massacred by their fellow countrymen in Northern Nigeria, or expelled from that region, because of what they had achieved in life. In other words, they were being punished for being successful.

Instead of being an asset, their education and entrepreneurship became a liability. And it cost them thousands of lives in only a few weeks after the coup.

Had Yorubas also settled in the north in large numbers like the Igbos had done, they would have met the same fate as their southern compatriots, the Igbo. But, unlike the Igbos, Yorubas have traditionally remained and prospered in their home region, although a substantial number of them also live outside the southwest, their homeland.

The divergent paths the two regions – north and south – took in pursuit of education, or lack thereof, was put in proper perspective by Margery Perham – and this is only one example – when she stated:

"The people of the Hausa states and the Kanuri of the ancient northern kingdom of Bornu had their own

29

language, whereas in the south, English was increasingly the lingua franca of the people and opened them to the full impact of the new economic, political and religious influences.

A northern chief once reproached me about the failure of the British to spread the English language. I reminded him of the strong opposition to this and of an incident encountered in Bornu where there was great anger because the British would not give first place to Arabic in schools. 'Well,' he said, 'you should have forced us.'" – (Margery Perham, "Nigeria's Civil War," in Colin Legum and John Drysdale, *Africa Contemporary Record: Annual Survey and Documents 1968 – 1969*, London: Africa Research Limited, 1969, p. 4).

The English language, which increasingly became the lingua franca of many southerners, also opened up educational educational opportunities for them, as did conversion to Christianity, enabling them to attend mission and government schools founded by Europeans in the south; unlike in the north where the people had their own Islamic faith and Islamic schools in which Arabic and the Koran were taught more than anything else.

The result of this glaring contrast between the two regions was clearly evident in the differences in the level of education between the southerners and the northerners, with the latter lagging far behind their fellow countrymen. The led to mistrust and even animosity between them.

The mistrust between them was also a major factor in the January 1966 military coup. And it turned violent. As Northern Nigerians went on a genocidal rampage against the Igbos and other Eastern Nigerians living in Northern Nigeria, they tried to justify the killing frenzy by invoking images of a complete take-over of the country by the southerners. Isolated in the north, and defenceless, the Igbos and other southerners became even more vulnerable to attack by marauding gangs of bloodthirsty thugs full of hate. As the death toll continued to rise, northern authorities simply looked the other way and in many cases even encouraged the massacres. It was nothing short of ethnic cleansing. Many people saw in this the end of Nigeria as a country:

"The northerners in some of the towns, suspecting a complete Ibo take-over (after the coup), fell upon the scattered minorities and massacred some hundreds of them...(after) Ironsi, in Edict No. 34, announced (in May 1966) the abolition of the regions and therefore of the federation, in favour of a unitary government and also a unification of the civil service which would have very adversely affected the prospects of the northerners, more backward in modern education than their southern competitors.

Ironsi retracted his policy of unification but too late for his own safety. On July 29th, 1966, he and the military governor of the Western Region were murdered along with a number of Ibo (army) officers by northern soldiers.

This time there was no valid constitutional power left to act and after some confusion the young Chief of Staff, Colonel Gowon (33 years old), took over. He had the advantage not only of a good reputation, but, as a northerner who yet came from a Middle Belt small tribe, and was also a Christian, he seemed to bridge the fissures which had split Nigeria." – (Margery Perham, ibid., p. 6).

Gowon introduced his own measures to avert an even worse catastrophe involving more massacres and outright civil war. But nothing seemed to work, although some prisoners, including two prominent ones – Chief Obafemi Awolowo and Chief Anthony Enahoro – benefited from his policy of clemency:

"Colonel, later General, Gowon began by releasing prisoners, including two eminent ones, Awolowo and

Enahoro, who from this point played a major role.

He repealed the obnoxious Edict No. 34 and in September (1966) called a meeting of notables from all regions to discuss the future of Nigeria. All possible solutions were considered.

But even while the conference was sitting there was a new wave of massacres in the northern towns in which Igbos and other easterners were killed, often in the most revolting manner. Estimates of the number killed vary from three to thirty thousand and the survivors fled back to the east to inflame their families and clansmen with hatred for their oppressors and a desire to cut all links with the federation.

It was, therefore, not surprising that in the confusion of the moment, with the army and civil service tending to break up into their regional parts, and the east alienated by the successive massacres, little progress could be made in rebuilding the federation." - (M.Perham, ibid., 6 - 7).

Nigeria should probably have been restructured to form a confederation with extensive devolution of power to the regions to allay fears of domination of the country by some groups; a solution that may also be applicable in the case of Tanzania where the people of Zanzibar have always complained of marginalisation and domination by mainland Tanzanians.

With regard to Nigeria in 1966, there is the question of what could have been done immediately after the coup. The record shows that events unfolded in rapid succession thereafter. Could General Ironsi, who became the new head of state soon after the coup, have averted further tragedy – the massacre of Igbos and other easterners in Northern Nigeria by forming a truly national government instead of having one that was "dominated" by Igbos as Chief Enahoro and others claimed?

He probably would not have been able to prevent the tragedy. The ruling organ during that time, which was the

Supreme Military Council, was already, as the record shows, a nationally representative body and was *not* dominated by Igbos. Easterners on the ruling council were hopelessly outnumbered 3 to 9. Even the three from the Eastern Region were not all Igbos.

And the measures Ironsi tried to implement in pursuit of national reconciliation achieved nothing of the sort. Even his retraction of the policy to abolish the regions did not avert the catastrophe. And distrust and hatred of the Igbo among many northerners – by no means all – was nothing new.

Also, Ironsi's national tour during which he met with different traditional rulers and other leaders to discuss the country's future did not achieve anything in terms of restoring law and order or resolving ethno-regional rivalries.

There was nothing that could constrain the fury of the northerners against the Igbo and other easterners living in Northern Nigeria. Instead, more massacres took place, including Ironsi's assassination.

Although Ironsi was an Igbo and the highest-ranking military officer, Igbos did not control the Nigerian army as some people claimed. As Chief Anthony Enahoro himself conceded:

"It became clear after a few months that the country had no satisfaction from the events of January 15, 1966.

Once again, conditions were ripe for change. In the last week of July 1966, the change came....

Some of the senior army officers of non-Ibo origin were now holding some key positions in the army and still prevented an all-Ibo command at the top of the Nigerian military administration.

There were also rumours of a counter-coup to reverse the effects of the January 15 coup...A mutiny started at the army barracks in Abeokuta in the former Western Region in the morning of July 29....An officer of northern origin...asked all soldiers from other (non-Ibo) ethnic groups to take up their arms....Disorders spread to other barracks in the rest of the country and continued through the weekend.

Major-General Aguiyi-Ironsi, who was then visiting Ibadan (capital of the Western Region), and his host, the military governor of the West, Lieutenant-Colonel Adenkule Fajuyi, were kidnapped at the Government House in Ibadan.

The net result of this was another coup. Following the coup, Major-General – then Lieutenant-Colonel – Yakubu Gowon succeeded Major-General Aguiyi-Ironsi on 1st August (1966) as head of the federal military government." – (Anthony Enahoro, in a statement to the OAU conference on the Nigerian civil war, Addis Ababa, Ethiopia, 12 August 1968, reproduced in *Africa Contemporary Record*, ibid., p. 676).

With the assassination of General Ironsi on 29 July 1966, Nigeria had experienced its second coup in only six months. And there is no doubt that northerners were behind it.

Ironsi also sealed his own fate when he chose northern soldiers as his bodyguards to show that he trusted them as fellow Nigerians and did not favour his fellow Igbos.

One of the soldiers he trusted to protect him was the younger brother of Lieutenant-Colonel James Pam who was killed in the January coup. Other northern soldiers responsible for his personal security were Major Theophilus Yakubu Danjuma who was based in Ibadan where Ironsi was killed; and three lieutenants – Sani Bello, Titus Numan and William Walbe.

Troops commanded by Danjuma surrounded the residence of the Western Military Governor Francis Adenkule Fajuyi, where Ironsi was staying, ready for a counter-coup and for the assassination of the visiting military head of state and his host. There were also reports that Danjuma received a telephone call from Lieutenant-Colonel Gowon, who was the chief of staff at the federal army headquarters in Lagos, and told Gowon that he was going to capture Ironsi.

Instead, Ironsi ended up dead, killed at the residence of the Western military governor, his host. Other people were also killed.

Ironsi's northern bodyguards who were inside the house with him were part of the coup plot and worked in coordination with the northern soldiers outside who had surrounded the house under the leadership of Danjuma. He had trusted the wrong people for his personal security and they ended up betraying him.

Danjuma and his troops eventually entered the house and kidnapped Ironsi and his aide Captain Andrew Nwankwo, his host Fajuyi, and Lieutenant Sani Bello who was one of his security men. They all had their hands tied behind their backs when they were taken out of the house. It was a death sentence. They were reportedly stripped naked and brutally beaten by their captors before being executed.

Captain Nwankwo – with the help of one of his northern captors – escaped after he and the other captives were taken into the bush and their captors were so focused on Ironsi and Fajuyi, torturing them. It was he, together with Lieutenant Bello who also survived, who provided a first-hand account of what happened on that day.

There were also reports that Fajuyi tried to persuade Danjuma not to kill Ironsi but Danjuma refused to spare Ironsi's life. Fajuyi then reportedly told Danjuma that if Ironsi was going to be killed, then they should kill him first; they did.

The July 1966 coup had profound implications for the future of Nigeria. Four of the Northern Nigerian army officers who participated in coup became heads of state at different times: Murtala Mohammed, Mohammed Buhari, Ibrahim Babangida, and Sani Abacha.

The coup enabled northern soldiers to take full control of the Nigerian army, the most powerful institution in the country, once again guaranteeing northern domination of the federation.

Danjuma at one time became the army chief of staff, a position also once held by Gowon, another northerner who also became head of state. Although Gowon did not take part in the July 1966 coup, he knew northern army officers were making plans to launch a counter-coup.

Northern military officers virtually constituted Nigeria's ruling class for decades and were responsible for instituting militocracy in Africa's most populous nation. And it all started with the July 1966 military coup.

There is no question that the July 1966 coup was led by northern army officers – Hausa-Fulani and others – in retaliation against the Igbos for launching the first one and for killing Northern Nigerian leaders and army officers, including the premier of Northern Nigeria and the prime minister of the Nigerian Federation who was also a northerner. The leader of the coup was Lieutenant-Colonel Murtala Muhammed who was the inspector of signals in the federal army.

Northern Nigerian leaders, together with the northern army officers, wanted the Northern Region to secede but were dissuaded by some influential Nigerians and British as well as American diplomats from doing so.

Besides the two northern politicians – Federal Prime Minister Tafawa Balewa and Northern Premier Ahmadu Bello – other prominent northerners killed were four of the most senior army officers from that region: Brigadier Zakariya Maimalari (the highest-ranking northern military officer who was reportedly shot by southern coup leader Major Emmanuel Ifeajuna in Ibadan when he tried to escape during the coup); Colonel Kur Mohammed, Lieutenant-Colonel James Pam, and Lieutenant-Colonel Abogo Largema.

The killings were carried out by Igbo army officers in

an army that was predominantly northern. About 75 per cent of the soldiers in the entire Federal Nigerian army were northerners, far outnumbering their their southern counterparts. So northerners, by sheer numbers, had ample leverage to tip scales in their favour in a counter-coup.

General Ironsi's fate – including the national tour which cost him his life – and the fate of other Igbos in general was determined by what turned out to have been a conspiracy by northerners, not only to retaliate against the Igbos and avenge the murder of Northern Nigerian leaders and army officers but mainly to regain control of the federation they had lost in the first coup. Northerners regained control of the federation and retained their dominant position for decades.

All of Nigeria's military heads of state since the assassination of Ironsi were northerners, except Olusegun Obasanjo, a Yoruba from the southwest. And one civilian president, Shehu Shagari elected in 1979, was also a northerner.

It was not until 1999 that a southerner became president when Olusegun Obasanjo won the election after he came out of prison where he was locked up by the military head of state, General Sani Abacha, a northerner, on false charges of treason. But even *he* was elected with the support of northern generals including former military head of state Ibrahim Babangida. He was elected on 27 February and assumed office on 29 May 1999.

Obasanjo was also supported by northern political heavyweights and businessmen; thus ensuring continued domination of the federation by northerners from behind the scenes, although they did not succeed in all areas during his reign. Obasanjo did not turn out to be the puppet they thought he would be, manipulated at will by powerful northerners.

But even throughout that turbulent period in Nigerian history since independence when the majority of the military officers were southerners – mostly Igbos and

37

Yorubas – most of the enlisted men were northerners, thus tipping scales in favour of the north in case of any conflict between the regions which was best demonstrated during the Nigerian civil war when Hausa soldiers wreaked havoc in the secessionist region of Biafra.

Some of the brutalities by northern soldiers during the war were motivated by resentment. They resented what they considered to to be the "privileged" position of educated southerners – the Igbos in this particular case – in the federation who now had to be "punished" for having enjoyed life at "their" expense before the civil war.

There is no question that Igbos had incurred the wrath of Northern Nigerians because of what happened in the first coup. They masterminded it. But they had never won endearment from the northerners even in the past, as the massacres of hundreds of Igbos in Jos in 1945 and in Kano in 1953 clearly show.

And the virtual absolute power northerners had over the federation – because of their superiority in numbers – even when Ironsi was head of state; and especially their dominant position in the military where they flexed muscles – again because of their vastly superior numbers in the armed forces – in defence of Northern Nigeria's hegemonic control of the country, meant that the course of events during those tragic years would hardly have been any different even if all Igbos were saints.

That is why Ironsi's tour of the nation to try and discuss the future of the federation was so fruitless, and tragic. As Ojukwu stated:

"Firm assurances of personal safety for our people in Northern Nigeria had been given by the Supreme Military Council itself (in which Eastern Nigerians were outnumbered), and by the Sultan of Sokoto and the Emirs of the North. On the strength of these assurances, we appealed to our people who had left their stations to return to Northern Nigeria. They did.

At this point Major-General Aguiyi-Ironsi undertook an extensive tour of Northern and Mid-Western Nigeria, and arranged to round off his tour at Ibadan in Western Nigeria with a meeting of traditional rulers and chiefs from all over Nigeria to seek advice on matters affecting the future of the country. The meeting was scheduled for July 29, 1966.

But in the morning of that day, a well-organized group of northern soldiers kidnapped the supreme commander and his host, Lieutenant-Colonel Adenkule Fajuyi, the military governor of Western Nigeria, and subsequently murdered them in very gruesome circumstances. The cruel massacre of over 200 Eastern Nigerian army officers and men also took place." – (Ojukwu, *Africa Contemporary Record*, ibid., p. 656).

Lieutenant-Colonel Yakubu Gowon, later Major-General, succeeded Major-General Aguiyi-Ironsi on 1 August 1969 as head of the federal military government. In a broadcast to the nation that morning, he promised to bring disorders in the army under control, stop further bloodshed, restore law and order and confidence in all parts of the country with minimum delay, and seek a new basis for unity.

He also analysed the roots of the Nigerian crisis and announced that a unitary form of government – formed by his predecessor General Ironsi – did not provide a basis for Nigerian unity and stability. He promised that with the concurrence of the regional military governors – North, East, West, and Mid-West – and other members of the Supreme Military and Federal Executive Councils, a decree would soon be issued to lay a sound foundation for Nigerian unity.

July 29th was welcomed by the nation, particularly because of the ensuing events after the coup which marked another turning point in Nigerian history.

On assuming office, Gowon set in motion the

machinery for finding a lasting solution to Nigeria's problems. He ordered:

(a) the release of Chief Obafemi Awolowo who was the leader of the opposition in the federal parliament until his imprisonment in 1963; Chief Anthony Enahoro and other political prisoners and detainees;
(b) an immediate return to the federal system of government;
(c) the summoning on 12th September, 1966, of an *ad hoc* conference on constitutional proposals comprising representatives of all the regions of the federation. This conference was preceded by consultative conferences in all areas in the regions. At these consultative conferences, the issue of the creation of more states in the federation was revived and memoranda were submitted demanding that the basic cause of dissatisfaction - i.e. - the imbalance in the federal structure should be removed.

Although one of the first things Gowon did when he became head of state was to grant pardon to a number of prisoners the most prominent of whom were two Yorubas, Awolowo and Enahoro, the pardon was not a blanket clemency. However, the two Yoruba leaders went on play prominent roles in the new Nigerian government. Awolowo became vice chairman of the Federal Executive Council which was the government and whose chairman was Gowon himself. Therefore Awolowo was Nigeria's vice president under Gowon. He also served as finance minister at the same time.

Enahoro served as labour and information minister and as head of the Nigerian delegation to the peace talks under the auspices of the Organisation of African Unity (OAU) held in Addis Ababa, Ethiopia, in August 1968, aimed at resolving the Nigerian conflict.

Besides releasing the nation's two most well-known prisoners, Gowon also made another momentous decision

40

which had a profound impact on Nigeria's future by placating the north. In September 1966, within two months after Ironsi was assassinated, he repealed the decree, known as Edict No. 34, which had infuriated Northern Nigerians so much by abolishing the regions and unifying the civil service.

During the same month, he also called a meeting of all prominent Nigerians – including traditional rulers, religious leaders, and academics – in the nation's capital to discuss the future of Nigeria. All options were considered, including dissolution of the federation. Forming a loose federation or a confederation or even a system entirely new and unique to Nigeria were also among the options considered. As Gowon stated at the *ad hoc* conference which began in Lagos on 12 September 1966, Nigerians should seriously consider the following forms of government for Nigeria:

"A federal system with a strong central government; a federal system with a weak central government; a confederation; or an entirely new arrangement which may be peculiar to Nigeria." – (Gowon, *Africa Contemporary Record*, p. 658).

Forming a unitary republic was out of the question. The violent reaction by Northerners to Ironsi's unification policy which created a unitary state ruled that out.

But even when this conference was going on, the massacre of Igbos and other Eastern Nigerians living in Northern Nigeria continued unabated. Thousands were killed in the most gruesome way, dismembered or disemboweled, or burned alive. Many others were clubbed or hacked to death, hundreds of them at bus and train stations as they tried to flee the north and return to their home region.

More than 2 million easterners, mostly Igbo, were forced to flee back to Eastern Nigeria after losing tens of thousands of their kinsmen in the massacres in the north. With their fellow easterners back home, they vowed to sever all ties with the federation and stay in their native region. Many openly advocated secession. Expelled from Northern Nigeria, that is the trajectory their lives took, propelled towards secession by forces beyond their control.

The future of Nigeria remained uncertain as each region seemed to be going in its own way. There was a very strong possibility that the federal army and the government itself would split along regional lines resulting either in a loose federation or in a complete break-up of the country if nothing was done to contain the situation. And the situation could not be contained without the full participation of all the parties involved. For example, Ojukwu did not attend the national conference fearing for his safety.

Had he gone to Lagos or any other meeting place such as Benin City in Mid-West, he probably would not have returned alive. Instead, arrangements were made for him to attend a peace conference in Aburi, Ghana, with the other military governors of Nigeria including the head of state General Gowon. The Ghanaian military head of state, Lieutenant-General Joseph A. Ankrah who replaced Dr. Nkrumah after Nkrumah was overthrown, hosted the conference. The future of Nigeria was at stake:

"With the army and the civil service tending to break up into their regional parts, and the east alienated by successive massacres, little progress could be made in rebuilding the federation. Ojukwu feared for his safety if he should go to Lagos to confer.

It was therefore decided to hold a meeting in Ghana, at Aburi, near Accra, on January 4th and 5th, 1967, to which delegates could easily go by plane." – (Margery Perham, *Africa Contemporary Record*, ibid., p. 7; *Ghanaian Times*, January 3 – 6, 1968).

What happened at the Aburi meeting is one of the subjects we are going to address when we look at some of the major events which took place in Africa in 1967.

Perhaps what happened in Nigeria during the sixties – the massacres, the secession of the Eastern Region, the clamour for self-determination from different ethnic groups across the country – might have been avoided if the Nigerian leaders themselves had decided to delay independence for a few years, may be for five or even seven years, until they had restructured the federation to reflect the ethnic composition and diversity in the allocation of power and resources, instead of having it dominated by the three major ethnic groups: the Hausa-Fulani, the Igbo and the Yoruba. That would have entailed breaking down the three massive regions into several and probably autonomous or semi-autonomous states to accommodate the interests of all the ethnic groups especially smaller ones which were dominated by the big three.

It was done after the coup and after the massacres when the federation was broken down into 12 states by Gowon on 27 May 1967. But it was too late by then. It was also done without consultation, thus infuriating Igbos among other groups.

There also seems to have been a consensus among Nigerian leaders during the tragedy of the sixties that they probably had demanded independence too soon, much sooner than they should have, given the volatile ethnic mix and numerical disparity of the country's ethnic groups in the structurally flawed federation. As Chief Enahoro stated during that time when the civil war was going on:

"Unfortunately, during the years of British occupation, Nigeria did not produce one nationalist movement in the classic sense, as was the case in India and Ghana, to mention only two former British colonial territories.

Instead, Nigeria produced three nationalist movements which, unfortunately, were based on the three major tribal groupings.

The major political parties grew out of these movements, and political developments during the struggle for independence therefore took the shape of compromises between these political parties which were different in their outlook and programmes and which were regionally entrenched.

The only common factor among them was the struggle for independence. In their common desire to win independence, many vital problems were left unsolved. One of these outstanding problems was the creation of more states which would have provided a more lasting foundation for stability of the Federation of Nigeria.

The British government pointed out at the time that if new states were to be created, the new states must be given at least two years to settle down before independence could be granted. On reflection, Nigerian leaders have admitted that the British were right and they were wrong on this vital issue in hurrying to independence without solving the problem of the federation." – (Anthony Enahoro, *Africa Contemporary Record*, ibid., p. 673).

Despite the flawed structure of the federation which threatened the very existence of Nigeria as a single political entity, as the secession of the Eastern Region tragically demonstrated, the composition of the country's diverse ethnic groups was itself enough threat to the survival of Nigeria as much as it is to the rest of the African countries almost all of which are plagued by ethnic and regional tensions only in varying degrees.

The only difference is that in the case of Nigeria the problem is much more complex because her population is much bigger – the largest of any African country – in an area smaller than Angola, Mali, Niger or Tanzania; and her ethnic composition is one of the most diverse on the continent, including groups which virtually constitute nations within a nation – the Hausa-Fulani, the Igbo, and Yoruba – and whose separate populations exceed the population sizes of a number of African countries. For example, there are more than 36 million Yorubas in Nigeria.

That alone, compounded by differences in cultural and historical backgrounds for all the groups in Nigeria, fueled demands for secession through the years.

Even Northern Nigerians who dominated the federation wanted, more than once in the 1950s and the 1960s, to secede; so did Eastern and Western Nigerians.

Chief Obafemi Awolowo threatened in 1953 to pull Western Nigeria out of the federation if the federal territory, Lagos, was not incorporated into the region which – as Yoruba territory – was considered by Yorubas to be an integral part of their region. And in 1954, the Western Region again threatened to secede.

And Eastern Nigerians, mostly Igbos, made the most determined attempt to secede – and in fact succeeded in doing so – in the sixties when they established the Republic of Biafra which lasted for about two-and-a-half years from 30 May 1967 to 15 January 1970 when the secessionist forces capitulated to federal might.

But it was Northern Nigerians who had a much longer history of making secessionist threats. Even in the 1950s when southern politicians in Eastern and Western Nigeria were making a concerted effort to win independence for Nigeria as a single nation, northerners wanted to secede. As Professor Ali Mazrui stated in his article "Black Africa and the Arabs" in *Foreign Affairs*:

"Whereas the spread of Islam through East and West Africa provides a cultural bond, it also, in some cases serves to reinforce separatist tendencies. In Nigeria in the last decade before independence, Muslim Northerners, fearful of the political militancy of Christian Southerners – talked seriously of secession....

Ironically, separatism moved southward after independence, into Azikiwe's community, for it was Ibo Christians rather than Hausa Muslims who eventually sought to break up Nigeria.

And many Christian missionary organizations moved to the support of Biafra, almost seeming to regard the Nigerian Civil War as a re-enactment of the crusades – a religious war rather than an ethnic confrontation. In reality the religious factor in the civil war was not fundamental." - (Ali Mazrui, *Foreign Affairs*, July 1975, p. 737).

Religion did play a role, and probably more than the subsidiary one Mazrui assigns it. But it is true, as he stated, that it was not fundamental.

However, the magnitude of its significance and impact was evident in the denunciations exchanged in religious terms between the northerners and the easterners during the civil war.

Many Igbos denounced the Hausa-Fulani as "Muslim hordes" bent on the elimination of the "Christian Igbo." And Ojukwu, in one midnight broadcast from Biafra's radio station in Enugu, which was then the capital of the secessionist region, pleaded:

"Holy Archangel Michael, defend us in battle." – (Ojukwu, quoted by Colin Legum and John Drysdale, eds., *Africa Contemporary Record: Annual Survey and Documents 1968 - 1969*, p. 553).

What Ojukwu said was an invocation reminiscent of the Crusades, thus validating the contention that religion was also a factor in the Nigerian civil war especially between the predominantly Muslim Hausa-Fulani of Northern Nigeria and the predominantly Christian Eastern Nigerians, especially the Igbos.

From the northerners came denunciations of southern "infidels."

But despite the fact that the Nigerian head of state during the civil war, General Yakubu Gowon, was a Christian although a northerner yet not a northern Muslim, there is enough evidence to show that regional ties transcended religious bonds.

The majority of Northern Nigerians, including many Christians most of whom came from smaller tribes in what was then known as the Middle Belt and other parts in the north as opposed to the Hausa-Fulani who are overwhelmingly Muslim, also supported the expulsion of the Igbos from the north just like their Muslim counterparts did. And the vast majority of them also supported the war against Biafra.

Northern Muslim leaders were also emphatic in their determination to embrace northern Christians at all cost for no other reason than that they were fellow northerners; even if it meant giving them money from the Northern Nigerian government to help them start businesses to replace the Igbos and other southerners – most of whom were easterners – who were being expelled from Northern Nigeria. As long as they were southerners, and Christian, they had to go. As one representative in the Northern Regional Assembly, A.A. Abogede representing Igala East, stated during the February-March 1964 session:

"I am very glad that we are in Moslem country, and the government of Northern Nigeria allowed some few Christians in the region to enjoy themselves according to the belief of their religion, but building of hotels should be taken away from the Ibos and even if we find some (northern) Christians who are interested in building hotels and have no money to do so, the government should aid them, instead of allowing Ibos to continue with the hotels." – (A.A. Abogede, *Africa Contemporary Record*, p. 664).

Another member of the Northern Regional Assembly, Alhaji Usman Liman representing the Sarkin Musawa constituency, won sustained applause from the other representatives in the same session when he said:

"What brought the Ibos into this region? They were here since the colonial days. Had it not been for the colonial rule there would hardly have been any Ibo in this region. Now that there is no colonial rule the Ibos should go back to their region. There should be no hesitation about this matter.

Mr. Chairman, North is for Northerners, East for Easterners, West is for Westerners and the Federation is for us all (Applause)". – (Alhaji Usman Liman, *Africa Contemporary Record*, p. 665).

Even the powerful Northern premier, Sir Ahmadu Bello, who virtually controlled the Nigerian Federation and who was also known as the Sardauna of Sokoto, was hostile towards the Igbos. As he bluntly stated during the same February-March 1964 session in the Northern House Assembly:

"It is my most earnest desire that every post in the region, however small it is, be filled by a northerner (Applause)." – (Ahmadu Bello, *Africa Contemporary Record*, ibid.).

He was also roundly applauded. And from members of the Government Bench in the Regional Assembly came shouts of "Good talk," and "Fire the Southerners," following blistering attacks on and denunciations of the Igbos by northern representatives in the northern legislature.

The tragedy that befell Nigeria in the sixties was not totally unexpected. There had been warnings through the years that a catastrophe was in the making, even if it was not imminent. Right from the beginning when Nigeria was established as one colony in 1914, uniting the north and the south, northerners openly contended that the amalgamation was "a mistake."

And in 1964, almost two years before the first military coup and the massacre of the Igbos in Northern Nigeria, the Northern premier, Sir Ahmadu Bello, ridiculed those who talked about Nigerian unity and the existence of Nigeria as a single political entity. As he bluntly stated:

"Politicians always delight in talking loosely about the unity of Nigeria. Sixty years ago there was no country called Nigeria.

What is now Nigeria consisted of a number of large and small communities all of which were different in their outlooks and beliefs. The advent of the British and Western education has not materially altered the situation and these many and varied communities have not knit themselves into a complete unit." – (Ahmadu Bello, *Africa Contemporary Record*, ibid., p. 670).

Soon after the assassination of Ironsi on 29 July 1966 in the second military coup staged by northern Nigerian soldiers led by Major Murtala Muhammed, Major Theophilus Yakubu Danjuma, and Major Martin Adamu, northern military officers and politicians demanded dissolution of the Nigerian federation and total independence for each of the three massive regions – North, East and West. And they got a lot of support from fellow northerners. In fact, before May 1966, Northern Nigerian leaders were contemplating secession within months:

"It was well-known before May, 1966, that there were very powerful moves in Northern Nigeria for secession from the federation....(Northern) traditional rulers, politicians, civil servants and intellectuals were known to have planned and led the riots of May (in which thousands of Igbos were massacred in the north) and the rebellion of July (in which Ironsi was overthrown and killed by Northern Nigerian soldiers). Their July putsch was given the code name *araba* or secession." – (Ojukwu, *Africa Contemporary Record*, p. 657).

Even the Nigerian military head of state, General Yakubu Gowon expressed serious doubt about the continued existence of the federation, especially as it was then structured. He bluntly stated in his first broadcast to the nation as head of state on 10 August 1966:

"The base for unity is not there." - (Yakubu Gowon, *Africa Contemporary Record*, ibid.).

And in a memorandum submitted to the *ad hoc* conference on the Nigerian constitution in Lagos in September 1966, the Northern Nigerian delegation hardly expressed any confidence in the viability of the Nigerian federation, stating unequivocally:

"We have pretended for too long that there are no differences between the peoples (of Nigeria). The hard fact which we must honestly accept as of paramount importance in the Nigerian experiment especially for the future is that we are different peoples brought together by recent accidents of history. To pretend otherwise will be folly." – (*Africa Contemporary Record*, p. 670).

At the same constitutional conference, Northern Nigeria again threatened to secede. It was a thinly veiled threat contained in the memorandum Northern Nigerian leaders submitted to the conference, arguing that Nigeria should be split into:

"a number of autonomous states...that is to say, Northern Nigeria, Eastern Nigeria, Western Nigeria, Mid-Western Nigeria, or by whatever name they may choose to be called...(under) a Central Authority (whose powers are to be) delegated by the component states except that powers connected with the external or foreign affairs and immigration can be unilaterally withdrawn by the State Government....

Nigerian citizenship (should be abolished and replaced by an) Associate citizenship....Any Member State of the Union should reserve the right to secede completely and unilaterally from the Union and to make arrangements for cooperation with the other members of the Union in such a manner as they may severally or individually deem fit." – (Ibid., p. 658).

What the Northern Nigerian leaders proposed at the constitutional talks in Lagos in September 1966, as shown in the preceding quotation, struck at the very core of the union, threatening to dissolve some of the very ties which made its existence possible as a federation.

Any territorial unit which controls its own foreign affairs and immigration policy is, at the very least even without international recognition, a sovereign entity short of diplomatic representation.

Those are some of the key areas which fall under the jurisdiction of the national government; not of the component units of a unitary state like Ghana or Kenya or of a federation like Nigeria.

Even in a confederation, member states or provinces or regions don't conduct their own foreign affairs or formulate their own immigration policy. Quebec, for example, with all its separatist tendencies, does not have its own foreign or immigration policy separate from what is carried out or approved by the Canadian national government, although the province may have some different requirements for admission of immigrants as long as there is no conflict of interest between the provincial government and the national government.

What Northern Nigerians presented to the constitutional conference in Lagos in September 1966 was a specific agenda for dissolution of the Nigerian federation. Had any of the major items in their memorandum been adopted by the national delegates, or had they been incorporated into the conference's final resolutions, that would have been the end of the Nigerian federation.

Even a confederation, of whatever configuration, would not have been consummated given the concerted effort by northerners to separate from the rest of Nigeria or remain an integral part of this sovereign entity only if they could dominate it perpetually.

Western Nigerians also communicated an implied threat to secede, forcefully articulated in their memorandum to the constitutional conference in Lagos. They proposed a "Commonwealth of Nigeria" if other regions did not accept federalism:

"The Commonwealth of Nigeria (shall comprise) the existing regions and such other regions as may be subsequently created. The government of each state within the Commonwealth shall be completely sovereign in all matters excepting those with respect to which responsibility is delegated to the Council of State." – (Ibid.).

No one would seriously argue that the British Commonwealth, now simply known as the Commonwealth – consisting of former British colonies except Cameroon and Mozambique which once were French and Portuguese colonies, respectively; and Rwanda, a former Belgian colony – is a single political entity like Brazil, Ghana, China, Iran, Zimbabwe, Tanzania, Argentina, South Africa or any other sovereign state.

If the member states in the proposed Commonwealth of Nigeria were to be sovereign as proposed by the Western Nigerian delegation to the 1966 constitutional conference, Nigeria would have ceased to exist as a single sovereign nation had the proposal been implemented.

And probably that is exactly what the Western Nigerian leaders had in mind, dissolution of the federation, when they presented their memorandum proposing the establishment of a Nigerian Commonwealth.

They were already frustrated by their inability to end northern domination of the federation; they also wanted to manage their own affairs as an autonomous entity or in pursuit of self-determination; and they were bitter for having been excluded from the central government when Eastern and Northern Nigeria formed an alliance to establish the first African government at independence in 1960.

It seemed as if the two regions – North and East – had conspired against one region, the West, to exclude it from power. Western Nigerians never forgot that. So, ending the federation would not have been much of a loss to them.

Therefore, as the record shows, Northern and Western Nigerians threatened to break up the Nigerian federation far more often, and for a much longer period since the 1950s, than Eastern Nigerians did and whose secessionist threat and attempt was made only once and at a much later date in 1967.

And while northerners and westerners were making all those secessionist threats in 1966, massacres of the Igbos in Northern Nigeria continued unabated.

By October in the same year, more than 30,000 Eastern Nigerians, mostly Igbo, had been massacred in Northern Nigeria over a five-month period. The pogroms continued while the Federal authorities and the Northern Nigerian government looked the other way or simply ignored the tragedy. Some of the officials even encouraged the killers to commit more atrocities.

Seven months later, in May 1967, Eastern Nigeria seceded from the federation and declared independence as the Republic of Biafra. Another tragedy began. We will examine that later when we look at what happened in Africa in 1967.

The Nigerian military coup on 15 January 1966 was followed by another tragedy on the continent only about a month later. It was also a military coup. It took place in Ghana on 24 February 1966. And it marked the end of the political career of one of Africa's most prominent leaders, and probably the most influential, Dr. Kwame Nkrumah. The coup was engineered and masterminded by the CIA.

When Dr. Nkrumah's reign came to an abrupt end, several reasons were given for his ouster. His critics accused him of dictatorship. But that is not why the CIA orchestrated his downfall.

The United States has always supported and propped up dictators around the world, including some in Africa such as Mobutu Sese Seko for 32 years, as long as the despots serve American and Western interests. Nkrumah did not and incurred the wrath of the United States and other Western governments.

The United States was no more interested in helping the people of Ghana establish democracy than they were in helping the people of Iraq and Afghanistan establish democracy when she invaded those countries.

In the case of Iraq, it was oil more than anything else that triggered the invasion. In the case of Afghanistan, the invasion was "justified" by the Americans on grounds of national security to neutralise terrorists who were radical Islamists.

Other geopolitical interests of the United States were at stake. Yet, in both cases, American leaders claimed they wanted to help the people in those two countries establish democracy.

If the United States wanted to help the people who live

under dictatorial regimes institute democracy, she would have helped to overthrow *all* dictators, not just some.

In Africa, the United States supported not only Mobutu but the apartheid regime of South Africa. It was a tyrannical regime. For some inexplicable reason, American leaders felt that black people and other non-whites in South Africa did not want to live under democracy, although the majority of South Africans made it clear that they did not want to live under apartheid or to be denied basic human rights.

Yet, the United States found it necessary to overthrow a democratically elected government in Ghana under Nkrumah on the spurious grounds that it was helping to establish democracy in that country. Why in Ghana and not in South Africa, in Zaire under Mobutu, in Rhodesia and in the Portuguese colonies of Angola, Mozambique and Guinea Bissau if the United States was really interested in helping Africans establish democracy?

Several factors converged through the years Nkrumah was in power which made him a target for coups by both internal and external forces.

His Pan-African militancy and relentless support for African liberation movements, and his quest for genuine political and economic independence not only for Ghana for the entire African continent, antagonised the West; prompting Lyndon Johnson who was the American president when Nkrumah was overthrown to say that Nkrumah – among all African leaders – was the biggest threat to American interests in Africa. He inspired, educated and influenced others by example. And the United States was not going to tolerate that.

It is true that assumption of virtual dictatorial powers by Nkrumah solidified opposition to his rule in Ghana. Yet, it was the people of Ghana themselves who, in a national referendum in July 1964, voted to transform Ghana into a one-party socialist state. Also, the establishment of authoritarian rule and introduction of the

Preventive Detention Act by Nkrumah to keep a tight reign on some of his opponents who were his political enemies determined to destroy him should be viewed in its proper historical context.

Curtailment or abrogation of freedom is deplorable. But those who criticise Nkrumah for muzzling his critics and detaining his political enemies by using the Preventive Detention Act should also concede that Nkrumah was compelled to invoke such powers – even if he may have exceeded or violated his mandate in some cases – because of the constant threats against his life.

Bombs had been thrown at him; also bombs had been planted on different occasions to blow him up or blow up his car and his entourage. Even some members of his own security force tried to kill him.

He survived several assassination attempts by his enemies within Ghana who worked in collusion with external forces, especially with the CIA, to eliminate him.

Under those circumstances, it is not difficult to understand why he had to take draconian measures to protect himself and his government.

That does not justify dictatorship. But it puts things in proper perspective in the context of Ghana under Nkrumah. He was forced to live in a state of emergency and under very difficult conditions created by his enemies including the CIA and other Western intelligence services.

Yet, his critics don't blame the CIA for threatening his life. And they don't blame some of his fellow countrymen who tried to kill him.

Nkrumah was overthrown almost nine years after he led Ghana to independence, the first black African country to emerge from colonial rule. He blazed the trail for the African independence movement. He was determined to help liberate the rest of Africa.

And he believed that the colonial rulers were not really interested in relinquishing power but wanted to reassert their control over their former colonies in an indirect way or by putting puppets in power whom they could manipulate at will. It was he who coined the term "neo-colonialism" to define this insidious phenomenon. The term became an integral part of the English vocabulary.

None of that won him accolades or genuine friendship among Western leaders and other powerful political and financial interests in the metropolitan powers. They were determined to remove him from office by any conceivable means including undermining his government; sabotaging Ghana's economy to turn the people against him and then blame him for it; and by simply killing him.

In his book, *Neo-Colonialism: The Last Stage of Imperialism*, Nkrumah exposed the insidious forces at work in African countries in pursuit of American imperialist goals and other Western interests.

Western embassies in Africa were hotbeds of intrigue. Covert activities by Western intelligence services were conducted from those diplomatic missions using diplomatic cover to undermine truly independent nationalist governments which refused to bend to Western wishes.

Nkrumah also bluntly stated that Africans must be vigilant against imperialist machinations and local elements working in collusion with external forces to undermine genuine leadership in African countries in order to enable Western powers to perpetuate their domination and exploitation of Africa through multinational corporations and other means.

The United States was determined to establish hegemonic control over Africa, using economic muscles and political power to impose a stranglehold on African countries not only to exploit the continent but to promote American geopolitical and strategic interests as well. And Nkrumah accused the CIA of fomenting trouble on the continent, including overthrowing governments the United States did not like.

After the book was published in 1965, the United

States government sent a note of protest to Nkrumah and immediately cancelled a $35 million aid-programme to Ghana. A few months later, he was overthrown in a military coup.

His ouster was one of the most dramatic demonstrations of power projection capabilities by the United States in the African continent. And it was a warning to others: If you don't toe the line, America will get you. Might is right. That is the imperial dictum. As Dr. John Prados of the National Security Archive at George Washington University states in his book, *Safe for Democracy: The Secret Wars of the CIA*:

"The CIA's role in Ghana seems to have flowed from both Washington and the field. A nationalist hero and first president of independent Ghana, Nkrumah had an uneasy relationship with the United States. Educated in missionary schools and in the segregationist America of the thirties and forties, he learned his Marxism there, influenced by the racial attitudes of the day. He was no Moscow puppet. Nkrumah called his program 'African Socialism'....

Ghana's economy went into deficit as prices for its cocoa plunged. Nkrumah attributed the hardship to the former colonial power, Great Britain, and to the United States. Washington blamed Nkrumah for anti-American agitation in Ghana. American aid for a dam on the Volta River and to develop new economic resources in aluminum hung in the balance.

Nkrumah attributed the January 1964 assassination attempt to the CIA. The Johnson administration stepped carefully around this thorny question, with U.S. Ambassador William P. Mahoney assuring LBJ that his country team – including CIA – was fully under control, and the CIA denying any role. In February 1964 Nkrumah sent Johnson a letter asserting that there were 'two conflicting establishments' representing the United States, the diplomatic mission and the CIA, which 'seems to devote all its attention to fomenting ill-will, misunderstanding and even clandestine and subversive activities among our people, to the impairment of the good relations which exist between our two governments.'

Johnson conveyed reassurances on the CIA both in his response and through Ambassador Mahoney, who reportedly told Nkrumah that the five CIA officers in the station at Accra were under his strict supervision." – (John Prados, *Safe for Democracy: The Secret Wars of the CIA*, Ivan R. Dee, Publisher, Chicago, Illinois, USA, 2006, pp. 328 – 329).

Denial by American officials of CIA involvement in covert and subversive activities in other countries is a standard response. Even Prados states that official documents don't show any direct connection between Washington and the coup in Ghana. Yet some CIA agents admitted CIA involvement in Nkrumah's ouster. And there is enough evidence, including circumstantial, to show that the coup was the work of the CIA working with the army and police officers who overthrew Nkrumah, although Prados gives a slightly different version with regard to American involvement in the coup. He goes on to state:

"But Washington's record was not entirely innocent. As early as February 6, 1964, Dean Rusk asked John McCone about suitable candidates to head a post-Nkrumah government, and they discussed the very general who was eventually to move against the Ghanaian (president). The two men speculated on the possibility of concocting a covert operation in concert with the British. When the State Department proposed an action program it had the explicit purpose of slowing Nkrumah's leftward political evolution. The proposal was to actively undermine him by threatening to halt aid to the Volta River project, recognizing opponents, and using psychological warfare and other means to diminish his support. President Johnson deliberated on this program at the exact moment Nkrumah sent his letter protesting CIA subversion.

LBJ went ahead with the Volta dam aid, but he may well have approved undermining Nkrumah. During a home visit in March 1965 Ambassador Mahoney met with Director McCone and AF Division deputy chief John Waller. They specifically discussed a coup plot in Ghana hatched by police and military figures, including Gen. Joseph A. Ankrah, the same man McCone and Rusk had considered a year earlier.

Evidence indicates the Ghanaian military's plans were well-known to the CIA, which reported on them more than half a dozen times in 1965. As yet there is no evidence of direct CIA involvement from documents. What we do have is a series of confident predictions of a coup from the ambassador – who accurately foresaw that Nkrumah would be replaced by a military junta within a year – and NSC staffer Robert W. Komer. That summer Nkrumah detected the coup plot and cashiered Ankrah. The Ghanaian generals, their peripatetic plots more than a year old, were temporarily stymied." – (Ibid., p. 329).

They were now waiting for the best opportunity to carry out the coup. Colonel Akwasi A. Afrifa who led the coup stated in his book, *The Ghana Coup*, that it would have been very difficult if not impossible to overthrow Nkrumah when he was still in Ghana. The best time to overthrow him was when he was out of the country. And that is exactly what the coup plotters did:

"Kwame Nkrumah strove for a role on the world stage, trying to be a peacemaker and help end the Vietnam War. This annoyed Washington, especially when Nkrumah tried to intercede between the British and Guyana's Cheddi Jagan. He also made unwelcome overtures in the Middle East. In the summer of 1965 Nkrumah sent diplomatic envoys to North Vietnam, suggesting that he himself visit early the following year. He tacked on visits to Burma and the People's Republic of China. According to CIA political operative Miles Copeland, under whom the agency had begun an effort to plant astrologers on world leaders known to favor the occult, a CIA occult agent may have had a role in convincing Nkrumah to plan the trip.

In 1965, Nkrumah published a book, *Neo-Colonialism: The Last Stage of Imperialism*, which must have raised hackles in Washington. Then came an overt move toward Moscow – Nkrumah accepted Soviet arms and training for his presidential guard. The last straw may have come when the CIA reported that a Soviet arms shipment was on its way to Ghana.

William Mahoney left Accra for good in the summer of 1965, and for eight months there was no U.S. ambassador. Station chief Howard T. Bane had a much freer hand. Bane proposed the CIA sponsor a coup. The views of Africa Division chief Glen Fields are not known, but he had been amenable to the Congo, and his deputy John Waller had made his mark in the 1953 CIA coup in Iran. The Special Group turned them down. Bane thought that shortsighted, and as a colleague later put it, he had 'no patience for management of which he was not a part.'

Howard Banes, another man who came to Africa from the DO Far East Division, had an affinity for the military and determination to go with it. A knuckle-dragger, in Korea he had run a net to rescue downed fliers. In India he had backstopped the Tibet project, insulating it from the jaundiced Harry Rositzke. He wet his teeth in Africa heading the CIA station in Kenya.

Not phased by the Special Group's rejection, the tobacco-chewing, cigar-smoking Bane took advantage of his instructions to keep a close watch on the Ghanaian military. With a complement variously reported at ten or up to three dozen case officers, Bane exploited his military contacts.

61

A few winks and nods from Bane betokened U.S. support to Ghanaian soldiers. With just a pair of brigades, both based in Accra, there were not that many to convince. Bane had time to suggest that Langley send a few officers from the CIA Special Operations Division, who could not only concretize the impression of support but use the coup to purloin documents and code materials from the Chinese embassy in Accra, a unilateral operation under cover of the coup. Headquarters spurned him again.

But in mid-January 1966 Bane reported that a rash of coups elsewhere in Africa had reenthused Ghanaian officers, and on February 17 came concrete indications of a plot, Operation Cold Chop. Twenty-four hours before the coup, Bane reported the military planned it for the time Nkrumah was out of the country. President Nkrumah left Ghana on February 22, the coup occurred on the 24th. General Ankrah returned to head the resulting junta....Langley credited Accra station with an assist. Howard Banes wound up as chief of operations for the AF Division.

In Tanzania, meanwhile, Che Guevara tarried for months after leaving the Congo. There he turned his diaries into a narrative, seeking to understand what had gone wrong. He stayed in Dar-es-Salaam until early 1966, when a top DGI official came to give Guevara the latest assessment of prospects for revolution in each Latin American country.

Guevara really wanted to fight in Argentina, but security services there had suppressed dissident networks. In Peru the CIA and the government had foreclosed that option. That left Bolivia as the major prospect.

Che's hope lay in what he called a *foco*, literally a focus or a lighthouse, in practice an exemplar activity that could lead the masses to rally to the revolution, much as Castro's small July 26th Movement had brought the end of Batista."
– (Ibid., pp. 329 – 331).

As in Ghana, the Americans had also accomplished their mission in the former Belgian Congo. Together with the Belgians, they succeeded in getting rid of Patrice Lumumba whom they considered to be a threat to Western interests. After Lumumba's assassination, supporters of Lumumba, including Cubans led by Che Guevara, used Tanzania as a rear base and as a conduit for the shipment of weapons to Lumumbist forces in Congo, a role that earned President Nyerere enemies in Washington who wished he had been overthrown as well.

And there is question that the United States played the biggest role in Nkrumah's ouster from power. Other Western countries also played a big role. The British, the French and West German governments, together with the United States, conspired to sabotage Ghana's economy in preparation for the coup.

They lowered the price of cocoa, Ghana's biggest foreign exchange earner, on the international market in order to squeeze Nkrumah. They also denied him much-needed economic assistance.

Their intelligence agencies also worked together with the CIA to undermine him. Britain's MI6, not just the CIA, played a significant role in his ouster; so did other Western intelligence services, especially German and French. Nkrumah himself, in his book *Dark Days in Ghana*, named West Germany as one of the countries which played a role in overthrowing his government.

Declassified documents available in the United States since 1999 clearly show that the American government played the biggest role in overthrowing Nkrumah.
They constitute an indispensable work, entitled *Covert Foreign Relations of the United States* from 3 January 1964 to late 1968, published by the Historian's Office of the US State Department. That was the period when Lyndon Johnson was president of the United States.

But even before the intelligence reports were partially declassified, testimony given to the US Senate Foreign

Relations Committee under the chairmanship of Senator Frank Church of Idaho in 1975 showed that the CIA played a major role in overthrowing Nkrumah; although not much information was made public during that time in terms of details on what the CIA exactly did to undermine and overthrow Nkrumah.

The hearing focused on the CIA's illegal activities which included assassination of foreign leaders, among them Patrice Lumumba.

There were other African leaders who were on the CIA's hit list. Julius Nyerere was another leader the CIA tried to overthrow in the mid-sixties. Nkrumah, in *Dark Days in Ghana*, discussed the CIA's involvement in his ouster and in a plot to overthrow Nyerere.

And in his book *Freedom and Socialism*, Nyerere also mentioned American involvement in a plot against his government. As he stated in 1966:

"We have twice quarrelled with the US Government; once when we believed it to be involved in a plot against us, and again when two of its officials misbehaved and were asked to leave Tanzania....

The disagreements certainly induced an uncooperative coldness between us, thus suspending and then greatly slowing down further aid discussions. A comparison of American aid to Tanzania and other African countries supports the contention that at any rate our total policies (including support of the African liberation movements) have led to a lower level of assistance than might otherwise have been granted." – (Julius K. Nyerere, *Freedom and Socialism: A Selection from Writings and Speeches 1965 – 1967*, Dar es Salaam, Tanzania: Oxford University Press, 1968, pp. 201, 202, and 203).

Although Nkrumah survived many assassination attempts, at least seven, he was such a towering personality that one of the three solders who led the coup,

Major Akwasi Amankwa Afrifa, in his book *The Ghana Coup*, conceded that had Nkrumah been in the country during the coup, he and his co-conspirators would probably not have been able to overthrow him.

The leader of the trio was Colonel Emmanuel Kwasi Kotoka. The other officer who was one of the three leaders of the military coup against Nkrumah was Colonel Albert Kwei Ocran. They knew that the best time to execute the coup was when Nkrumah was out of the country.

And that is exactly what they did when he was in Peking on his way to Hanoi on a peace mission to help end the Vietnam war; and no wonder with encouragement from President Lyndon Johnson who wished him "good luck," knowing what was going to happen in Ghana when Nkrumah was not there. In fact, President Johnson sent him a message in the first week of February 1966 – when Nkrumah was preparing for the trip – to assure him of a safe landing in Hanoi. As June Milne, Nkrumah's former research and editorial assistant, stated in her article, "The Coup That Disrupted Africa's Forward March," in the *New African* :

"Contemplating the years between 1957, Ghana's independence, and 1972 when Nkrumah died, I have been re-reading some of my notebooks written during those years when I was Nkrumah's research and editorial assistant. I wrote daily accounts of our many meetings both before 1966, the year of the coup, and afterwards. The value I attach to the notebooks is because they were written at the time. Not from memory or hindsight.

A notebook entry made during the first week in February 1966 is significant because it was made only three weeks before the coup. It was at a time when Nkrumah was preparing to travel on the peace mission to Hanoi. I was with him in his office in the Osu Castle in Accra. He was checking the page proofs of his book, *Challenge of the Congo*. Occasionally he asked if I thought he had used the most appropriate word in a particular context. 'It is your language, not mine.'

We were suddenly interrupted by the appearance of Foreign Minister, Quaison Sackey, to report that he had just received an urgent message from the Ghanaian ambassador in Washington. The US president, Lyndon Johnson, wished to assure Nkrumah that America would stop the bombing of Hanoi to allow his aircraft to land safely. He could, therefore, travel to Vietnam with his peace proposals 'in perfect safety.'

Why were the Americans so anxious for Nkrumah to leave Ghana – especially when he had suggested peace talks could be held in Accra: For some months, Nkrumah had been working on a peace plan. But a coup to remove him from power was in the final stages of planning. For it to succeed, it was imperative that he was out of the country, and as far as possible to ensure he would be unable to make a quick return....

When news of the coup reached him, Nkrumah was in Peking (today's Beijing) en route to the Vietnamese capital, Hanoi, with plans to end the American war in Vietnam. He was too far away for a quick return to Ghana where he may have been able to end the military action.

Leaders of four African countries sent Nkrumah immediate messages of support and invitations. They were the presidents of Egypt (Gamal Abdel Nasser), Mali (Modibo Keita), Guinea (Sekou Toure), and Tanzania (Julius Nyerere). Nkrumah decided to accept Sekou Toure's invitation." – June Milne, "The Coup That Disrupted Africa's Forward March," the *New African*, London, 6 March, 2007).

This brings to mind what British Prime Minister Edward Heath said to Dr. Milton Obote and two other African leaders in January 1971.

At a Commonwealth meeting in Singapore, Nyerere, Kaunda and Obote told Edward Heath that their countries would withdraw from the Commonwealth if Britain proceeded with the sale of arms to the South African apartheid regime. In the ensuing debate, Heath is reported to have told the three leaders:

"I wonder how many of you will be allowed to return to your own countries from this conference?"

It was an ominous warning, confirmed shortly thereafter, when Obote learned in Nairobi, Kenya, on his way back to Uganda from the conference that he had been overthrown. And it directly implicated Britain in the coup. Britain's involvement in the coup was further confirmed only a few days later when the British government became the first to recognise Amin's military regime exactly one week after he seized power.

Obote never returned to Uganda after the Commonwealth conference. He was overthrown by Idi Amin. But it was the British – and the Israelis – who were behind Obote's downfall and simply used Idi Amin to get him out of power; so it was with Nkrumah in Ghana: the same trick, and same approach, in this case masterminded by the CIA.

In the case of Obote, it was Britain's M16 together with Mossad, Israel's intelligence service, which masterminded the coup against him. The CIA was also involved in Obote's ouster. In fact, one of Amin's close friends, when Amin was in power, was a CIA agent. As one of Amin's sons, Jaffar Amin, stated in an interview with the *Mail*, London, 13 January 2007:

"That year (1975) my father took us to Angola. It was a really nice day trip. My father was friends with a CIA agent who had new equipment from the US, including planes for our trips." – Jaffar Amin, in "Mad Ugandan Dictator's son reveals all about his 'Big Daddy'," the *Mail*, London, 13 January 2007).

Britain's and Israel's involvement in Obote's downfall was an open secret. As David Hebditch and Ken Connor state in their book, *How to Stage a Military Coup: From Planning to Execution*:

"Beverly Barnard's plan went smoothly. Amin's troops sealed off Kampala airport at Entebbe and tanks and infantry took to the streets of the capital. The presidential palace was seized and vehicle checkpoints set up on all major routes. And the plotters didn't forget to take over the radio station!....

British High Commissioner Richard Slater rushed around to Amin's office. There, with his feet metaphorically on the general's desk, was the Israeli Defence Attaché Colonel Bar-Lev....In a recently declassified cable to London, Slater stated: '....The Israeli defence attaché discounts any possibility of moves against Amin'....

Amin showed his appreciation by making his first official overseas visit to Israel, where he alarmed Prime Minister Golda Meir by demanding enough munitions to keep her country's arms industry busy for a decade. Within months 'The Strangler' was having lunch with the Queen at Buckingham Palace. God only knows what they chatted about.

Not in the dark about developments in Uganda was a colourful Kenyan businessman-politician and World War II fighter called Bruce McKenzie. McKenzie had astutely backed jailed opposition leader Jomo Kenyatta during the build-up to independence and was later rewarded with the influential post of minister of agriculture. He was the ultimate wheeler-dealer....

When in the UK, McKenzie was a regular house-guest of Maurice Oldfield, Barnard's ultimate boss as 'M', the director-general of MI6. Indeed he had also been McKenzie's 'boss' since 1963 when the businessman had signed up as an agent of the Secret Intelligence Service.

Alarmed by the threat of Obote's policy of nationalising foreign businesses, McKenzie was a keen supporter of 'Amin for president' and those views were undoubtedly impressed on Oldfield and Prime Minister Harold Wilson. When he lost his job as agriculture minister in 1970, he remained the most influential white man in East Africa." – (David Hebditch and Ken Connor, *How to Stage a Military Coup: From Planning to Execution*, New York: Skyhorse Publishing, 2009).

American officials shared the same position with their British counterparts on Obote and equally wanted him out of power. However, the biggest players who orchestrated Obote's downfall were the British and Israeli intelligence officers including Israeli military officers in Uganda. Still, Americans supported the coup and were aware of it from the beginning when it was being planned.

But it was in Ghana where the CIA's role in overthrowing an African government became so sinister, and so tragic for Africa, as it was earlier in the case of Congo under Lumumba. And Nkrumah's indictment against the CIA – which was also Africa's indictment – for its role in fomenting trouble and undermining African governments American leaders did not like, was not simply paranoia. It was grounded in reality and backed up by empirical evidence. The tentacles of the CIA reached far and wide.

When I was a student at Wayne State University in Detroit in the state of Michigan in the United States in the early and mid-seventies just a few years after Nkrumah was overthrown, I remember reading an article about the CIA's interest in recruiting African students in that state to work for the intelligence agency. The article was published in one of the country's leading newspapers, the *Detroit News*.

It said the CIA was active on university campuses

recruiting foreign students, targeting those it considered to be potential leaders when they returned to their countries. It also tried to identify those it felt were sympathetic towards the United States.

The article named the University of Michigan and Michigan State University as the CIA's main recruiting grounds in the state of Michigan because of the large number of foreign students attending those schools. It concluded by saying: "The emphasis is on the emerging nations of Africa."

That was the kind of treachery Nkrumah warned against when he said the CIA and other Western intelligence agencies always tried to find "quislings and traitors in our midst," as he put it, to work for the enemies of Africa. And he became one of the first and biggest casualties of such machinations by the CIA when some of his fellow countrymen conspired against him and removed him from office.

Another traitor was Nkrumah's black classmate at Lincoln University, a predominantly black school in Pennsylvania in the United States, in the 1940s. His name was Franklin H. Williams. He was the American ambassador to Ghana when Nkrumah was overthrown. He was appointed by President Lyndon Johnson in 1965 and served as ambassador to Ghana until 1968 when he returned to the United States.

The CIA's plot to overthrow Nkrumah was executed from the embassy with the full knowledge and participation of the ambassador. As Nkrumah stated in his book *Dark Days in Ghana*, it was impossible for Ambassador Williams not to have known what the CIA was doing at the embassy of which he was in charge. In fact, as the head of the American embassy in Ghana from which plots were hatched and executed to overthrow Nkrumah, it was his job to know what was going on.

In an article in a black American publication, *Jet* magazine, 20 August 1970 (pp. 20 – 22), Williams contended that he did not play any role in Nkrumah's downfall. The article was entitled, "Did Not Aid in Nkrumah's Ouster."

But evidence demonstrated otherwise.

The coup was masterminded by the CIA and the American embassy in Ghana was in touch with Washington when the coup was being planned. It is impossible for Ambassador Williams not to have known that. And as Marvin Wachman, a white American who was president of Lincoln University when Nkrumah was overthrown and who knew Nkrumah, stated in his book, *The Education of a University President*:

"In February 1966, Nkrumah was on his way to Hanoi to visit North Vietnam's president, Ho Chi Minh, 'with proposals for ending the war in Vietnam.' When he stopped in Peking en route to Hanoi, he was greeted with the news that his regime had been overthrown.

In *Dark Days in Ghana*, a book he wrote while in exile in Conakry, Guinea, Nkrumah strongly implies that America's CIA masterminded the coup. He was particularly vituperative about the alleged role of Ambassador Franklin H. Williams in bribing Nkrumah's enemies to carry out his overthrow.

'It is particularly disgraceful that it should have been an Afro-American ambassador who sold himself out to the imperialists and allowed himself to be used in this way,' Nkrumah wrote. 'However, his treachery provides a sharp reminder of the insidious ways in which the enemies of Africa can operate. In the U.S.A. The 'Uncle Tom' figure is well known. We have mercifully seen less of him in Africa. The activities of the C.I.A. no longer surprise us.'

Franklin Williams, a 1941 Lincoln University graduate, was so upset by this charge that he asked me to intercede for him with Nkrumah and explain that he had nothing at all to do with the coup. I did write to Nkrumah but did not hear from him." – (Marvin Wachman, *The Education of a*

University President, Philadelphia, Pennsylvania, USA: Temple University Press, 2005, p. 82; Kwame Nkrumah, *Dark Days in Ghana*, New York: International Publishers, 1968, p. 49).

Kevin K. Gaines, in his book *American Africans in Ghana: Black Expatriates and the Civil Rights Era*, states that Nkrumah did respond to Wachman:

"The president of Nkrumah's alma mater, Lincoln University, Dr. Marvin Wachman, informed Nkrumah of Williams's assurance that he had not been a party to the Ghanaian coup.

In an otherwise cordial letter to Wachman, Nkrumah wrote, 'I have noted what you say about Franklin Williams' (Wachman to Nkrumah, July 21, 1969, Nkrumah to Wachman, August 10, 1969, in *Kwame Nkrumah: The Conakry Years, His Life and Letters*, comp. June Milne [London: PANAF, 1990], 321, 325)." – (Kevin K. Gaines, *American Africans in Ghana: Black Expatriates and the Civil Rights Era*, Chapel Hill, North Carolina, USA: The University of North Carolina Press, 2008).

Franklin H. Williams' predecessor as ambassador to Ghana, William P. Mahoney, played a critical role – with the US State Department, the White House and the CIA – in drafting an eight-point "Proposed Action Program for Ghana" devoted to psychological warfare and other tactics to be used against Nkrumah to bring about his downfall. As the document stated:

"Intensive efforts should be made through psychological warfare and other means to diminish support for Nkrumah within Ghana and nurture the conviction among the Ghanaian people that their country's welfare and independence necessitate his removal."

The document was dated 11 February 1964, 13 days before Nkrumah was overthrown. Authorship of the document is credited to William C. Trimble, then director of the Office of West African Affairs at the State Department and his deputy director Leon G. Dorros, as well as William P. Mahoney.

It was addressed to G. Mennen Williams who was the assistant secretary of state for African affairs, a post he assumed in 1961 in the Kennedy administration after serving as governor of Michigan for 12 years; he decided not to run in 1960 for another term as governor.

Here is the full document:

"The course of action outlined below is based on the following assumptions:

(1) By his present actions, Nkrumah is daily rendering our position in Ghana more difficult. He sees us as an ideal scapegoat to cover his domestic shortcomings and a handy whipping boy to promote his extreme brand of Pan-Africanism. In contrast to his leftist advisors, it is doubtful, however, that he wishes us to leave. He probably desires to retain the Volta aid and also some connection with the West to give him a posture of neutrality. But his present conduct can only lead to circumstances under which our position could well become untenable.

(2) The U.S. should make a determined effort to remain in Ghana. Voluntary withdrawal of our representation would be interpreted both there and elsewhere in Africa as a defeat for the U.S. and a victory for the Communists. It also would encourage the Communists and leftist elements in other parts of Africa to adopt the same tactics they have been following in Ghana. The Soviet bloc desires us to leave Ghana and is actively engaged in promoting this end.

(3) Nkrumah is convinced that the U.S. is the principal obstacle to his program for African unity. He is also convinced that through the CIA we are seeking to engineer his downfall. He is living in a state of fear induced by the several assassination attempts and an overriding sense of insecurity, and consequently is increasingly irrational and irresponsible.

(4) Nkrumah's popularity has markedly declined in the past 18 months, especially among civil servants, police, businessmen, university students and the professions. Though he still enjoys a considerable following among the rural masses, the more politically-minded urban population has lost confidence in him.

(5) Time is not on our side. The Parliament, judiciary and police have been emasculated; a purge of the universities is now under way and one of the civil service imminent. Although moderate elements still exert a slight influence on Nkrumah, he increasingly depends for advice and counsel on the small group of leftists in his immediate entourage. Nkrumah is consciously and deliberately creating a police state based on national Marxist principles.

(6) Although Nkrumah's leftward progress cannot be checked or reversed, it could be slowed down by a well conceived and executed action program. Measures which we might take against Nkrumah would have to be carefully selected in order not to weaken pro-Western elements in Ghana or adversely affect our prestige and influence elsewhere on the continent.

(7) U.S. pressure, if appropriately applied, could induce a chain reaction eventually leading to Nkrumah's downfall. Chances of success would be greatly enhanced if the British could be induced to act in concert with us.

(8) Failure to act can only result in a further deterioration of the situation to the point where we may feel compelled to leave Ghana, thereby facilitating the chance of Soviet success.

B. Summary of Proposed Actions

(1) Postponement of Ambassador Mahoney's Return to Accra

Ambassador Ribeiro should be called to the Department and informed by Governor Williams that in view of the Ghanaian Government's expression of regret at the demonstrations before the American Embassy and the Foreign Minister's assurance that they would not re-occur, it had been decided that Ambassador Mahoney would return to Accra on February 14. Because of the subsequent expulsion of American professors at the University of Ghana and vicious attacks on an officer of our Embassy, we now intend to postpone the Ambassador's return. The same statement should also be made to Botsio by our Charge at Accra.

(2) Award of Medal of Freedom to Adger E. Player

Congressmen Oliver P. Bolton and Zablocki have proposed that the Medal of Freedom be awarded to Mr. Player for his action in preventing desecration of the American flag. The White House has asked for the Department's views on the proposal. Our response should indicate that a decoration is fully justified, and suggest that it be either the Medal of Freedom or the Legion of Merit. Mr. Player's valorous conduct has been widely reported in the American press, and the award would constitute tangible evidence of the country's gratitude and admiration. It would also underscore our contempt for the controlled Ghanaian press in seeking to besmirch Mr. Player's character.

(3) Representations to Nkrumah by Ambassador Mahoney

The Ambassador should see Nkrumah as soon as possible after his return to Accra and make clear to him our concern at the course of developments in Ghana and their seriously adverse implications for U.S.-Ghanaian relations. He should indicate that as Ghana has failed to carry out the understandings set forth in the 1961 exchange of correspondence between President Kennedy and Nkrumah, we may be forced to reexamine our commitments to Ghana. He should also express our shock that no action has been taken against the leaders of the demonstrations. The impact of the Ambassador's remarks would obviously be enhanced if he were in a position to state that he had seen the President just before leaving Washington and had discussed the Ghanaian situation with him. It is felt that the Ambassador should not bring a letter from the President to Nkrumah since it might (a) serve further to inflate Nkrumah's ego; (b) encourage him to initiate an exchange of correspondence with the President and (c) be quoted out of context by Nkrumah to serve his own purposes.

(4) Visit by Edgar Kaiser

Mr. Edgar Kaiser should be encouraged to seek an interview with Nkrumah in the near future at which he would stress the unfavorable reaction in the U.S. to recent events in Ghana and indicate that they are causing serious misgivings among the Directors of Kaiser Industries on the desirability of proceeding with the VALCO project.

(5) IBRD Review of Its Support of Volta

76

The recommendation should be made to the IBRD, preferably through the Secretary of the Treasury, that it send a team to Ghana to study the desirability of continuing its support of the Volta project in the light of Ghana's adverse financial situation.

(6) Slow-down in Payments on the Volta Dam Project

AID and the Eximbank should delay action on pending and future requests for draw downs of loan funds by the Volta Dam. (This course of action is possible only until around July 1, 1964 when the lake starts to form and further delays in construction might cause serious flooding and loss of life.) Because of the IBRD's direct involvement in the project, it should be informed in advance of any such action.

(7) Termination of NIH Facility

The Bureau of the Budget is anxious to close down the NIH research facility at Accra as part of its program to reduce the balance of payments deficit. Although useful, the facility has been unable to fully realize its potential as a source of data on tropical diseases because of the uncooperative attitude of the leftist Director of the Ghanaian Institute of Health. Although of marginal value, early announcement of our intention to terminate the facility would be interpreted in Ghana as an indication of our displeasure at recent developments there but should not alienate pro-Western groups. If feasible, the operation possibly on a reduced scale, in deference to Budget's B/P concerns, should be shifted to Sierra Leone thus making the point entirely clear to Nkrumah and at the same time achieving a favorable impact with moderate African leaders.

(8) Psychological Warfare

Intensive efforts should be made through psychological warfare and other means to diminish support for Nkrumah within Ghana and nurture the conviction among the Ghanaian people that their country's welfare and independence necessitate his removal. Themes which might be exploited include:

(a) The strong non-Ghanaian element among Nkrumah's closest advisors and their Communist backgrounds;

(b) Suppression of civil liberties as exemplified by the Preventive Detention Act, purge of the judiciary, etc.;

(c) Perversion of the trade union movement without regard to the interests of the working people;

(d) Announced intention to destroy civil service leadership;

(e) Parliament is no longer responsive to public opinion;

(f) Threat to academic freedom as evidenced by expulsion of eight professors, invasion of the campus by the mob, campaign to place political commissars in institutions of higher learning, removal of the respected headmaster of Achimoto, etc.;

(g) Decline in Ghana's international prestige and increasing alienation of sister African nations;

(h) Introduction of Soviet security agents among the President's household;

(i) Serious deterioration in Ghana's financial position resulting from Nkrumah's irresponsible policies;

(j) Creation of a police state;

(k) Likelihood that Nkrumah's policies will result in Soviet bloc domination of Ghana, thereby substituting one form of colonialism for another; and

(l) Increasingly precarious position of the ordinary Ghanaian citizen.

(9) Nkrumah an African Problem

We must bring home to other African leaders that Nkrumah is a problem which they must face up to in their own national interest." – (*Foreign Relations of The United States, 1964 – 1968, Volume XXIV, Africa, Document 237*. **Memorandum From the Director of the Office of West African Affairs (Trimble) to the Assistant Secretary of State for African Affairs (Williams).** Source: Department of State, Central Files, POL 1 GHANA–US. Secret. Drafted by Trimble, Mahoney, and Deputy Director of the Office of West African Affairs Leon G. Dorros).

All that was an integral part of the revelations from declassified documents released by the US State Department in 1999 which clearly show what the United States did to get rid of Nkrumah.

Franklin Williams was appointed ambassador to Ghana in 1965, obviously to oversee the execution of a coup against his former classmate and black "brother," Kwame Nkrumah. Nkrumah's ouster had been contemplated earlier. It was discussed by American officials and their allies, especially the British and the French.

In fact, the discussion to overthrow him started as far back 6 February 1964. That was when US Secretary of State Dean Rusk and CIA Director John McCone met and chose Joseph A. Ankrah, a general in the Ghanaian army, as the best man who should replace Nkrumah after Nkrumah was overthrown.

The interest to overthrow him was further fuelled by the publication of Nkrumah's book that was highly critical of the United States and other Western powers. The United States sent him a strong note of protest after his book,

Neo-Colonialism: The Last Stage of Imperialism, was published in the same year, coincidentally or not, Williams was appointed ambassador to Ghana:

"In his book, *Neo-Colonialism: The Last Stage of Imperialism*,[1] Ghana's first president, Dr. Kwame Nkrumah, addressed the subject in a pan-African context, warning of the danger the United States posed to Africa by trying to establish hegemonic control over the continent, using American economic muscles to impose a stranglehold on African countries in order to exploit the continent and promote American geopolitical and strategic interests. He also accused the CIA of fomenting trouble on the continent, including overthrowing governments the United States did not like.

After the book was first published in 1965, the United States government sent a note of protest to Nkrumah and immediately cancelled a $35 million aid-programme to Ghana. A few months later, Nkrumah was overthrown in February 1966 in a military coup masterminded by the CIA." – (Godfrey Mwakikagile, Pretoria, South Africa: New Africa Press, *Africa is in A Mess: What Went Wrong and What Should Be Done*, 2006, pp. 128 – 129. See also Kwame Nkrumah, *Neo-Colonialism: The Last Stage of Imperialism* (New York: International Publishers, 1965)).

Besides denying his involvement in the plot to overthrow Nkrumah, Franklin Williams even blamed Hershey's, the giant chocolate manufacturer, in a conversation with one African American scholar, Professor Nathan Hare; according to what Hare said in one of his messages posted on an African discussion group, Mwananchi, in 2005.

Hare said Franklin Williams told him that it was Hershey's, not the United States government, who overthrew Nkrumah. And there were many other denials by Williams even before then. But facts do not bear him out.

The United States had been wary of Nkrumah from the time he became prime minister of Ghana when the country won independence from Britain on 6 March 1957. He became president in March 1960 when the country became a republic. Attempts to undermine his government started in the early sixties, fueled by his strong support of Lumumba in 1960 and his opposition to American intervention in Congo. From then on, American leaders started to watch him closely.

But it was not until 1964, even before the publication of his book *Neo-Colonialism: The Last Stage of Imperialism* which infuriated American officials and other Western leaders, that a concerted effort was launched to overthrow him. And to send a powerful message to Nkrumah and his supporters as well as other African leaders who tried to emulate him or pursue truly independent policies, he was overthrown almost exactly one month after he inaugurated the Akosombo Dam which had been built with American help.

The dam was officially opened on 26 January 1966. Nkrumah was overthrown on February 24th. The timing was not coincidental. It was a demonstration of American power at its worst in the Ghanaian context. It was also a warning to other African leaders who were fiercely independent-minded like Nkrumah. As the American declassified document cited earlier states:

"We must bring home to other African leaders that Nkrumah is a problem which they must face up to in their own national interest."

Other American declassified documents also show that American officials started plotting against Nkrumah in February 1964, almost two years before he was overthrown. US Secretary of State Dean Rusk and CIA Director John McCone met and felt that Major-General

Joseph Arthur Ankrah would be a suitable choice to replace Nkrumah after the coup.

A series of events took place after that meeting including participation by Britain and France, together with the United States, in a plot to sabotage Ghana's economy in order to inflame passions among Ghanaians against Nkrumah. And many of them were alienated when life became harder because of the economic squeeze on the Ghanaian economy when the three Western powers implemented their nefarious scheme.

It was a scheme of economic strangulation of a country whose leader was a shining example of African independence and manhood in a world dominated by Western powers and who was determined to see Africa free politically and economically. He had to be destroyed, lest others try to emulate him.

Coco farmers earned less and less for their export crop and blamed Nkrumah and his government for that. As history has shown, economic mismanagement, and discontent among the masses, is one of the main reasons used by soldiers and others to justify military coups not in only Africa but in other countries as well. And this was a perfect setup against Nkrumah. It was only a matter of time when he would fall, given the big powers behind the plot against him.

Documents declassified by the US State Department show that on 6 February 1964, US Secretary of State Dean Rusk and CIA Director John McCone had a meeting to review what they described as "an anti-American agitation in Ghana" which they attributed to "Nkrumah's anti-American push." McCone suggested to Rusk that "the substantial aid programs, including the Volta Dam and the Aluminum Project [being financed by the United States] should be reviewed in view of Nkrumah's attitude."

As the conversation went on, Dean Rusk asked McCone if General Joseph Ankrah, who had recently retired as Nkrumah wanted him to, could take over after

Nkrumah was overthrown. According to McCone's Memorandum, the CIA director said:

"We [have] no indication, observed the General [has] no political ambition and [I think] that if it [is] desired to develop something, we might work with the British on a joint program."

Rusk then asked McCone to further "explore this prospect fully" and report to him. He also suggested that the subject should "be discussed with Home [British Premier Alec Douglas-Home] and [his Foreign Secretary] Butler" when they come to Washington. They had been scheduled for an official visit to the White House in about a week's time, and they did go to Washington.

Other officials attended the meeting, including the US State Department director of the West African desk, William C. Trimble who wrote the memo, "Proposed Action Program for Ghana" to the assistant secretary of state for African affairs, G. Mennen Williams (who besides having served as governor of the state of Michigan from 1949 – 1961, was also once the US ambassador to the Philippines from 1968 – 1969), which stated:

"Although Nkrumah's leftward progress cannot be checked or reversed, it could be slowed down by a well conceived and executed action programme. Measures which we might take against Nkrumah would have to be carefully selected in order not to weaken pro-Western elements in Ghana or adversely affect our prestige and influence elsewhere on the continent.

US pressure, if appropriately applied, could induce a chain reaction, eventually leading to Nkrumah's downfall. Chances of success would be greatly enhanced if the British could be induced to act in concert with us.

Intensive efforts should be made through psychological warfare and other means to diminish support for Nkrumah within Ghana and nurture the conviction among the Ghanaian people that their country's welfare and independence necessitate his removal."

The British were not only induced to conspire with the Americans against Nkrumah; as the former colonial rulers of Ghana, they felt that they had an obligation to play an active role in his ouster.

According to declassified documents, a meeting of American and British officials – as well as intelligence officers – was held at the White House on 12 February 1964 to discuss Nkrumah's ouster. It was also attended by President Lyndon Johnson who chaired the meeting.

Others who attended the meeting included Secretary of State Dean Rusk; US under-secretary of state, Averill Harriman, who later served as American ambassador to Nigeria under President Johnson; and special assistant to the president on national security affairs, McGeorge Bundy.

The British delegation to the meeting was led by Sir Alec Douglas-Home, the prime minister. He was accompanied by his foreign secretary, Richard Austen Butler, who served in that capacity from October 1963 to October 1964.

According to released documents, the American under-secretary of state, Averill Harriman, said when the meeting started: "Nkrumah blames the United States for all his troubles, including the attempt at assassination." President Johnson responded: "His behavior has become intolerable."

Some of the American officials at the meeting wondered if it would not be a good idea to cut off financial assistance to Nkrumah which was critical to the successful completion of the Volta Dam project and which Nkrumah valued so much in his quest for industrialisation in Ghana; many industrial projects would depend on cheap electricity generated from the Volta River after the dam was completed. That was one of Nkrumah's most ambitious projects during his presidency.

In response to that, according to the minutes taken at the meeting:

"The [British] Prime Minister said he was worried about Ghana. Nkrumah has gone very close to being Communist. If the United States took away its aid to the Volta project, it was his opinion that Ghana would go right over to the Russians who would supply the money for the Volta dam."

The Americans and the British ruled against that option at the meeting but agreed to continue applying pressure on Nkrumah in different ways to weaken him, while being friendly towards him and pretending that they were on his side.

The British foreign secretary, Richard Butler, remarked at the meeting:

"One could not be sure how long Nkrumah would last."

But whatever doubts and suspicions some of them may have had at the meeting were soon dispelled as a concerted effort got underway to overthrow the Ghanaian president.

Two weeks later on 26 February 1964, another strategy session was convened at the White House to discuss the same subject: how best to eliminate Nkrumah from power.

At the meeting was CIA Director McCone and his close friend Edgar Kaiser who was working with Nkrumah on the Volta River Project which led to the construction of the Akosombo Dam and creation of Lake Volta, the largest man-made lake in the world.

The meeting was also attended by the American ambassador to Ghana, William P. Mahoney. He served as ambassador from 1962 – 1965.

According to records of the meeting extracted from declassified documents, McCone was quoted as saying:

"I asked Ambassador Mahoney if he felt that the CIA was operating independently of his office [in Accra]. Mahoney answered absolutely and positively no."

It would, of course, have made no sense for the CIA to engage in a clandestine operation in pursuit of American interests without the full knowledge of the ambassador.

He was the head of the US diplomatic mission from which the operation against Nkrumah was being launched, hence the highest representative of the American government in Ghana where his government had targeted the Ghanaian president for elimination because he was perceived as a threat to American interests.

It was also, coincidentally or not, on the same day that Nkrumah wrote President Johnson to express his concern about covert activities against him and his government by CIA agents in and outside Ghana.

He was aware of the pressure that was being applied on him by Western powers in collusion with local elements and had this to say in his formal letter – partly reproduced – to the American president dated 26 February 1964, the same day the American and British officials were having another meeting at the White House in Washington, D.C., in a conspiracy against him:

"...I must express some concern about that which has come to my notice within recent times as a result of the activities of certain United States citizens in Ghana.

There appears to be two conflicting establishments representing the United States in our part of the world. There is the United States Embassy as a diplomatic institution doing formal diplomatic business with us; there is also the CIA organisation which functions presumably within or outside this recognised body.

This latter organisation, that is, the CIA, seems to devote all its attention to fomenting ill-will, misunderstanding and even clandestine and subversive activities among our people, to the impairment of the good relations which exist between our two Governments.

If my analysis of this situation is correct, and all the indications are that it is, then I could not, Mr. President, view this without some alarm. Neither will any other Government in a developing State, however weak its economic position, accept this situation without demur.

We of the Independent African States wish to be left alone to pursue policies and courses which we know to be in the best interests of our people, and at the same time conducive to the maintenance of good relations with other governments of the world."

President Johnson denied those charges by Nkrumah and attempted to allay his fears by reassuring him that the United States wanted to maintain good relations with Ghana on the basis of mutual respect; while it was at the same time busy, working round the clock, to undermine him.

After the February 26th meeting at the White House, Ambassador Mahoney returned to his post in Accra, Ghana, and went to see Nkrumah on 2 March 1964, coincidentally or not, just four days before Ghanaians were to celebrate their seventh independence anniversary on March 6th. After meeting with Nkrumah, he sent a message to President Johnson and other high-ranking American officials at the state department and at the White House stating:

"I said [to Nkrumah] that I am in full control of all US government activities in Ghana. I could assure him without hesitation that during my incumbency absolutely nothing has been done by any US agency, which could be construed in any way as being directed against him or his government. Nkrumah replied with words to the effect: 'I will take your word for it.'

I repeated that there had been no conceivable activity on our part to subvert or overthrow him. I pointed out how inconsistent our entire aid effort, aimed at assisting and strengthening his government is, with wild accusations in [the] Ghanaian press that the US [is] acting against him. I added that, speaking frankly, our main intelligence effort is to keep an eye on his Soviet and Chinese friends, whose activities are really large scale.

[A] beginning has been made in effort to dispel some of Nkrumah's misconstructions on [the] role of CIA, [but] pressure should be kept up."

Nkrumah's vulnerability to CIA machinations was compounded by his dependence on American economic assistance especially involving the Volta River Project more than anything else.

When Dwight Eisenhower was still president of the United States, Nkrumah asked him to use his personal influence to persuade Henry Kaiser to put together a consortium of aluminium companies to build an aluminium smelter in Ghana. Kaiser and the consortium were willing to build the aluminium smelter only if the price of electricity was extremely low. Later the low price was criticised as exploitative but it had to be low enough to induce the aluminium producers to build the smelter in the first place. Without such an inducement, the smelter would not have been built.

It was also Eisenhower who authorised funding of the Volta River Project. When Ghana's finance minister, Komla Gbedemah – who, by the way, was once denied service at a Howard Johnson's restaurant in the state of Delaware in the United States together with his African American secretary because the restaurant did not serve blacks, an incident which made headlines around the world – met with Eisenhower and requested funding for the project. Eisenhower asked his vice president, Richard Nixon, to help arrange financing of the project. Gbedemah was the second most powerful man in Ghana after Nkrumah.

Yet, while the United States was doing all this, it was also busy trying to undermine Nkrumah at the same time and used the economic assistance it provided as a smokescreen to hide its real intentions towards him: which was to get him out of power.

A lot of this activity was directed from the American embassy in Ghana where the American ambassador played a critical role in fomenting trouble against Nkrumah. On 23 March 1964, Ambassador Mahoney sent another telegram to Washington, stating:

"I believe someone has to keep hammering him [Nkrumah]."

The assistant secretary of state, G. Mennen Williams, followed the advice of Ambassador of Mahoney and on 9 April 1964 wrote a memo to the under-secretary of state, Averill Harriman, stating that the American government should continue to exert pressure on Nkrumah to maintain his relations with the United States on a tolerable basis:

"The United States should] keep continuing pressure on [Nkrumah] to maintain his relations with the US on a tolerable basis... We shall consult with the British in the next few days to discuss what contribution they may be able to make in this area."

Almost by mid-March 1965, the plot against Nkrumah had reached critical stage. CIA Director John McCone held a meeting in his office on 11 March 1965 which was attended by Ambassador Mahoney and other high ranking officials to discuss what to do next.

The topic of discussion was "Coup d'etat Plot: Ghana."

Also at the meeting was the deputy chief of the Africa division at the CIA whose name was not declassified when the intelligence documents were released to the public in 1999.

According to what was discussed at that meeting, Ambassador Mahoney told CIA Director McCone that pressure exerted on Nkrumah by Western powers was working. He went on to say there was dissatisfaction with his leadership among many people in Ghana because of the deteriorating economic situation as a result of various measures taken by the United States, Britain, France and other Western countries to sabotage Ghana's economy and encourage his enemies to launch a coup.

But Mahoney was still not quite convinced that the coup that was being planned by Acting Police Commissioner John W.K. Harlley, General Ankrah who was chief of defence staff and his deputy Major-General Stephen J.A. Otu, would necessarily take place. But he was sure that Nkrumah would be overthrown within a year. As he bluntly put it:

"One way or another Nkrumah [will] be out within a year."

And he was.

When, at the meeting at the White House before the coup, McCone asked Mahoney who would succeed Nkrumah, Mahoney said a military junta would probably take over. He also made it clear that a coup d'etat was already "being planned by Acting Police Commissioner Harlley and Generals Otu and Ankrah."

Another person who attended the meeting was Robert W. Komer who had replaced George McBundy as President Johnson's adviser on national security. He was a veteran CIA officer and agreed with Mahoney's assessment of the situation in Ghana and said at the meeting:

"We may have a pro-Western coup in Ghana soon. Certain key military and police figures have been planning one for some time, and Ghana's deteriorating economic condition may provide the spark. The plotters are keeping us briefed, and State [Department] thinks we're more on the inside than the British.

While we're not directly involved, (I'm told) we and other Western countries (including France) have been helping to set up the situation by ignoring Nkrumah's pleas for economic aid. All in all, looks good."

In early January 1966, Ambassador Mahoney was recalled to Washington after he finished doing what he was supposed to do to prepare for the coup against Nkrumah. And President Johnson appointed Franklin Williams as the new American ambassador to Ghana just in time for the coup.

American officials felt that Nkrumah would trust him since he was his classmate at Lincoln University (the class of 1941), and was also a fellow black. Therefore he would not suspect him of being involved in any plot against him and would believe him if he told him that the CIA was not plotting to overthrow him. But Nkrumah knew better than that.

Within two months or so after Williams assumed his post as the American ambassador to Ghana, Nkrumah was overthrown. And he knew Williams was involved in the plot. His appointment as ambassador was perfect timing for him to oversee the execution of the coup against his former classmate and fellow African - American officials saw him as one, hence his appointment for him to work with his own kind but against them!

Nkrumah never forgave Williams for what he did to him and to Africa as a whole. In his book *Dark Days in Ghana*, Nkrumah said Ambassador Williams' treachery provided a sharp reminder of the insidious ways in which the enemies of Africa can operate.

Williams said he knew nothing about the coup and was not involved in it. Nkrumah did not believe him. As he said to his research assistant, June Milne, who also became a publisher of some of Nkrumah's works:

"It is extremely unlikely that Williams did not know what was going on in the embassy with CIA officers operating from there."

When Dr. Marvin Wachman was about to end his tenure as president of Lincoln University, he wrote Nkrumah on 21 July 1969 – Nkrumah was then living in exile in Conakry, Guinea – stating:

"As I prepare to leave, I would like to write a word on behalf of Franklin H. Williams of the Class of 1941... Mr Williams is a very bouncy and vigorous individual, and I have never seen him so crushed as he has been, concerning your feelings that he was involved in some way in the episodes in Ghana. He has assured me, personally, that he had no knowledge of the coup."

Ironically, Nkumah's assessment of CIA's involvement in his ouster and interference of external powers in African affairs also got support from an unlikely source, his political adversary Felix Houphouet Boigny, former president of the Ivory Coast, who said in an interview with the French magazine *Jeune Afrique*, 4 February 1981:

"Destablisation is not a new thing. Did you know why Idi Amin made his coup in 1972? It was not he who did it, but the British. He did not even know what he wanted himself.

It was the same in Ghana when the military overthrew Nkrumah. They [the Ghanaian coup makers] came to see me. I asked them why. They replied: 'All is not well any more.' 'Is that all?' [I asked them]. I also asked them what they were going to do; they did not know. People outside knew it for them."

Outsiders who were behind the *coup d'etat* did not even try to hide their feelings as they gleefully congratulated those who executed it and celebrated Nkrumah's downfall. As President Johnson's special assistant on national security, Robert W. Komer, stated in his message to the president concerning the coup:

"The coup in Ghana is another example of a fortuitous windfall. Nkrumah was doing more to undermine our interests than any other black African. In reaction to his strongly pro-Communist leanings, the new military regime [in Accra] is almost pathetically pro-Western."

It shows how much respect they had for their puppets in Ghana. It was pathetic how subservient the coup makers were to the West even according to the assessment of their masters, as Komer put it, describing them as "almost pathetically pro-Western."

Even their own intelligence officers, although years later, proudly talked about the role they played in overthrowing Nkrumah.

Howard Banes, the CIA station chief at the American embassy in Accra, Ghana, who masterminded and directed the entire operation – obviously with the full knowledge of the black American ambassador Franklin Williams – was awarded an Intelligence Star, and got double promotion, for his role in Nkrumah's downfall. As Paul Lee stated in "Documents Expose US Role in Nkrumah Overthrow":

"Declassified National Security Council and Central Intelligence Agency documents provide compelling, new evidence of United States government involvement in the 1966 overthrow of Ghanaian President Kwame Nkrumah.

The coup d'etat, organized by dissident army officers, toppled the Nkrumah government on Feb. 24, 1966 and was promptly hailed by Western governments, including the U.S.

The documents appear in a collection of diplomatic and intelligence memos, telegrams, and reports on Africa in Foreign Relations of the United States, the government's ongoing official history of American foreign policy.

Prepared by the State Department's Office of the Historian, the latest volumes reflect the overt diplomacy and covert actions of President Lyndon B. Johnson's administration from 1964-68. Though published in November 1999, what they reveal about U.S. complicity in the Ghana coup was only recently noted.

Allegations of American involvement in the *putsche* arose almost immediately because of the well-known hostility of the U.S. to Nkrumah's socialist orientation and pan-African activism.

Nkrumah, himself, implicated the U.S. in his overthrow, and warned other African nations about what he saw as an emerging pattern.

'An all-out offensive is being waged against the progressive, independent states,' he wrote in *Dark Days* in Ghana, his 1969 account of the Ghana coup. 'All that has been needed was a small force of disciplined men to seize the key points of the capital city and to arrest the existing political leadership.'

'It has been one of the tasks of the C.I.A. and other similar organisations,' he noted, 'to discover these potential quislings and traitors in our midst, and to encourage them, by bribery and the promise of political power, to destroy the constitutional government of their countries.'

A Spook's Story

While charges of U.S. involvement are not new, support for them was lacking until 1978, when anecdotal evidence was provided from an unlikely source – a former CIA case officer, John Stockwell, who reported first-hand testimony in his memoir, *In Search of Enemies: A CIA Story.*

'The inside story came to me,' Stockwell wrote, 'from an egotistical friend, who had been chief of the [CIA] station in Accra [Ghana] at the time.' (Stockwell was stationed one country away in the Ivory Coast.)

Subsequent investigations by *The New York Times* and *Covert Action Information Bulletin* identified the station chief as Howard T. Banes, who operated undercover as a political officer in the U.S. Embassy.

This is how the ouster of Nkrumah was handled as Stockwell related. The Accra station was encouraged by headquarters to maintain contact with dissidents of the Ghanaian army for the purpose of gathering intelligence on their activities. It was given a generous budget, and maintained intimate contact with the plotters as a coup was hatched. So close was the station's involvement that it was able to coordinate the recovery of some classified Soviet military equipment by the United States as the coup took place.

According to Stockwell, Banes' sense of initiative knew no bounds. The station even proposed to headquarters through back channels that a squad be on hand at the moment of the coup to storm the [Communist] Chinese embassy, kill everyone inside, steal their secret records, and blow up the building to cover the facts.

Though the proposal was quashed, inside the CIA headquarters the Accra station was given full, if unofficial credit for the eventual coup, in which eight Soviet advisors were killed. None of this was adequately reflected in the agency's records, Stockwell wrote.

Confirmation and Revelation

While the newly-released documents, written by a National Security Council staffer and unnamed CIA officers, confirm the essential outlines set forth by Nkrumah and Stockwell, they also provide additional, and chilling, details about what the U.S. government knew about the plot, when, and what it was prepared to do and did do to assist it.

On March 11, 1965, almost a year before the coup, William P. Mahoney, the U.S. ambassador to Ghana, participated in a candid discussion in Washington, D.C., with CIA Director John A. McCone and the deputy chief of the CIA's Africa division, whose name has been withheld.

Significantly, the Africa division was part of the CIA's directorate of plans, or dirty tricks component, through which the government pursued its covert policies.

According to the record of their meeting (Document 251), topic one was the 'Coup d'etat Plot, Ghana.' While Mahoney was satisfied that popular opinion was running strongly against Nkrumah and the economy of the country was in a precarious state, he was not convinced that the coup d'etat, now being planned by Acting Police Commissioner Harlley and Generals Otu and Ankrah, would necessarily take place.

Nevertheless, he confidently – and accurately, as it turned out – predicted that one way or another Nkrumah would be out within a year. Revealing the depth of embassy knowledge of the plot, Mahoney referred to a recent report which mentioned that the top coup conspirators were scheduled to meet on 10 March at which time they would determine the timing of the coup.

However, he warned, because of a tendency to procrastinate, any specific date they set should be accepted with reservations. In a reversal of what some would assume were the traditional roles of an ambassador and the CIA director, McCone asked Mahoney who would most likely succeed Nkrumah in the event of a coup.

Mahoney again correctly forecast the future: Ambassador Mahoney stated that initially, at least, a military junta would take over.

Making it Happen

But Mahoney was not a prophet. Rather, he represented the commitment of the U.S. government, in coordination with other Western governments, to bring about Nkrumah's downfall.

Firstly, Mahoney recommended denying Ghana's forthcoming aid request in the interests of further weakening Nkrumah. He felt that there was little chance that either the Chinese Communists or the Soviets would in adequate measure come to Nkrumah's financial rescue and the British would continue to adopt a hard nose attitude toward providing further assistance to Ghana.

At the same time, it appears that Mahoney encouraged Nkrumah in the mistaken belief that both the U.S. and the U.K. would come to his financial rescue and proposed maintaining current U.S. aid levels and programs because they will endure and be remembered long after Nkrumah goes.

Secondly, Mahoney seems to have assumed the responsibility of increasing the pressure on Nkrumah and exploiting the probable results. This can be seen in his 50-minute meeting with Nkrumah three weeks later.

According to Mahoney's account of their April 2 discussion (Document 252), 'at one point Nkrumah, who had been holding face in hands, looked up and I saw he was crying. With difficulty he said I could not understand the ordeal he had been through during last month. Recalling that there had been seven attempts on his life.'

Mahoney did not attempt to discourage Nkrumah's fears, nor did he characterize them as unfounded in his report to his superiors.

'While Nkrumah apparently continues to have personal affection for me,' he noted, 'he seems as convinced as ever that the US is out to get him. From what he said about assassination attempts in March, it appears he still suspects US involvement.'

Of course, the U.S. was out to get him. Moreover, Nkrumah was keenly aware of a recent African precedent that made the notion of a U.S.-organized or sanctioned assassination plot plausible – namely, the fate of the Congo and its first prime minister, his friend Patrice Lumumba.

Nkrumah believed that the destabilization of the Congolese government in 1960 and Lumumba's assassination in 1961 were the work of the 'Invisible Government of the U.S.,' as he wrote in *Neocolonialism: The Last Stage of Imperialism*, later in 1965.

When Lumumba's murder was announced, Nkrumah told students at the inauguration of an ideological institute that bore his name that this brutal murder should teach them the diabolical depths of degradation to which these twin-monsters of imperialism and colonialism can descend.

In his conclusion, Mahoney observed: 'Nkrumah gave me the impression of being a badly frightened man. His emotional resources seem be running out. As pressures increase, we may expect more hysterical outbursts, many directed against US.'

It was not necessary to add that he was helping to apply the pressure, nor that any hysterical outbursts by Nkrumah played into the West's projection of him as an unstable dictator, thus justifying his removal.

Smoking Gun

On May 27, 1965, Robert W. Komer, a National Security Council staffer, briefed his boss, McGeorge Bundy, President Johnson's special assistant for national security affairs, on the anti-Nkrumah campaign (Document 253).

Komer, who first joined the White House as a member of President Kennedy's NSC staff, had worked as a CIA analyst for 15 years. In 1967, Johnson tapped him to head his hearts-and-minds pacification program in Vietnam.

Komer's report establishes that the effort was not only interagency, sanctioned by the White House and supervised by the State Department and CIA, but also intergovernmental, being supported by America's Western allies.

'FYI,' he advised, 'we may have a pro-Western coup in Ghana soon. Certain key military and police figures have been planning one for some time, and Ghana's deteriorating economic condition may provide the spark.'

'The plotters are keeping us briefed,' he noted, 'and the State Department thinks we're more on the inside than the British. While we're not directly involved (I'm told), we and other Western countries (including France) have been helping to set up the situation by ignoring Nkrumah's pleas for economic aid. All in all, it looks good.'

Komer's reference to not being told if the U.S. was directly involved in the coup plot is revealing and quite likely a wry nod to his CIA past.

Among the most deeply ingrained aspects of intelligence tradecraft and culture is plausible deniability, the habit of mind and practice designed to insulate the U.S., and particularly the president, from responsibility for particularly sensitive covert operations.

Komer would have known that orders such as the overthrow of Nkrumah would have been communicated in a deliberately vague, opaque, allusive, and indirect fashion, as Thomas Powers noted in *The Man Who Kept the Secrets: Richard Helms and the CIA.*

It would be unreasonable to argue that the U.S. was not directly involved when it created or exacerbated the conditions that favored a coup, and did so for the express purpose of bringing one about.

Truth and Consequences

As it turned out, the coup did not occur for another nine months. After it did, Komer, now acting special assistant for national security affairs, wrote a congratulatory assessment to the President on March 12, 1966 (Document 260). His assessment of Nkrumah and his successors was telling.

'The coup in Ghana,' he crowed, 'is another example of a fortuitous windfall. Nkrumah was doing more to undermine our interests than any other black African. In reaction to his strongly pro-Communist leanings, the new military regime is almost pathetically pro-Western.'

In this, Komer and Nkrumah were in agreement. 'Where the more subtle methods of economic pressure and political subversion have failed to achieve the desired result,' Nkrumah wrote from exile in Guinea three years later, 'there has been resort to violence in order to promote a change of regime and prepare the way for the establishment of a puppet government.'"

Attempts were made by some military officers to reinstate Nkrumah. The first casualty in one of those attempts was Lieutenant-General Emmanuel Kwasi Kotoka, chief of the defence staff, who – together with Akwasi Amankwaa Afrifa – led the coup against Dr. Nkrumah; it was also Kotoka who announced on the radio that Nkrumah had been overthrown and the armed forces had taken over the government.

Kotoka was killed on 17 April 1967 in an abortive counter-coup masterminded by Lieutenant Samuel Arthur who together with two of his colleagues, Lieutenant Moses Yeboah and Second-Lieutenant Osei-Poku, wanted to return Nkrumah to power. The attempted counter-coup was code-named Operation Guitar Boy.

Lieutenant Arthur and Lieutenant Yeboah were tried by a six-man military tribunal and sentenced to death by firing squad, while Second-Lieutenant Osei-Poku received a 30-year prison sentence. Arthur and Yeboah were executed on 26 May 1967 before a crowd of about 20,000 people in the nation's capital Accra.

The ouster of Nkrumah was one of the most tragic events in the history of post-colonial Africa.

Nkrumah was the strongest proponent of immediate continental unification, a stand which put him in a class almost by himself.

He was also, together with leaders such as Nyerere, Sekou Toure, Modibo Keita, Obote and Kaunda one of the strongest supporters of African unity and of the African liberation movements and an uncompromising opponent of interference in African affairs by world powers and other external forces. And that made him an enemy of the West.

He became prime target for the CIA and other Western intelligence services including Britain's MI6. As he himself stated in *Dark Days in Ghana*:

"In Ghana, the embassies of the United States, Britain, and West Germany were all implicated in the plot to overthrow my government.

It is alleged that U.S. Ambassador Franklin Williams, offered the traitors 13 million dollars to carry out a *coup d'état*. Afrifa, Harlley and Kotoka were to get a large share if they would assassinate me at Accra airport as I prepared to leave for Hanoi.

I understand Afrifa said: 'I think I will fail,' and

101

declined the offer. So apparently did the others." – (Kwame Nkrumah, *Dark Days in Ghana*, London: Panaf Books, 1968, p. 49. See also *Black World/Negro Digest*, Chicago, Johnson Publishing Company, May 1969, pp. 71 – 72).

Nkrumah was the most prominent African leader who was ousted in a military coup in the sixties. Nyerere and Sekou Toure survived. The United States and other Western powers were disappointed that the two leaders had not been removed from office in military coups which came to characterise transfer of power across the continent during that turbulent decade.

Even years before the coup that ousted him from office, Nkrumah was not trusted by the Americans. They were also concerned about his ideological orientation which they felt would threaten the interests of the United States on the African continent.

American leaders, CIA agents and State Department officials including ambassadors who dealt with Africa were also arrogant and racist, clearly demonstrated by their attitude towards Nkrumah, Nyerere and Sekou Toure, leaders they did not like.

Their condescending attitude towards these leaders and Africans in general, and the disparaging remarks they made about them, obviously played a major role in the formulation of American policy towards Africa.

Americans did not consider Africans to be their equal intellectually and in terms of sophistication; an assessment that can not be reconciled with reality in the case of highly intellectual and knowledgeable leaders such as Nyerere and Nkrumah and can be nothing other than a product of racial arrogance on the part of Americans and other Westerners who had very low regard for Africans in general.

Besides President Lyndon Johnson who was in office when Nkrumah was overthrown, his predecessor, John F.

Kennedy, was also suspicious of Nkrumah as someone who was taking Africa in the wrong direction. Compounding the problem for Nkrumah was the fact that most African leaders did not like him. They were concerned about his subversive activities in their countries. He supported dissidents from a number of countries across the continent who wanted to overthrow their home governments. Nkrumah's critics also felt that he was megalomaniac and wanted to rule Africa. As Professor Larry Grubbs of Georgia State University states in his book, *Secular Missionaries: Americans and African Development in the 1960s*:

"If Africans lacked emotional stability and maturity, their passionate attachment to novel concepts and ideologies, or political causes such as the liberation of Southern Africa from colonialism and apartheid, need not be seriously engaged at an intellectual level. One scholar noted that 'the emergence of African states has not been universally received with respect for the integrity of Africans,' as Westerners at times dismiss African nationalism 'as little more than grotesque comedy.'[51]

U.S. Intelligence analysts considered Pan-Africanism 'a mystical concept, glorifying racial kinship and the African personality and culture' whose 'chief target is 'neocolonialism'[52]....

When asked by President Kennedy if Nkrumah was a 'Marxist,' Ambassador William Mahoney declared Ghana's leader 'a badly confused and immature person who is not quite sure of what he wants except that he wants to lead all of Africa.'[54]

African critics, too, questioned Nkrumah's sanity, often to flatter Americans. Senghor told Kennedy that the Ghanaian leader 'required the attentions of a psychiatrist' to cure him of his stupendous dreams of leading Africa and his absence of principles.[55]

As for Guinea's nationalist leader, Sékou Touré,

American observers repeatedly belittled his economic decisions, and a Central Intelligence Agency report insisted he lacked 'any grasp of the economy and how it functions, even less of development and how it is achieved.'

While his long rule over Guinea certainly failed to produce great economic growth, Touré did devote three books of over 1,000 pages to discussion of socialism and development." – (Larry Grubbs, *Secular Missionaries: Americans and African Development in the 1960s*, University of Massachusetts Press, 2009, pp. 155, and 156).

Grubbs goes on state:

"The main American concerns seemed to have less to do with the credentials of the African leaders than the ideology they espoused or specific policy disagreements.[56] U.S. Officials believed it would be difficult to speak with Touré about details of the aid he had received from the Communist Bloc not only because of his secretiveness but also because, as a White House aide put it, 'apparently Touré himself is totally ignorant about foreign assistance to Guinea, whether it be Bloc or non-Bloc – he simply does not and will not understand it.'[57]

Attwood's successor in Conakry reported 'Touré's unhappiness over the US aid program in Guinea,' though he claimed 'that the issue is being resolved' and that 'the major problem...is educating Touré' on how U.S. aid works.[58]

Julius Nyerere, according to an American diplomat in Tanganyika, though a good political leader, had proven a 'poor administrator' who 'has no head for complex economic development programs.'[59] By the mid-1960s the CIA regarded him as 'enigmatic.'

At a time when Tanzania courted Communist China's support for the construction of a railroad that would permit

Zambia to transport goods without going through white-ruled Rhodesia, Nyerere became increasingly less identified with the West. CIA analysts sneered at his 'newly-found mission as the prime mover in the 'liberation' of southern Africa,' as well as his efforts to help Congolese rebels gain access to 'Communist arms' in their struggle against the American-backed regime.

The United States provided a small $6 million annual aid program, and 'the Peace Corps largely staffs Tanganyikan secondary schools,' yet Nyerere complained the volunteers spread anti-government propaganda.

Speculating that he now believed the Americans would not help him fight colonialism and apartheid, 'and that Communist China represents the wave of the future,' CIA analysts predicted that, under his 'weak and ineffectual leadership,' radicals and Communists would grow increasingly influential. Rather than stop there and chalk up Nyerere's views and behavior to a political or ideological conflict, the CIA report groped for ways to neutralize his intransigence.....

When Nyerere responded to the U.S. airlift in the Congo by writing to President Johnson, the U.S. Ambassador called the letter a product of 'emotionalism, suspicions, and fear,' rather than the understandable concerned reaction of an African nationalist. Unable to understand him as anything other than a typically emotional African, the United States came to hold the view that 'under the mercurial and fiercely independent leadership of Nyerere, Tanzania is the bastion of radicalism in East Africa'[61]....

Americans' only real regret about the wave of African coups was that Sékou Touré and Julius Nyerere were not among its victims....

A State Department review of CIA activities noted that, in the Congo, the agency had covertly helped Adoula and Tshombe 'to buy the support of political and military leaders.'" – (Ibid., pp. 156, and 157).

Nyerere himself knew that the Americans tried to undermine him. As he stated in June 1966:

"We have twice quarrelled with the US Government; once when we believed it to be involved in a plot against us, and again when two of its officials misbehaved and were asked to leave Tanzania." – (Julius Nyerere, "Principles and Development," in Julius K. Nyerere, *Freedom and Socialism: A Selection from Writings and Speeches 1965 - 1967*, Oxford University Press, Dar es Salaam, Tanzania, 1968, pp. 202 – 203).

The U.S. State Department even wanted the United States to provide arms to some people in Tanzania who wanted to overthrow Nyerere. The Secretary of State during that time was Dean Rusk who was first appointed by President John F. Kennedy and who continued to serve in the same capacity under Lyndon Johnson. As John Prados states in his book, *Safe for Democracy: The Secret Wars of the CIA*:

"The Special Group (at the CIA) reportedly considered a State Department proposal to supply arms to certain groups in Tanzania, where secret-war wizards saw President Julius Nyerere as a problem, in the summer of 1964....Like Nyerere, Washington viewed Ghana's leader Kwame Nkrumah as a troublemaker." – (John Prados, *Safe for Democracy: The Secret Wars of the CIA*, Ivan R. Dee, Publisher, Chicago, Illinois, USA, 2006, p. 328).

The assessment of African leaders by the CIA, American ambassadors and other American leaders was not realistic. And it was clearly biased, a product of preconceived notions and expectations by Americans of what African leaders should be. In many cases, they grossly underestimated them; for example, Nyerere's commitment to African liberation. As Professor Piero Gleijeses of Johns Hopkins University states in his book, *Conflicting Missions: Havana, Washington, and Africa, 1959 – 1976*:

"Of all the African leaders who proclaimed their support for the liberation struggle in Africa – Nkrumah, Nasser, Ben Bella, Sekou Toure – he (Nyerere) was the most committed. And by the second half of 1964, spurred by events in Zaire and the obvious failure of peaceful attempts to end white rule in southern Africa, this commitment, and his a disappointment with the Western powers, was increasingly evident.

By the time Che arrived (in 1965), Dar es Salaam had become the Mecca of African liberation movements....Dar es Salaam 'has become a haven for exiles from the rest of Africa,' the CIA lamented in September 1964. 'It is full of frustrated revolutionaries, plotting the overthrow of African governments, both black and white'....

In September 1964, Frelimo, the movement against Portuguese rule in Mozambique, had launched the opening salvo of its guerrilla war from bases in southern Tanzania, its only rear guard.

Following Stanleyville, Nyerere had thrown his full support to the Simbas, and Tanzania had become their main rear guard and the major conduit of Soviet and Chinese weapons for them.

It was also the seat of the Liberation Committee of the OAU. The head offices of Frelimo and a host of other movements struggling against the white regimes in South Africa, Namibia, and Rhodesia were in Dar es Salaam.

The Cuban embassy there was, the CIA reported accurately in March 1965, 'the largest Cuban diplomatic station in sub-Saharan Africa.' The ambassador, Captain Pablo Ribalta, was a close friend of Che Guevara.

In early 1964 Ribalta had been the commander of the Libertad air force base near Havana. 'One day,' he told me,

'Che arrived and said, 'Listen, Fidel wants to send you to Tanzania.' He told me I had to establish good relations with the liberation movements there. So they sent me to the Foreign Ministry to learn about Africa, and especially about Tanzania.'

Ribalta arrived in Tanzania on February 25, 1964, with four trusted aides from Libertad...." – (Piero Gleijeses, *Conflicting Missions: Havana, Washington, and Africa, 1959 – 1976*, The University of North Carolina Press, 2002, pp. 84 and 85).

Sometimes even when American diplomats and CIA agents are right on the spot where they make assessments of African leaders and conditions prevailing in a given country, they are dead wrong in their assessments and reports although they have ample time and enough resources, and access to sources they can use to verify and support their conclusions.

One typical example involved Tanzania's First Lady, Salma Kikwete, the wife of President Jakaya Kikwete. Shabyna Stillman, a senior diplomat at the American embassy in Dar es Salaam, Tanzania, wrote in a confidential cable to Washington on Thursday, 5 May 2005, stating that Salma Kikwete was a cousin of the late Rwandan president, Juvenal Habyarimana, without verifying the information although there were numerous people in Dar es Salaam she could have contacted to verify that.

The diplomat was dead wrong. Salma Kikwete came from Lindi in southern Tanzania and was not a Hutu. She was a member of an ethnic group, Ndengereko, indigenous to that part of Tanzania. As Stillman stated:

"For years, observers of the Great Lakes conflicts have considered Kikwete to be virulently pro-Hutu. Rumors that he was facilitating arms transfers to Burundian Hutu rebels (when he was minister of foreign affairs) persisted, but have never been substantiated. Kikwete's marriage to a cousin of former Rwandan President Juvénal Habyarimana may have fueled these rumors." – (Shabyna Stillman in CONFIDENTIAL SECTION 01 OF 02 DAR ES SALAAM 000888 SIPDIS DEPARTMENT FOR AF/E E.O. 12958: 5/5/15 TAGS: PGOV TZ. SUBJECT: It's Kikwete: the CCM Party Chooses a Presidential Candidate. The cable was released by Wikilleaks.org/cable/2005/05/05DARESSALAAM888.html).

The report that Salma Kikwete was a cousin of the late Rwanda president, Habyarimana, was probably a product of propaganda by the Rwandan government under President Paul Kagame which was at war with Hutu extremists and which perceived Kikwete, rightly or wrongly, to be pro-Hutu when he was Tanzania's minister of foreign affairs and probably thought he would continue to be that way when elected president of Tanzania.

The cable by the American embassy was an update of the political situation in Tanzania during the selection of the presidential candidate for the ruling Chama Cha Mapinduzi (CCM) which, in Kiswahili, means the Party of the Revolution or the Revolutionary Party.

Just as the Americans were wrong about Salma Kikwete being a cousin of Habyarimana, they were equally wrong in their assessment of a number of African leaders in the sixties. They grossly underrated them and made disparaging remarks about them which did not correspond to reality; for example doubting or questioning the leadership qualities of Nkrumah, Nyerere, and Sekou Toure.

They even doubted Nyerere was a strong nationalist leader. Yet his stature as an ardent nationalist and Pan-Africanist has been vindicated by history; so has Nkrumah's and Sekou Toure's.

Like Nkrumah and Sekou Toure, Nyerere was also

underestimated as a leader capable of understanding complex issues of development.

Simply because these leaders pursued policies Americans did not like and sought solutions – to African problems – which did not reflect American thinking does not mean they did not understand the nature of underdevelopment and what needed to be done; nor does it mean they did not understand complex issues of global significance including Cold War rivalry which had direct impact on the African continent itself, tragically demonstrated by the Congo crisis in the bleeding heart of Africa.

They may not have been trained economists, and they may not have had a full grasp of abstract economic concepts, but they understood the nature of underdevelopment and the problems their countries faced in the quest for development. As Professor Gerry Helleiner of the University of Toronto stated in "The Legacies of Julius Nyerere: An Economist's Reflections":

"I spent some of the best years of my life working in Dar es Salaam in the late 1960s when Mwalimu Julius Nyerere was its inspiring young President.

In later years, I worked for shorter periods in Tanzania – under each of its Presidents – and had many occasions to reflect on the longer-term role that Nyerere played in his own country. Internationally, too, I have frequently had the honour and privilege of working in Mwalimu's ambit, most notably through the South Commission and the South Centre.

I believe I may be the only economist to speak at this conference. (In fact, it is quite possible that I am the only economist in attendance.) Much of the economics profession has taken rather a dim view of the legacy of Julius Nyerere. (I won't dignify with quotation or repetition some of the things I have heard said about him in the World Bank.)

It is precisely *because* I am an economist – and Mwalimu so evidently was not – that I want to put my profound admiration of his record and his legacy on the record.

It is undoubtedly in the field of economics that Julius Nyerere has received his worst press, and in which his legacy has been seen as most negative. The heading for his obituary in the (London) *Financial Times* read 'Man of integrity whose policies hurt his country.' That in *The Economist*, while generally friendly, concluded: 'He was a magnificent teacher: articulate, questioning, stimulating, caring. He should never have been given charge of an economy.'

Personally, I see his legacy in the realm of economic and development policy rather differently.

Mwalimu's grasp of the traditional tenets of economic theory was probably weak and so was that of his closest advisors and speechwriters (although there were those within government of whom this could certainly not be said).

Most of the criticism coming from economists relates to his 'socialist' policies. But his government's most damaging economic policy errors, in my view, had little to do with socialism *per se*. They came relatively late in his Presidency and were on the relatively non-ideological issue of exchange rate policy; they were errors shared by many other low-income countries in the early 1980s.

As for his "socialism", some elements can be faulted as far more serious in their negative economic consequences than others. Nationalizations and restrictions on competition (including price controls) in the trading, industrial, agricultural and financial sectors were far beyond governmental management capacities and proved costly. Widespread (and even forced) 'villagization' in the rural sector was not only economically costly but also deeply unpopular.

The 'basic industry' policy – to the extent that it was

part of Nyerere's 'socialism' – was also mistaken in that it was premature and inappropriate for so economically small a country; it too proved costly.

All of these 'socialist' policies could be foreseen (and were) as likely to slow overall economic growth and development both immediately and over the longer run. (My personal anxieties in this regard, circa 1969-70, may be found in an article in the *Journal of Development Studies*, Vol. 8, no. 1, January, 1972.) Arguably, none seemed likely, of themselves, however, to create the degree of economic collapse that occurred in the early 1980s. Nor, in my view, did they. Severe macroeconomic shocks – oil prices, weather, and war against Amin – and their serious domestic mismanagement were required for that.

In the early 1980s, as the UK White Paper on international development put it in its commentary on African experience, the 'worldwide international climate ... left little margin for policy errors' (*Eliminating World Poverty: A Challenge for the 21st Century, White Paper on International Development*, November 1997, p. 9).

In Tanzania, there undoubtedly were such policy errors. Again, my view is that Tanzania's economic dislocations in the early 1980s were only partially attributable to its efforts to restructure the economy towards socialism. Far more serious were the errors in macroeconomic policy in the face of severe shocks (as well as, of course, the shocks themselves).

It is important for critical economists (and others) to recall that there were other elements in Nyerere's socialist programme – increased equity in the distribution of income; an attempt at a direct assault on bottom-end poverty (including provision of primary education and clean water); a 'leadership code' for politicians and civil servants; major reform of the educational syllabus; and (at least rhetorical) emphasis on self-reliance and reduced aid dependence.

112

These elements of Nyerere's 'socialist' programme excited widespread admiration and support (ultimately too much support of an unhelpful kind) from many academics and policymakers in the capitalist West, particularly in the Nordic countries and the Presidency of the World Bank. So compelling was this side of his socialist aspirations and practice that, for some time, admirers were prepared to give Tanzania the benefit of the doubt on the less propitious elements of its 'socialist' development policy and its economic sustainability.

Sadly, as Tanzania's resource constraints tightened and macroeconomic policies faltered in the late 1970s and early 1980s most of these supporters lost confidence in the overall Nyerere socialist vision. Their withdrawal of financial support then worsened what had already become a crisis situation.

The first serious external pressures upon the Government of Tanzania to reform its economic policies were related primarily to its macroeconomic management policies, *not* to its socialism, and they came, of course, from the IMF. According to the IMF tenets of the times, what Tanzania most required in the late 1970s and early 1980s was across-the-board governmental austerity and severe currency devaluation.

It was the effort at imposition of such IMF conditionality that prompted Nyerere's famous public outburst (in 1981): 'Who elected the IMF to be the Finance Ministry for every country in the world?' (or words to that effect).

There followed an almost total breakdown in Tanzania-IMF relations. Julius Nyerere may be said to have fired the first African salvo in the great debate over the role of the IMF in Africa. (By a quirk of chance, it was at about the same time, 1980 that the annual meetings of the IMF were to be chaired by Amir Jamal, Tanzania's then Minister of Finance. I remember his recounting his surprise when, upon his arrival in Washington for the meetings, IMF staff presented him with a draft of his introductory remarks. He thanked them for their thoughtfulness he delighted in recalling, but told them he had brought his own speech.)

At this point (1980-81), Nyerere and Tanzania were still sufficiently respected that the then-President of the World Bank, Robert McNamara, initiated a mediation effort to seek an accommodation between the IMF and the Tanzanians. This was to be attempted through the provision of technical assistance for the preparation, in Tanzania, of an alternative to the IMF's stabilization and structural adjustment plan; the Government of Tanzania was given a voice (and indeed veto power) over the composition of the three-person team which was given the ultimate responsibility for the task.

With both expatriate and local staff working together in Dar es Salaam for a year, an alternative structural adjustment programme was tortuously constructed. Anticipating later African debates, it called for much greater emphasis upon supply-side expansion than demand-side restraint; much greater care over the distributional effects of required macroeconomic adjustment (with conscious effort to maintain equity of sacrifice); and a more gradual programme for the implementation of reforms.

The effort failed, however, when neither the Government of Tanzania nor the IMF found the programme satisfactory. (This is probably the appropriate point to recount another anecdote, one of my favourite Mwalimu stories.

Upon personally welcoming the agreed three-person team to Tanzania as it embarked on its task, the President followed his initial niceties to the group, each of whom he knew, with the prescient introductory substantive comment: 'You know, gentlemen, I asked for money, not advice!' A more succinct statement of the problem of conditionality has probably never been made.)

A major 'sticking point' in the failure to agree on what

114

was, for its time, a highly innovative programme (as well as a potentially important model for IMF-member country dispute resolution), though not the only one, was the Government's (mistaken) reluctance sufficiently to devalue its currency. I am personally convinced that, like so many laymen, Mwalimu did not understand the role of the exchange rate; some (not all) of his advisors gave him very bad advice.

As the Government went ahead on its own more and more donors (including now the World Bank) lost faith in Tanzanian macroeconomic management, the economy spiralled further downward, corruption grew, and all-around confidence in the entire Nyerere vision was lost.

The advent of Reagan-Thatcher influences on economic policy throughout the world and in the Bretton Woods institutions (McNamara left the World Bank in 1981) furthered darkened external views of the Tanzanian situation.

The necessary policy turnaround – now in much more dire economic circumstances, and with both much more external policy leverage and, significantly, a degree of non-governmental (mainly university) technical influence – finally began in 1986, *after* Nyerere's departure.

When the turnaround came, except for exchange rate action, which, by its nature, had to come more swiftly (in effect, it began with the 'own funds' import programme in 1984), it came fairly *gradually* and slowly. By the mid-1990s, the economy had significantly recovered and donors had returned. Remarkably, political stability had been a constant.

By this time, however, Tanzania was in trouble over other issues. Corruption had reached the highest levels of the Government and party (attracting public criticism from, among others, the now-retired Mwalimu, who now also supported competitive elections in a multi-party system); the central economic policymaking machinery was demoralized and in disarray; and, partly in consequence, aid donors were almost totally 'driving' such development efforts as were under way (outside the private sector).

Economic growth was taking place but there was a notable absence of any public 'vision,' such as had characterized the Nyerere years, as to where the country was going and why. Economic policy was seen as dictated by the international financial institutions and the aid donors. (For an account, see the Helleiner Report, *Report of the Group of Independent Advisers on Development Cooperation Issues Between Tanzania and Its Aid Donors*, Gerald K. Helleiner, Tony Killick, Nguyuru Lipumba, Benno J. Ndulu and Knud Erik Svendsen, Royal Danish Ministry of Foreign Affairs, June 1995.)

The Government of Benjamin Mkapa, newly elected in 1995, set out with the encouragement of some of the major aid donors, to restore ownership of its own development programmes, fight corruption, and recreate a sense of vision of the country's direction.

While much remains to be done, to a remarkable degree, it seems to me, it has been succeeding. It reached an important agreement, in principle, with the aid donor community on appropriate aid relationships – and, again, while much remains to be done, there can be no doubt that ownership of economic policy and programmes is returning to Tanzania.

The Government has prepared its own policy framework paper (PFP) and its own long-term vision statement (both with non-governmental inputs), led its own public expenditure review (PER) and the new Tanzania Assistance Strategy (TAS), and will now develop its own Poverty Reduction Strategy Paper (PRSP). Increasing (though still too small) proportions of aid expenditure are flowing through (or at least reported in) the national budget as the central economic administration strengthens.

Tanzanian-led sectoral strategies and policies are being

developed and implemented in health, roads and education. Prime emphasis throughout these efforts is to address the principal problems of poverty and to do so under Tanzanian, not donor, leadership. (More details on all this can be found in a paper prepared for the May 1999 meeting of the Consultative Group for Tanzania: Gerry Helleiner, "Changing Aid Relationships in Tanzania, December 1997 through March 1999", Dar es Salaam, mimeo, 1999.)

One senior (and informed) World Bank official has remarked (to me privately) that, despite all the favourable press on Uganda, Tanzania is actually about four years or more ahead of it in terms of truly nationally-owned (and thus sustainable) economic policy for overall development. Tanzania may seem to move more slowly, he noted (and I agree), but it does so on a firmer and more stable base.

This base was established, I would argue, in the time of Julius Nyerere – a politically unified country; shared values as to equity in income distribution and political participation; and determination to develop and implement one's own policies and programmes.

Because Tanzania now has in place all of the key elements for sustained development – macroeconomic stability; broadly sensible incentive structures; broad political participation and stability; growing national self-confidence, ownership and capacity – I believe it is likely that, barring calamities of weather or the terms of trade, Tanzania will soon be everyone's favourite African 'success story' (and model).

It is now 'conventional wisdom' in Washington (even in the IMF, at least in terms of its rhetoric) and in donor capitals that poverty needs to be addressed as a matter of highest priority; that political stability and good governance (notably reduced corruption) are prerequisites for development; and that national ownership of programmes is critical to their success.

It has taken them a long time to reach these positions. But Julius Nyerere was espousing them and trying to build practice upon them 30 years ago. His slogan of 'socialism and self-reliance,' if transmitted today as 'equity, honesty and ownership,' would win universal assent. He was decades ahead of his time in these matters.

Today's key Tanzanian policymakers – both politicians and technocrats – grew up and were educated in the Nyerere years. They have undoubtedly learned from earlier economic and other policy mistakes. (Mwalimu was himself a learner and pragmatist, who often changed policy positions when the evidence as to the failure of previous approaches seemed clear.)

I believe that the respect, which Mwalimu enjoyed in his own country right up until his death indicates that they also retained much that Mwalimu had taught. They now can build 'humane governance' on the political and value base he constructed. (The apt concept of 'humane governance' has recently been developed to encompass sound and equitable economic *and* political governance, including responsive and participatory institutions, respect for human rights, and special provision for the most needy and most vulnerable. See *Human Development in South Asia, 1999*, Mahbub ul Haq, The Human Development Centre and Oxford University Press, Pakistan, 1999.)

Whatever his other mistakes in the realm of economics, in one area of economic policy Mwalimu was dead right – and, again, ahead of his time.

Both in his anguished cry about the IMF in 1981 and in his subsequent work in the South Commission and the South Centre, he steadily maintained the need for fairer international (or global) systems of economic governance, particularly in the financial sphere.

It is important to underline his consistent emphasis upon *equity* in global economic governance arrangements because there is every sign that current reform efforts in the international financial arena are overly focussed upon efficiency considerations and the avoidance or minimization of the effects of systemic crises.

This focus has resulted in some effort to incorporate some of the interests and concerns of the newly emerging countries and the largest of the poor countries and this certainly constitutes important progress in global economic and financial governance; but it leaves out the poorest and weakest. The latter are unrepresented - either in the new Financial Stability Forum or in the even newer Group of Twenty (G20), chaired by the Canadian Finance Minister. (The G20 has also contrived to exclude all of the so-called "like-minded" countries, who might be expected to take a deeper interest in the problems of the poorest countries and peoples, as they have done in the past on debt relief and other issues.)

Nyerere's activities in the international/global sphere included efforts to bolster analysis, both economic and political, to inform those who speak for the developing countries, especially the poorest among them, in international negotiations and organizations. The developing countries are still woefully weakly equipped to deal with the batteries of well-funded economists, lawyers and lobbyists who defend Northern interests in international discussions and the media.

He was among those who saw, far ahead of others, that there is ultimately no substitute for one's own technical, professional and institutional strength. Today it is known as 'capacity building,' and it has entered 'conventional wisdom' as to what is to be done not only in Africa but throughout the developing world.

Yes, Julius Nyerere made some economic policy mistakes. In this he was certainly not alone. He also left a country capable of learning from its experience with a minimum of political ruckus, a country now moving forward economically on a firm political and value base. That is a significant legacy.

At the international level the fruits of his efforts are

probably more distant. I expect, however, that one day they too will come." – (Gerry Helleiner, "The Legacies of Julius Nyerere: An Economist's Reflections," University of Toronto, 2000. See also Gerry Helleiner in Godfrey Mwakikagile, *Tanzania under Mwalimu Nyerere: Reflections on an African Statesman*, New Africa Press, 2006, pp. 199 – 207).

As Nyerere was grappling with economic problems, he also faced another major problem, probably the biggest threat to his government since independence.

In October 1969, a coup attempt masterminded by Tanzania's former minister of foreign affairs, Oscar Kambona, who also had been one of Nyerere's closest colleagues, was foiled by the nation's intelligence service. As I state in one of my books, *Nyerere and Africa: End of an Era*:

"In spite of his immense popularity, President Nyerere was not immune from subversion. He became a target of a number of attempts, from within and without, to oust him from power. There were also many attempts to destabilize and weaken his government which his enemies and detractors hoped would eventually lead to his downfall.

He was fiercely independent, a stance that rankled Western powers as he went on to forge links with Eastern-bloc countries including the People's Republic of China and the Soviet Union, but especially with China, while maintaining ties with the West in pursuit of his policy of non-alignment. And his strong support for the African liberation movements was not endorsed by Western powers which wanted to perpetuate white minority rule in Africa for hegemonic control of the continent by the West.

So, Western powers wanted him out. Apartheid South Africa and other white minority regimes on the continent including Rhodesia and the Portuguese colonial governments - hence their mother country Portugal – also wanted him out. They did everything they could, including infiltrating and bombing Tanzania, to destabilize his government. One of the attempts to undermine his government involved the United States in the mid-sixties. As Nyerere himself stated in June 1966:

'We have twice quarrelled with the US Government, once when we believed it to be involved in a plot against us, and again when two of its officials misbehaved and were asked to leave Tanzania....The disagreements certainly induced an uncooperative coldness between us.'

Dr. Kwame Nkrumah, in his book *Dark Days in Ghana*, also discusses attempts by the CIA and the American government to undermine and overthrow Nyerere. He himself was ousted from power in a coup engineered and masterminded by the CIA in February 1966.

The most dramatic attempt to overthrow Nyerere came to public attention in October 1969 when the accused conspirators were brought to court in Tanzania's most celebrated treason trial. There was another treason trial in 1983. But it was not as dramatic as the other one mainly because of the people involved, although the plot in 1982 to overthrow the government led to the arrest of 600 soldiers and about 1,000 civilians in January 1983 for their alleged involvement in and support of the coup attempt.

The 1969 treason case involved some of Tanzania's most prominent politicians, including luminaries in the independence movement and two former cabinet members. The leader of the treasonous coterie was Oscar Kambona, Tanzania's former minister of foreign affairs who earlier had also served as minister of home affairs and then as minister of defence. He was also one of the country's three most influential and powerful leaders, together with President Nyerere himself and Vice President Rashidi Kawawa, who spearheaded the independence movement in Tanganyika; Kawawa was vice president of Tanganyika until April 1964 when he became second vice president after Tanganyika united with Zanzibar, and the president of Zanzibar, Abeid Karume, became first vice president.

In July 1967, Kambona left Tanzania and went into self-imposed exile in London, Britain. He continued to exercise some influence on his supporters in Tanzania, disgruntled with Nyerere's socialist policies and one-party rule, but gradually faded into obscurity as a "potent" force on the nation's political scene. His opposition to Nyerere's leadership and socialist policies reached a dramatic point towards the end of January in Arusha just before the adoption of the famous Arusha Declaration which became Tanzania's economic blueprint and political manifesto, covering all aspects of national life across the spectrum including foreign affairs and the liberation of Africa from colonialism and imperialism.

At the centre of the socialist transformation of Tanzania was the establishment of ujamaa villages (*ujamaa* means familyhood in Kiswahili or Swahili). It was a massive exercise in social engineering unprecedented in the history of post-colonial Africa.

Nyerere himself wrote the Arusha Declaration which, even years later just before he died, he said he would not change except for a few words here and there in its Swahili version. As Arthur Wille, a Catholic priest who knew Nyerere well and was close to him since the 1940s, stated:

'When the TANU National Executive Committee met in Arusha January 26 - 29 it turned out to be a stormy session. At this meeting Nyerere proposed that *Ujamaa* become the official policy of the government. Oscar Kambona objected strongly to this policy. Twice during these sessions, the Executive Committee adjourned in order to allow their three leaders, Nyerere, Kambona and

Kawawa to go into private session. Each time that they returned to the Executive Committee it was apparent that Kawawa had supported Nyerere to defeat Kambona. The result was that the Arusha Declaration was adopted.'

The Arusha Declaration was adopted on February 5, 1967. It was the most ethical economic and political document ever written by an African leader. As Andrew Nyerere, Mwalimu Julius Nyerere's eldest son with whom I was in regular contact when I worked on the second edition of this book, stated in his comments in August 2003 when he looked at my work in progress:

'The Arusha Declaration forbade leaders to have two salaries. And there is one African businessman who told me that when Nyerere did this, when he restrained his colleagues from becoming rich, that is how we came to prominence; by that, he meant a whole generation of noveau rich people. The man who told me this has since died. He was suffering from a terminal illness. He spoke to me a few months before he died.'

Kambona left Tanzania about five months after the Arusha Declaration was adopted and continued to criticize Nyerere from Britain. And following Tanzania's recognition of Biafra in April 1968, a move that infuriated the Nigerian federal government, Nigerian leaders invited Kambona to Nigeria to lecture. He took this opportunity to denounce Nyerere and pursue his political ambitions. The Nigerian government also immediately broke off diplomatic relations with Tanzania because of her recognition of Biafra as an independent state, the first country to recognize the secessionist region of Eastern Nigeria as a sovereign entity.

Kambona left Tanzania via Kenya where some of his supporters lived and used Kenya's capital Nairobi as one of their operational bases in their conspiracy to overthrow

Nyerere. But even in Kenya itself, a neighbouring country whose policies were different from Tanzania's - Kenya was capitalist and pro-Western, Tanzania socialist and non-aligned - there were many people who saw Kambona as a spent force fading into oblivion, although he could not be entirely dismissed as a non-entity. As the *Kenya Weekly News* stated on July 26, 1968, almost exactly one year after Kambona went into voluntary exile in Britain:

'Every lost turning, every sign of human weakness and failing will be exploited by people like Mr. Kambona. While this might be legitimate political opposition at home, it smacks of straw-clutching and opportunism coming from abroad. This is Mr. Kambona's problem; but it is unlikely to dissuade him from seeking to exploit every twist and turn in Tanzania's politics. It is the only way he can remain in business.'

One year and three months later, Kambona was accused of treason. The charges against him and his alleged conspirators were brought before the High Court of Tanzania in Dar es Salaam presided by Chief Justice Phillip Telfer Georges from Trinidad, who later served in the same capacity in newly independent Zimbabwe under President Robert Mugabe, himself with strong ties to Tanzania before and after he became the leader of his country. The prosecution team was led by Attorney-General Mark Bomani, and later by Senior State Attorney Nathaniel King, also from Trinidad, who almost single-handedly handled the case for the government.

I was a student then, at Tambaza High School in Dar es Salaam, in Form VI, or standard 14, and attended the treason trial with some of my schoolmates; the high court was only within walking distance from our school. I had just reached the age of 20 in October, the same month the treason charges became known to the public in 1969, four months after I was first hired as a reporter by the *Standard*, the country's largest English newspaper, in the nation's capital. But the trial did not start until June 1970. I went to the high court, not as a reporter, but simply as a spectator following the proceedings of the most important case in the history of Tanzania since independence in 1961. It was also the country's first treason trial, but not the last.

Kambona sought help from the CIA to overthrow Nyerere, just as Simon Kapwepwe did in his attempt to oust Zambian President and his childhood friend Kenneth Kaunda. But neither got the help they needed, at least not enough of it to carry out a coup. The immense popularity of both leaders, their high international stature as highly respected statesmen, and their incorruptible nature, made it highly unlikely that their ouster would be accepted domestically or internationally; thus making it very difficult for their would-be successors to win support and recognition. As Andrew Nyerere stated in his written remarks to me on what I said about the CIA in this chapter when he read my manuscript:

'We were discussing it at Msasani (where President Nyerere and his family lived on the outskirts of Dar es Salaam) one day, the supposed CIA infiltration of our government. We were talking about it with my mother, and Mwalimu Nyerere was present. And my mother said, there was much confusion nowadays. Everyday one hears of more government leaders who are on the payroll of the CIA. And I said that surely there is a misunderstanding concerning this, because the CIA argue with those whom they consider to be the enemies of the United States, and this had nothing to do with us. And I saw that this statement made my mother calm.'

Some observers have emphasized the integrity of the two leaders, as incorruptible individuals, as the prime factor in the refusal or unwillingness of the CIA to support coup attempts against them. As Ben Lawrence, a Nigerian, stated in his article, "Privatization: Nigeria's New Gold Rush":

'The survival of Kenneth Kaunda and Julius Nyerere for so long in power was because of their alliance with the masses. When Oscar Kambona of Tanzania and Kapwepwe of Zambia requested the Central Intelligence Agency's (CIA) help to overthrow their former friends, they were plainly told that those leaders were impregnable because they were incorruptible and had no loot stashed in foreign vaults.'

But none of this was enough to dissuade Kambona from pursuing his goal of trying to overthrow Nyerere. What I wrote about the CIA in this chapter inspired more remarks from Andrew Nyerere who said the following in his comments to me:

'One day Mwalimu Nyerere was speaking in praise of various US presidents, and then he lowered his voice and spoke in a very hushed tone referring to President Ronald Reagan, saying that, now they have elected this murderer, that is Ronald Reagan. Now that the American people have elected this murderer, there is much chaos in the world. But I do not think that Mwalimu Nyerere meant that he feared his life was in danger. I think he was just wondering how he was going to get aid from the United States now that there was a hostile government in power. Or maybe he was half-hoping that Jimmy Carter would be re-elected and that he would be able to make another visit to the White House. Because he had been very pleased with that visit he made to the White House, he put the picture on the wall at Msasani.'

In the treason trial which began in June 1970, it was alleged that Kambona was the mastermind behind the coup attempt. The coup was to take place in October 1969.

The conspirators wanted not only to overthrow the government but also to assassinate President Nyerere. I remember during the proceedings when Senior State Attorney Nathaniel King asked one of the accused, John Lifa Chipaka what he meant when he said they wanted to 'eliminate' the president. Chipaka responded by saying they wanted to 'eliminate him politically, not physically.' But the evidence presented in court demonstrated otherwise.

The accused were Colonel William Makori Chacha, a senior army officer in the country's army, the Tanzania People's Defence Forces (TPDF), who, not long before the treason trial, was a military attache at the Tanzania embassy in Peking in the People's Republic of China; John Dustan Lifa Chipaka, 38, former secretary-general of the defunct African National Congress (ANC) led by Zuberi Mtemvu in the 1960s. In the 1990s, after he was released from prison, Chipaka was still active in politics and became one of the opposition leaders in Tanzania and once led a party founded by Oscar Kambona after Kambona returned to Tanzania from Britain where he had lived in self-imposed exile for 25 years.

Others who appeared before the court on treason charges were: Michael Kamaliza, 46, a polio victim and former secretary-general of the National Union of Tanganyika Workers (NUTA) who also once served as minister of labour; Bibi Titi Mohammed, 45, a fiery orator, once a junior minister of labour and community development in the sixties and Tanzania's most prominent female politician who was head of the ruling party's women's movement known in Kiswahili as Umoja wa Wanawake wa Tanzania (UWT), translated as Women's Union of Tanzania; Gray Likungu Mataka, 34, a journalist; Captain Elia Dustan Lifa Chipaka, 32, of the Tanzanian army, the Tanzania People's Defence Forces (TPDF), and younger brother of one of the accused, John Dustan Lifa Chipaka; and Lieutenant Alfred Philip Milinga, 27, also of the Tanzania People's Defence Forces, and the youngest among the accused. They all denied all the charges brought against them.

One of the most remarkable things about this trial was the fact that some of the people involved in the coup attempt were once, or were supposed to be, some of the most loyal to the president. Before his departure from Tanzania in 1967, especially before 1966, the minister for foreign affairs, Oscar Kambona, was one of Nyerere's closest colleagues who even helped quell the army mutiny in 1964 when he went directly to speak to the mutinous soldiers and negotiate with them on their salary demands and insistence that the British army officers should be immediately replaced by indigenous ones.

He was also one of the founders of TANU, together with Nyerere and others, a party which led Tanganyika to independence. Another veteran politician and founding member of TANU, Bibi Titi Mohammed, also was known to be a close friend and very loyal supporter of Nyerere. So was former labour minister Michael Kamaliza, even if only by virtue of his position as a cabinet member under Nyerere. Colonel Chacha was also said to be a loyal supporter of President Nyerere.

Yet, they turned out to be the most prominent conspirators against him and his government. Ironically, not long before the treason trial, Nyerere himself had publicly stated in 1966 what turned out to be one of the most "prophetic" statements he had ever made during his presidency, unequivocally saying:

'I've been one of the luckiest presidents in Africa. My colleagues are very loyal to me.'

They proved him wrong; not all, but many of them, including those who lied to him throughout his tenure to promote their own interests. And others, of course, plotted to get rid of him right away, as the treason trial tragically

128

demonstrated.

The most ominous sign of things yet to come was the abrupt resignation of Oscar Kambona from his ministerial post and other positions in June 1967. This came only about four months after the adoption of the Arusha Declaration in February, the country's economic and political manifesto he strongly opposed. In July, he left the country. And within two years or so, he was accused of treason and of being the mastermind behind the coup attempt to overthrow and assassinate Nyerere, his erstwhile compatriot.

His attempts to undermine and oust Nyerere from power gained momentum soon after he settled in London where he launched a blistering attack on the president and his government in a concerted effort to win support and turn the people of Tanzania against him, but to avail. Nyerere's popularity was immense, even if his socialist policies and one-party rule weren't among a significant number of people; a disenchantment Kambona tried to capitalize on and use as a lightning rod to galvanize the opposition against Nyerere within the country.

However, there are different opinions on how much, if any, opposition to Nyerere's economic policies were generated or fuelled by the Arusha Declaration. As Andrew Nyerere stated in some of his comments to me on this second edition which he read when I was working on it:

'No one opposed the Arusha Declaration. There was only one problem in that the young students of primary school accepted it more readily than the older students of secondary school. The young were more idealistic.'

Safe in London, Kambona was not arrested for his involvement in the coup plot. But six of his fellow conspirators were arrested in October 1969. They were all arrested in Tanzania, with the exception of Gray Likungu

Mataka who once served as news editor of the TANU ruling party's daily newspaper, *The Nationalist*, a fiercely nationalistic and uncompromising publication whose managing editor, Benjamin Mkapa, became president of Tanzania from 1995 – 2005. Mataka was arrested in Nairobi, Kenya, where he had been acting as a conduit between Kambona and the other conspirators in Tanzania. It was one of the ironies of this trial that Mataka was not only once editor of the ruling party's newspaper but of a paper that was fiercely loyal to the president.

I also remember when I was a news reporter of the *Standard* in Dar es Salaam that we had a sort of an adversarial relationship with *The Nationalist* whose reporters, and sometimes even editorials, now and then lambasted us for working for "an imperialist newspaper." The *Standard* was then owned by Lonrho, until it was nationalized in 1970 when it became a state-owned newspaper and rechristened *Daily News*. President Nyerere became editor-in-chief of the *Daily News* but only as a ceremonial head. It was the editor of the paper who exercised power over us. Coincidentally, the treason trial started in the same year in which the paper was nationalized.

And in spite of its reputation as an 'imperialist' newspaper before it was nationalized, the *Standard* adhered to the highest journalistic standards in covering the treason trial. So did *The Nationalist,* without slanting facts in favour of the government, despite its strong nationalist bias and unswerving loyalty to President Nyerere.

The first accused was Oscar Kambona. There was speculation that the government would seek extradition of the former foreign affairs minister. But nothing was done, and he was tried in absentia. Andrew Nyerere remembers Oscar Kambona well, as much as he does the early days of independence when our country was still called Tanganyika, and had the following to say in his remarks to me when he read this chapter:

'I remember the day when we went to State House. Mr. Kambona took over the house that we were staying in, the one at Sea View, the residence of the Chief Minister. I gazed at him for a long time as the car sped away. He was taking charge of the house which was to be his new home. It is a pity that he turned out to be such a traitor. If Nyerere knew that he would turn out to be such a heinous traitor, he would not have given him all those responsible positions in government. But I went to his funeral. I felt that all these evils of the past should be forgotten.'

When I asked Andrew what he thought about Kambona since the early days of Tanganyika's independence in the sixties, in terms of what type of person he was, he responded by saying:

'He was a good man. But there was misunderstanding, and what happened, happened. For example, he strongly disagreed with Mwalimu Nyerere about Kassim Hanga, the Zanzibar (cabinet) minister who was sent back and killed. And Kambona was right about this. He did not want Hanga sent back to Zanzibar. And Mwalimu Nyerere said that, concerning Hanga, he sent him back, but he did not know that they were going to kill him.'

During the 1970 treason trial involving Kambona, it was alleged by the prosecution team that the conspirators intended to launch a military coup between October 10 and 15, 1969. During that time, President Nyerere and a large number of high ranking government officials including cabinet members, as well as the head of the Tanzania People's Defence Forces (TPDF), Major-General Mrisho Sarakikya, were out of the country. The plotters felt that this was the perfect time for a coup. Some people in Zanzibar were also implicated in the coup plot.

Geoffrey Sawaya, the director of the Criminal Investigation Department (CID), told the high court that Oscar Kambona sent large sums of money to the people in Tanzania who were to take part in the coup; and that all the conspirators used aliases.

One key figure in uncovering the plot was a South African freedom fighter living in exile in Tanzania, Potlako Leballo, the leader of the Pan-Africanist Congress (PAC), a black nationalist group which was formed in 1959 by members who left the African National Congress (ANC) over policy differences. The first leader of the PAC was Robert Mangaliso Sobukwe, a professor at Witwatersrand University and compatriot of Nelson Mandela. Mandela remained in the African National Congress and later became president of the organization which spearheaded the struggle against apartheid.

Leballo became head of the PAC after Sobukwe was sent to prison by the apartheid regime. And his testimony in Tanzania's first treason trial proved to be critical.

The coup plotters approached Leballo and enlisted his help in carrying out the coup, possibly with the help of his guerrilla fighters based in Tanzania, and he went along with the plan to gather intelligence for the government. Leballo met with the conspirators on a number of occasions. He had already informed the government and the conspirators were now under surveillance, with all their meetings being monitored by Tanzania's intelligence officers. Leballo became the government's key witness who unlocked all the secrets of the coup plotters. He also testified in court that Kambona had been given a lot of money to finance the coup. According to *Africa Contemporary Record*:

'The central prosecution witness was Potlako K. Leballo, a founder of the Pan-African Congress (Pan-Africanist Congress) of South Africa (PAC), which had its exile headquarters in Dar es Salaam.

The state maintained that seven defendants attempted to enlist Leballo in the plot but that he informed government officials and only appeared to go along with the plot in order to assist in capturing the conspirators.

Leballo testified that he frequently met with Kambona in London and that Kambona had shown him a cache of $500,000 and told him that he could 'get more where that came from' by contacting a U.S. Information Service 'friend' in London (*New York Times*, 19 July 1970, 12).

Leballo further testified that Kambona had an agreement with the South African foreign minister, Hilgard Muller, that South Africa would support the coup.

The defence charged that Leballo had a grudge against the Nyerere regime, which had cut off the funds it had given PAC, and that he would have been appointed a Bantustan leader in South Africa had the coup been successful.

Leballo denied that he was a South African spy, and the defendants called Leballo's evidence a fabrication. Some defendants (such as Bibi Titi Mohammed) denied any involvement in the plot, while others maintained that their opposition was by constitutional, not violent, means.

Chief Justice (Phillip) Telfer Georges and four others who conducted the trial found six of the seven guilty. Milinga was acquitted. Mattaka, the Chipaka brothers, and Bibi Titi were found guilty of treasonand sentenced to life imprisonment; Kamaliza and Chacha were convicted of misprison (misprision) of treason and sentenced to prison terms.' – (Colin Legum and John Drysdale, eds., *Africa Contemporary Record: Annual Survey and Documents 1970 – 1971*, London: Africa Research Ltd., 1971, pp. 170 – 171. See also Ronald Christenson, ed., *Political Trials in History: From Antiquity to the Present:*, Transaction Publishers, 1991, Piscataway, New Jersey, USA, pp. 235; and Oscar Kambona in Jacqueline Audrey Kalley, Elna Schoeman, Lydia Eve Andor, *Southern African Political history: a Chronology of Key Political Events from*

Independence to mid-1997, Greenwood Publishing Group, 1999, p. 594).

When Tanzania's Attorney-General Mark Bomani asked Tanzania's intelligence chief how he knew for sure that Leballo met the conspirators, Sawaya said whenever he knew in advance that there would be a meeting, he would assign his intelligence officers to monitor the proceedings in a clandestine operation the coup plotters never knew about. He also testified before the court that Leballo told him, in advance, about a trip to Nairobi, Kenya, on March 25, 1969; and that Leballo did go on that trip and returned to Dar es Salaam on April 1st .

Leballo told the director of intelligence the purpose of the trip was to meet with Gray Likungu Mataka, who then lived in Nairobi which was one of the operational bases for the coup plotters, to get confirmation of the coup plot as Mataka had explained to him earlier.

Sawaya went on to say that he already knew that Leballo and Colonel Chacha had a meeting and that Leballo had been introduced to Prisca (one of the code names used by one of the conspirators) and Bibi Titi Mohammed. Chacha and Leballo met at Twiga Hotel in Dar es Salaam. Leballo also met with Bibi Titi Mohammed at an Islamic Centre at Chang'ombe in Dar es Salaam and discussed how President Nyerere and other senior government officials including some cabinet members would be assassinated.

The director of intelligence further testified that on March 24, 1969, Leballo went to him and told him about the meeting he (Leballo) had with Chacha at Twiga Hotel. When Attorney-General Mark Bomani asked him how he knew the meeting had taken place, Sawaya said he sent his intelligence officers to Twiga Hotel on a surveillance mission after he was told about the meeting in advance. And they observed the meeting taking place.

On the following day, March 25, Leballo left for

Nairobi, the intelligence director said, and was 'escorted' by some intelligence officers who had been assigned by the director to accompany him.

Sawaya went on to tell the court that in April 1969, he went on a trip overseas. He said he met again with Leballo on May 2, 1969, and that Leballo told him that the plan for the coup as explained by Gray Mataka in Nairobi was very well received by Colonel Chacha, Michael Kamaliza and Bibi Titi Mohammed in a jovial mood. He also said Mataka had promised to ask for some money from Kambona to facilitate the operation. The intelligence chief further stated that Leballo produced a letter written to Prisca by Mataka, and that Mataka himself copied the letter in his own handwriting and gave the copy to Leballo.

Mark Bomani: Can you recognize the copy of this letter if you see it?

Intelligence director: Yes, I can.

Bomani: How can you recognize this letter?

Intelligence chief: I can recognize it by the name of Chaima.

Leballo: He (the intelligence director) told me that after I met with Mataka for the first time, the accused changed his name and gave himself the code name of Chaima.

Chief Justice: Was the letter translated?

Intelligence chief: Soon after the copy of the letter was made, it was translated so that I could understand what it said.

Bomani: Did you know the letter was delivered?

Intelligence chief: I was informed that it was being delivered.

The intelligence director went on to say that according to the information he got from Leballo, Chipaka, Titi, Kamaliza, Leballo and Prisca were going to have a meeting to discuss what they would be doing when they were waiting for some money from Kambona.

At that meeting, Kamaliza asked Leballo to go to London and ask Kambona to send more money. Kamaliza also asked Chipaka to write Kambona a letter and send him a 10-shilling note for Kambona to sign it. With Kambona's signature on the 10-shilling note, Kamaliza said the note would be passed around to convince some cabinet members and members of parliament to support Kambona in overthrowing the government.

It was also expected that the note would be used to raise more funds for the coup and get support from TANU leaders and workers and from the leaders and members of the country's labour union, the National Union of Tanganyika Workers (NUTA), to oppose the government; thus encouraging others to overthrow it.

Kamaliza told Leballo there was no doubt that the workers of Tanzania would support the coup because the president had removed him (Kamaliza) from the leadership of NUTA against the wishes of the workers.

Geoffrey Sawaya, the intelligence director, went on to say that Leballo met Titi (Bibi Titi Mohammed) at her house on June 23, 1969. She told him that she had been to Nairobi where she stayed for four days and made a telephone call to Kambona asking him to send one million shillings for overthrowing the government within two weeks.

Titi gave Leballo 400 shillings and said she had received 2,000 shillings, $1,000 for Colonel Chacha, for incidental expenses. Titi told Leballo she would give him 600 shillings in a few days, and did so on June 26. The money was presented in court as evidence.

On June 28, Colonel Chacha made arrangements to meet with Leballo on June 30 in order to introduce him to Major Herman. Chacha and Lieutenant-Colonel Marwa went to Leballo's residence at 3 a.m. on June 30. Chacha and Leballo went into the bedroom, leaving Marwa in the sitting room. There in the bedroom, Chacha told Leballo that he was ready to overthrow the government if he was paid 20 million shillings, and wanted Leballo to tell Kambona to send the money right away.

136

On July 3, Chacha and Leballo met again at the army headquarters at Chacha's request. Chacha told Leballo he was disappointed because the money was being delayed. And he wanted Leballo to go to the officers' mess at Lugalo Barracks where Captain Elia Dustan Lifa Chipaka would introduce him to Major Herman.

Leballo went there and found Captain Chipaka waiting for him. Captain Chipaka told Leballo that he did not trust Major Herman as someone who would be involved in overthrowing the government because he was a half-caste from Iringa (in the Southern Highlands of southwestern Tanzania); and that he would give him a list of army officers which would include the name of one officer from Zanzibar. From that list would be chosen a person who would lead the coup.

Afterwards, Captain Chipaka introduced Leballo to Major Herman.

After this meeting, Leballo met with John Chipaka and Michael Kamaliza in the main office of NUTA in Dar es Salaam. They had a discussion and agreed that Leballo should go to London and ask Kambona to send more money.

Around 4.15 p.m. on the same day, Leballo was again asked to go to the same office. He went and found Kamaliza alone in the office. Kamaliza told Leballo that he had sent someone to Kambona to get and bring the money. He also told Leballo that he personally would like Major Herman, and not Colonel Chacha, to lead the coup.

There were conspirators in Zanzibar but, because the former island nation was an autonomous entity with its own legal system even after uniting with Tanganyika to form Tanzania, the authorities in the isles dispensed swift justice against them. So, it was only the ones on the mainland who had to appear before the Tanzania High Court in Dar es Salaam presided over by the Trinidadian jurist Philip Telfer Georges.

The criminal investigation director (CID), Geoffrey

Sawaya, told the court that the coup did not take place because some of the conspirators were arrested and detained before the scheduled date for the takeover. He said some of them made statements after their arrest admitting most of the allegations about their involvement in the abortive coup attempt. And he produced evidence showing instructions on how strategic locations would be taken over. He also presented to the court lists of prominent people who were to be detained by the coup makers.

There were moonlight trips by dhow between Dar es Salaam and Zanzibar, made by the conspirators and their couriers. Secret meetings were held in expensive hotels in Nairobi, Kenya, in London, and in Dar es Salaam. Nightclubs were another hot spot where the coup plotters met to discuss their nefarious scheme which included a plot to assassinate President Nyerere. There was even a plan, for whatever reason they deemed appropriate, to bomb the University of Dar es Salaam; probably to cause panic while they executed the coup, or simply to wreak havoc and cause mayhem.

One of the most damaging pieces of evidence against the coup plotters presented in court was the 'wedding guest list' found at the residence of Captain Elia Dustan Lifa Chipaka. All 37 "guests" named on the list were army officers. Captain Chipaka told the court that the names were part of a list of the names of guests he was going to invite to his wedding. But, as Chief Justice Philip Telfer Georges said at the end of the trial, the list contained comments which an average person would consider to be totally irrelevant to preparation for a wedding. For example, against the name of one colonel was this comment: 'Dissatisfied, but his stand is not known.'

Other evidence included letters from Oscar Kambona written to the conspirators.

What the coup plotters did not know was that Potlako Leballo, the South African political exile and president of the Pan-Africanist Congress (PAC) was already working for the Tanzania intelligence service but gained their confidence. The outlandish claim by the that Leballo had manufactured the whole thing and was really a spy for the South African apartheid regime was dismissed as nonsense by the court.

In delivering the verdicts, the chief justice denied pleas for clemency made by the defence lawyers and made it clear that overthrowing governments was not an acceptable way to change leadership, emphasizing that the young African nations needed peace and stability to consolidate their independence and serve their people.

The trial lasted 127 days, the longest in the country's history. Chief Justice Philip Telfer Georges did not sentence the conspirators to death as he could have under the law, but nonetheless gave them stiff sentences as follows:

- Bibi Titi Mohammed: life imprisonment for treason.
- Gray Likungu Mataka: life imprisonment for treason.
- Elia Dustan Lifa Chipaka: life imprisonment for treason.
- Michael Kamaliza: ten years' imprisonment for misprision of treason.
- William Makori Chacha: ten years' imprisonment for misprision of treason.

Alfred Philip Milinga was acquitted of all charges, but after spending 16 months in detention under the Preventive Detention Act during the investigation and trial of the treason case. The act was passed by parliament to allow the government to detain people if they posed a threat to national security but was criticized by the chief justice during the treason trial for detaining people for too long before they were brought to court.

The ringleader and mastermind of the treasonous coterie, former foreign affairs minister Oscar Kambona, was tried in absentia. Only three years earlier, President Nyerere had said of his cabinet colleague and close political aide:

'Oscar is extremely loyal – to the party, to me, and to the people.'

President Nyerere could be extremely tough when you encroach on his authority. Yet he he also had a reputation for being very tolerant, kind, and forgiving. And he lived up to both. About seven years after the treason trial, Bibi Titi Mohammed received a presidential pardon in 1977 and walked out of prison in Dodoma, central Tanzania. She had written the president asking for forgiveness, but had no hope that she would get it.

On February 5, 1978, Otini Kambona, former education and information minister under Nyerere in the first independence cabinet, and Mattiya Kambona, the younger brothers of Oscar Kambona, were released from detention together with 22 other detainees and 7,000 petty criminals. They were all pardoned by President Nyerere. They were freed on the first anniversary of the founding of the ruling Chama Cha Mapinduzi (CMM), formed from a merger of the mainland TANU and its sister counterpart in Zanzibar, the Afro-Shirazi Party (ASP). February 5, 1978, was also the eleventh anniversary of the Arusha Declaration.

Otini and Mattiya Kambona were detained for more than 10 years. They were arrested and detained in December 1967 for supporting their brother's political activities and using a Kiswahili newspaper Otini Kambona published to help further his political ambitions, even if by making oblique references to his brother's agenda.

But more often than not, the newspaper *Ulimwengu* (The World) was explicit in its condemnation of the government. It published articles written by Oscar Kambona highly critical of the government. After the two brothers were arrested, the paper also immediately ceased publication.

Also released in 1972, like Bibi Titi Mohammed, was Eli Anangisye, former secretary-general of the TANU Youth League, who had been detained for his involvement in another plot to overthrow the government by trying to enlist the help of some army officers to carry out the coup. He was the alleged mastermind of this plot.

Why Nyerere freed all these people, despite their attempts to undermine his government, remained a mystery. And he gave no reason for setting them free, in spite of the overwhelming evidence implicating them in the plots. He was not ruthless but took a firm stand against his enemies. And he could have let them rot in prison, instead of pardoning them. Yet, he set them free, demonstrating one of his qualities as a compassionate man.

Kambona, of course, was never arrested. No extradition proceedings took place and he remained in Britain until he willingly returned to Tanzania in April 1992 after the country adopted the multiparty system which enabled him to form a political party and challenge the ruling Chama Cha Mapinduzi (Revolutionary Party) which had been in power since independence, first as TANU.

Ironically, multiparty democracy was introduced with the full support of former President Nyerere when he started questioning the functional utility of the one-party state of which he was the architect and which was officially adopted in 1965. But it had become corrupt, he said, and needed to be replaced. Yet his position on the multi-party system was not fully understood. As Andrew Nyerere stated in his written comments on my work in August 2003 when I was writing this expanded edition:

'Mwalimu Nyerere was chairman of the party. And he said, we have been discussing this multi-party democracy at the CCM meeting in Dodoma (Tanzania's new capital). We notice that in many countries there is much talk about the multi-party form of government. After discussing this, we have decided that there is no reason why this country should not follow this kind of multi-party democracy. So we invite everyone to discuss this.

In connection with this, I would like to make a comment about the notes which Mwalimu had been making for a speech which he was going to make, but which he never made, because death overtook him.

He wrote that he hoped he had made a good decision when he spoke in favour of multi-party democracy. This is good, in so far as Mwalimu hoped that all the decisions he had made during his life were good decisions.

But the mere fact that he wrote this meant that he did not see any necessity for a multi-party state, even as he did not see any necessity for a single party state. The only thing that mattered was that the government should serve the people well.'

Twelve years after the treason trial, Oscar Kambona gave an interview in April 1982 in which he explained why he was highly critical of Nyerere, and by implication tried to justify his attempt to overthrow the government, although nothing he said could justify that. As he stated in the interview with *Drum*:

'Nyerere and I go back a long way - we founded TANU. Nyerere was the chairman and I was the secretary-general.

Problems between us began in 1964 during the army mutiny. Nyerere and Kawawa hid themselves in a grass hut while I was left to face the music (Kambona was then minister of defence).

I negotiated with the army and managed to settle the uprising. When Nyerere returned, the army wanted to mutiny again - that was when we asked for military assistance from the British.

After the mutiny, some friends told him that he was

losing his grip on the country and I think he believed them.

When Nyerere visited China, he was very impressed with the glorification of Mao Tse-Tung. I think the seeds of a single, all-powerful individual, an autocrat, were sown in him on this trip. And when he came back, he wanted a one-party state.

I sat on the commission that looked at the question of a one-party state and produced a minority report in which I wanted to know what mechanism we had of changing government peacefully.

Nyerere persuaded me not to present my report and said that I should go along with the majority report which was in favour of a one-party state and that at the end of five years, we would review the situation and if we found any weaknesses we could put them right. I agreed, but I refused to sign as a member of the committee.

I think that *Ujamaa* was badly implemented and that is why it has been a failure. The government should have had pilot schemes which were successful so that people could go to see them.

The farmers in Tanzania are very conservative. They want to know what they get from their labour. If a man has a farm and earns 200 British pounds from it, and is then asked to go into an *Ujamaa* village and gets 20 pounds for the same work, he begins to ask: 'How is *Ujamaa* good for me?'

The system in Tanzania is such that Nyerere will continue to remain in power. The president chooses all the candidates for elections. Whichever way you vote, you still vote for his man.

In the presidential elections, there are only two boxes – one for Nyerere and the other against him. When you go into the polling booth, there is a soldier standing there. He tells you, 'If you want Nyerere, vote there, and if you are an enemy of the people, then vote in the 'no' box.'

Nyerere has been in power for 21 years now. And

nowadays he is always saying that he is going to resign. Then the parliamentarians stamp their feet and shout that he is their leader and Nyerere says: 'Well, what can I do? A captain cannot abandon his ship and let it sink.'

But why is it that during all this time he hasn't been able to find anyone who can rule the country besides himself?

I feel very sorry for the person who will take over because the country is bankrupt. If I took over I would change the economic policies and do away with detention for longer than ten days.'

But even after multiparty politics was introduced, Kambona was still not able to get significant support among the people after he returned to Tanzania in April 1992 from 25 years of exile in Britain." – (Godfrey Mwakikagile, *Nyerere and Africa: End of an Era*, New Africa Press, Dar es Salaam, Tanzania, pp. 361 – 375).

While Nyerere survived coup attempts, Nkrumah did not. And although Nkrumah was overthrown, he continued to be a towering figure. His influence and continental stature did not diminish. His ideas continued to have a major impact on political discourse on the future of Africa. And they still do today.

He was one of the most eloquent spokesmen for Africans and people of African descent worldwide and was admired by many people in the African diaspora as much as he was in Africa.

Although the year 1966 was marred by a number of tragedies in Africa including military coups and subsequent massacres in Nigeria; the ouster of Dr. Nkrumah in another military coup in Ghana; instability in Congo since the assassination of Lumumba; the Rhodesian crisis following the unilateral declaration of independence by the white minority government; and intensifying guerrilla warfare in southern Africa stretching from the

144

coast of the Indian Ocean in Mozambique to the Atlantic in Angola, among other events; it was also a year with some bright spots on the continent marked by the end of colonial rule in two countries.

On 30 September 1966, the British protectorate of Bechuanaland won independence. The new independent country was renamed Botswana.

Another country which won independence in 1966 was Basutoland. It was also a British protectorate and won independence on 4 October 1966. It was renamed Lesotho.

And the celebration of independence in both countries was, in a way, a celebration of the life and achievements of Dr. Kwame Nkrumah who was overthrown a few months earlier in that year but who will always be remembered for blazing the trail for the African independence movement when he led Ghana to become the first black African country to emerge from colonial rule. As he stated on Ghana's independence day on 6 March 1957:

"The independence of Ghana is meaningless unless it is linked with the total liberation of the African continent."

And as he stated on another occasion:

"The independence of Ghana, achieved on March 6, 1957, ushered in the decisive struggle for freedom and independence throughout Africa - freedom from colonial rule and settler domination.

On that day I proclaimed to the world, 'the independence of Ghana is meaningless unless it is linked with the total liberation of the African continent.'

Immediately, the beating drums sent this message across rivers, mountains, forests and plains. The people heard and acted. Liberation movements gained strength, and freedom fighters began to train. One after another, new African states came into being, and above the world's horizon loomed the African Personality.

African statesmen went to the United Nations; Africans proudly wore the ancient regalia of their ancestral land; Africans stood up and spoke on the rostrum of the world forum, and they spoke for Africans and the people of African descent wherever they might be."

Dr. Nkrumah became one of the strongest supporters of the African independence struggle, providing political and diplomatic support, as well as material and financial assistance to the liberation movements and individual leaders especially in the countries of southern Africa where the liberation struggle was most intense because of the refusal of the white minority regimes to relinquish power to the African majority.

He also forged links with the African diaspora more than any other African leader with the possible exception of Julius Nyerere.

One of Nkrumah's strongest admirers in the diaspora was Stokely Carmichael who later moved to Guinea and renamed himself Kwame Ture in honour of Kwame Nkrumah and Sekou Toure whom he equally admired. And, coincidentally, he was thrust into the international spotlight – as never before – in the same year Dr. Nkrumah was overthrown.

Carmichael said in an interview years later that before he settled in Conakry, Guinea, where Nkrumah also lived after he was overthrown, he wanted to go to Tanzania where he expected to forge links with the liberation movements based in Tanzania's capital Dar es Salaam. But he said Nkrumah asked him to stay and work with him in Guinea.

Carmichael moved to Guinea in 1967, a year that also witnessed some of the most dramatic events in the continent's history.

1967

THE year 1967 was, as were the last two years of that decade, dominated by the Nigerian civil war probably more than anything else. It was a conflict reminiscent of the Congo crisis in the early sixties, although the two crises were also different in some fundamental respects. Just as the secession of Katanga was at the centre of the Congo crisis, the driving force behind the Nigerian civil war was the secession of the Eastern Region which declared independence as the Republic of Biafra.

But the two secessions were fundamentally different.

The secession of Katanga was externally engineered, and manipulated, while the declaration of independence by Eastern Nigeria as the Republic of Biafra was an indigenous aspiration inspired by the injustices, including massacres, perpetrated against Eastern Nigerians, mostly Igbos, in Northern Nigeria and other parts of the country but mainly in the north. But before the leaders of Eastern Nigeria reached that momentous decision to secede, attempts were made to resolve the Nigerian crisis in order to end the bloodshed and save the federation.

The task was undertaken by the Nigerian military head of state General Yakubu Gowon and the military governors of Eastern, Northern and Western Nigeria, and of the Mid-West Region, who met at Aburi near Accra in Ghana on January 4th and 5th, 1967, under the auspices of Ghana's military head of state General Joseph Ankrah.

It was a solemn meeting. The military governors and General Gowon talked as fellow soldiers and as leaders of a nation they knew was on the brink of collapse. It was already faced with a catastrophe.

But there was not much agreement among the military governors except their shared contempt for the corrupt politicians who had brought so much grief upon their fellow countrymen. Ojukwu also carried the grief of millions of his fellow Igbos and other Eastern Nigerians who had been deeply wronged and who also felt, rightly or wrongly, that they had been expelled from the federation by the massacres perpetrated against them in Northern Nigeria.

Yet in spite of their position as leaders, all the military governors including Gowon himself, the military head of state, felt helpless in trying to command a federal army that had already split along tribal lines, hence into regional armies, each defending members of its regional tribes or ethnic groups. For example, it became impossible for Hausa enlisted men to take orders Igbo army officers, their arch-enemies during that time when the crisis which was triggered by the January 1966 military coup was still going on. They simply refused to do so and even threatened their officers who did not come from their region, especially the Igbos.

Obviously before then, they were not such bitter enemies – otherwise tens of thousands of Igbos would not have been able to live and work, and even intermarry with the indigenous people, in Northern Nigeria for years. But the military coup ended whatever peaceful co-existence there was between the two, although it was not necessarily under the best of circumstances because of the hostility between them through the decades, clearly demonstrated, for example, by the massacre of hundreds of Igbos in Northern Nigeria in 1945 and 1953 as we learned earlier.

During the crisis, the military governors not only felt helpless in trying to command a fragmented national army; it was also impossible for them to guarantee safety for the Igbos and other Eastern Nigerians in a country which seemed to be breaking up into its regional components.

The only place the easterners could be safe was in their home region, a restriction which made a mockery of the concept of federation as if Nigeria was no longer a federal state or one country. All Nigerians had the right to live and work anywhre in Nigeria and to be guaranteed safety in any part of the federation regardless of their origin, and not just in their home regions.

The federal crisis was also complicated by Ojukwu's relationship with Gowon. He did not accept Gowon's leadership as head of state or of the army like other military governors did. He accused him of not keeping his word on several promises and of not protecting the Igbos and other Eastern Nigerians since he came to power. He also accused him of killing Ironsi. As he stated at the OAU peace conference in Addis Ababa in August 1968:

"It is pertinent to state here categorically that we never recognized Gowon as head of the Nigerian military government. Gowon is a rebel. I made this point convincingly clear during the Aburi meeting of January 1967, and it was in acceptance of this fact that it was agreed at that meeting, that one of the first things to do on our return from Aburi should be the formal election of a commander-in-chief, whose duty would be to preside over meetings of the Supreme Military Council.

149

As the days passed by in August (1966), the wave of massacres in Northern Nigeria began to gain momentum. From even the remotest villages of the region, our people were fleeing for dear life to the bigger towns to return home.

At Kaduna on August 30, and in the early days of September, our people fleeing Northern Nigeria were again attacked – in the railway stations and motor parks where they had congregated in search of transport. Several hundred were killed. Those who escaped abandoned all their possessions.

In Minna and many other Northern Nigerian towns, the African Continental Bank and other businesses owned by our (Eastern Regional) Government and people were attacked and looted. Their agents and owners fled back to their homeland, determined never to return." – (Ojukwu, *Africa Contemporary Record*, op.cit., pp. 657 - 658).

They got no protection from the Northern Regional Government or from the Nigerian federal authorities, reinforcing the belief among the Igbos and other Eastern Nigerians that nobody cared about them or was concerned about their plight; and that they were therefore on their own and had to protect themselves by any means possible even if they had to secede and have their own country separate from the rest of Nigeria. The federation meant nothing to them.

There was yet another factor during the crisis which complicated the situation even further. Because of security problems, Ojukwu was virtually confined to his home region, Eastern Nigeria, making it impossible for him to work with the other military governors who together constituted the Supreme Military Council under Gowon. The two sides simply did not trust each other.

One side was represented by Gowon as head of the federation; the other by Ojukwu as the leader of those who felt they had been expelled from the federation; their

150

expulsion confirmed by the unwillingness of the federal authorities to protect them and stop the massacres in Northern Nigeria. Therefore war between the two sides seemed inevitable. It was only a matter of when.

There were also a number of important developments which took place after the Aburi meeting and before the war. After the meeting, Ojukwu returned to Enugu, the Biafran capital, and announced at a press conference that among several other things, it was:

"unanimously agreed (by the Supreme Military Council) that it was in the interests of the safety of this nation that the regions should move slightly further apart than before." – (Ojukwu, *Africa Contemporary Record*, ibid., pp. 645 - 646. See also the "Aburi Conference and Subsequent Developments," in *Africa Research Bulletin*, Vol. 4, Nos. 1 – 7, London, 1967; *Ghanaian Times*, January 1967; *West Africa*, February 1967).

Exactly three weeks later after the Aburi meeting, Gowon addressed a press conference in Lagos on 26 January 1967 stating that it had been agreed by the Supreme Military Council at the meeting in Ghana that there should be one Nigerian army under a unified command as presently constituted; but that the best way to achieve this goal was by organizing the army into area commands.

Most of the army personnel in each command would be drawn from the indigenous people of that area. Each command would be under an area commander who would receive operational instructions from the federal military headquarters which would be directly under Colonel Gowon as the supreme commander of the armed forces. He went on to say:

"Military governors can use the area commands for internal security purposes, but this will normally be done with the express permission of the head of the federal military government. We definitely decided against regional armies." – (Gowon, *Africa Contemporary Record*, ibid., p. 646; *Nigerian Times,* 27 January 1967; *West Africa*, February 1967; "Aburi Conference and Subsequent Developments," in *Africa Research Bulletin*, Vol. 4, Nos. 1 - 7, London, 1967).

One of the most divisive issues which sparked the violence against the Igbos and other Eastern Nigerians in Northern Nigeria was the centralisation of power by abolishing the regions and unifying the civil service; a decision that was agreed upon by all the military governors including Colonel Hassan Katsina of the Fulani royal family who was the governor of Northern Nigeria under General Ironsi and later under Gowon.

At the Aburi meeting, it was agreed by the Supreme Military Council of the military governors and Gowon that the country would have to go back to where it was before 17 January 1966 when the unification decree – Edict No. 34 – was issued by General Ironsi in his capacity as military head of state. Regions would be restored and no further changes in the structure of the federation would be introduced until a new constitution was written by the people of Nigeria themselves.

But that is *not* what Gowon did only a few months later. He went against the Aburi accords by creating states without the approval of the entire Supreme Military Council and before a new federal constitution was written as the agreements stipulated. However, on the unification decree which had caused so much bloodshed and suffering, he stated:

"(It had been agreed upon to return) to the status quo ante January 17th, 1966, and this is in keeping with my earlier public announcements that decrees or parts of decrees which tended towards over-centralization should be repealed." - (Gowon, ibid.).

After Gowon addressed the press conference on January 26th, 1967, Ojukwu also addressed one two days later on January 28th in Port Harcourt in Eastern Nigeria and warned that he would not attend any future meetings of the Supreme Military Council until the agreements reached at the Aburi conference were fully implemented. He also did not think it was safe for any of the Eastern Nigerian leaders to attend talks anywhere in the country unless the venue of the meeting was guaranteed security by implementing the Aburi accords. He said he had:

"a catalogue of agreements not implemented by Gowon. The crisis in Nigeria has turned out to be a brilliant essay in keeping bad faith." – (Ojukwu, ibid.).

Ojukwu explained that they had agreed at the Aburi meeting that all decrees which reduced the powers of the regions would be abrogated in January 1967, but Gowon "is not anxious to implement those decisions." He warned that any decree issued by Gowon without the approval of all the military governors would not be binding on Eastern Nigeria.

Exactly one month later on 28 February 1967, Gowon and all the military governors, except Ojukwu, met in Lagos and reaffirmed their belief in the continued existence of Nigeria as one country. They also agreed that a meeting of the entire Supreme Military Council should be held in the Mid-Western Region "to review the situation in the country."

The situation continued to deteriorate further. On 4 March 1967, Gowon addressed members of the diplomatic corps in Lagos stating that the agreement reached at Aburi not to use force in resolving the Nigerian crisis was valid "so long as there was no attempt anywhere on the part of anybody to disintegrate the country." Responding to

Ojukwu's ultimatum that he would take a unilateral action to implement the Aburi agreement if it was not implemented by the federal military government – the Supreme Military Council – before 31 March 1967, Gowon said:

"In the event of any section of this country acting unilaterally to the extent of destroying the constitution, we would have to take necessary police action to contain the situation and maintain the integrity of the nation....

I would like an assurance from your respective governments, through you individually, that in such extremities your governments will co-operate fully with us, and will do nothing whatsoever tending to give any form of recognition to such dissident elements opposed to my government." - (Gowon, *Africa Contemporary Record*, pp. 646 - 647).

Gowon did not explain why he would not implement any of the Aburi Agreements, in spite of the fact that they had been agreed upon by all the members of the Supreme Military Council including himself; any decree issued by him or even by a majority of the members of the Supreme Military Council was not binding unless it was approved by each and every member of the council.

Everyone of them had veto power; nor did Gowon state categorically that he would implement the agreement when Ojukwu said he would take unilateral action to implement it in his region if the federal government did not.

Gowon's response to Ojukwu's ultimatum was a concession, however inadvertently made if that was ever the case at all, that he would indeed not implement the accords exactly as Ojukwu charged.

On 1 March 1967, the Eastern Nigeria military government outlined its policy towards implementation of the Aburi accords. It said so long as the present situation in

Nigeria exists, Eastern Nigeria will not accept any fiscal arrangement which does not give each region control over its own resources.

Ojukwu's government went on to say that it would not "acquiesce in or operate" any decree issued after January 21st which was not in keeping with the Aburi Agreement; and that any executive act by the federal military government after that date which was not in accordance with the Aburi accords would not be accepted by the Eastern Nigerian military government.

The underlying principle of the Aburi accords was devolution, giving more to the regions, in order to save the federation. Centralisation of power had led to instability and threatened the very existence of the country as a single political entity.

Nigeria was going through a very difficult period, headed towards catastrophe. What was required to save the federation, and avoid war and disintegration, was major concessions to satisfy all the regions even if it meant having a weak central government. Unfortunately, Gowon refused to go that far. As Jimi Peters states in his book, *The Nigerian Military and the State*:

"In the circumstance in which the country found itself, it was felt that the only way to guarantee peace and stability was for the government to allow Nigerians drift apart slightly and for the Regions to be governed by indigenous representation. This position was justified by the fact that it would be impossible to find an individual who could command the loyalty of the various ethnic groups that made up the federation of Nigeria.

It is important to understand that Ojukwu's position was not entirely out of place. The leaders of the July 1966 counter-coup had themselves argued for the country to be split up. This was followed by the forced repatriation of Southerners from the North and *vice versa*. However, between the counter-coup and the Aburi meeting,

155

Northerners had been convinced of the need to stay within a united Nigeria. The portion declaring the secession of the North from the rest of Nigeria was hurriedly deleted at the last minute from Gowon's speech on his assumption of power on 1 August, 1966.

The decisions taken at Aburi, especially the question of whether Nigeria was to continue as a Federation or become a Confederation, was decided in favour of a loose Federation. It was Gowon's decision to go back on the agreements, after being briefed by the country's law officers on their constitutional implications, that was the final straw in the slide towards civil war.

Gowon was horrified to learn that the Aburi Accords gave Supreme Military Council (SMC) members, which also included all Military Governors, the right to veto any Federal legislation – including international custom – they opposed or felt was not in their own interests or Regions.

Once Gowon recognised the constitutional implications of the Aburi decisions and went back on them, Ojukwu decided to take counter-measures: 'If the Aburi agreements are not fully implemented by March 31st, I shall have no alternative but to feel free to take whatever measures to give effect in this Region to those agreements.'" – (Jimi Peters, *The Nigerian Military and the State, Volume 4*, International Library of African Studies, London: Tauris Academic Studies, I.B. Tauris & Co. Ltd., 1997, pp. 104 – 105).

The Eastern Nigerian government also said it would not recognise or deal with a Lagos High Court or a Supreme Court constituted "in the manner stipulated in the second draft decree"; nor will it permit the resources of Eastern Nigeria to be used "in the implementation of any decisions not taken in accordance with the Aburi agreements."

The position of the Easter Nigerian military government on all those issues was articulated in a White

Paper issued by the government in Enugu on 16 March 1967. The paper was also partly reproduced in *Africa Research Bulletin*, 1967, and cited in *Africa Contemporary Record: Annual Survey and Documents 1968 - 1969* (p. 647).

On the next day March 17th soon after Ojukwu spurned the federal authorities when he outlined his policy towards implementing the Aburi accords, the federal military government issued a new constitutional decree covering the whole country. It was approved at a meeting of the Supreme Military Council held in Benin, the capital of the Mid-West Region, on March 9th and 10th, 1967.

The meeting was attended by Gowon and the military governors of the North, West and Mid-West. Ojukwu did not attend the meeting and said he did not approve of the new decree.

The decree was, in fact, in clear violation of the Aburi agreements which explicitly stated that in order for any decree or decision to be binding on all the regions, it must be approved by all the members of the Supreme Military Council. Since Ojukwu did not approve of the new constitutional decree, he was not bound to obey it.

As the two sides moved towards confrontation, the Supreme Military Council – again without Ojukwu – announced on April 22nd a new states-structure to preserve the Federation of Nigeria as one country. Nigeria would be divided into 12 states which would replace the four regions – North, East, West, and Mid-West.

The Supreme Military Council also said it had taken the opportunity to review the latest actions of the Eastern Nigerian military governor, Lieutenant-Colonel Ojukwu, and had taken a number of decisions to protect the revenue and other commercial interests of the federation until such time as the military governor of the East could have second thoughts on his actions.

The Supreme Military Council had also authorised certain "stern measures" to be taken by the federal military government should Ojukwu continue what it called his "illegal actions."

Yet the decision to create states out of the existing regions was in violation of the Aburi agreements since it was not approved by all the members of the Supreme Military Council. Therefore Ojukwu was not bound to obey it. The Aburi agreements explicitly stated that the country would return to the status quo ante, as it was constituted before Ironsi issued the unification decree; which meant the regions would remain intact.

The accords also stated that the four regions – North, East, West, and Mid-West – should move further apart, not be broken down into states, some of which amounted to virtual "ethno-states"; a move in the right direction, especially for the smaller ethnic groups dominated by the big three – Hausa-Fulani, Igbo and Yoruba.

The problem was that the creation of the states violated both stipulations – loosening of the federation, with the regions moving apart, and the regions remaining the way they were instead of breaking them down into smaller components or states. The Aburi accords which were agreed upon and endorsed by all the military governors, and the military head of state himself, Gowon, did not state anywhere that the regions should be broken into states; nor did it give the military head of state the power to restructure the federation.

It was obvious that the nation was now headed towards another major crisis. On 27 May 1967, Gowon proclaimed a state of emergency. In a broadcast to the nation, he said the continued defiance of federal authority by the Eastern Region had produced uncertainty and insecurity generally, and "pushed the country with increasing tempo toward total disintegration and possible civil war...." He went on to say that Ojukwu had "continuously increased his demands, as soon as some are met, in order to perpetuate the crisis and move the Eastern Region out of Nigeria." – (*Africa Contemporary Record*, pp. 648 - 649).

He also explicitly stated that he was invoking full powers vested in him to maintain the territorial integrity of the federation at any cost:

"Faced with this final choice between action to save Nigeria and acquiescence in secession and disintegration, I am therefore proclaiming a state of emergency throughout Nigeria with immediate effect.

I have assumed full powers as commander-in-chief of the armed forces and head of the federal military government for the full period necessary to carry through the measures which are now urgently required." – (Gowon, ibid.).

Gowon went on to explain that the main obstacle to stability in Nigeria was the structural imbalance of the federation:

"Even Decree No. 8 or confederation or loose association will never survive if any one section of the country is in a position to hold others to ransom. This is why the first item in the political and administrative programme adopted by the Supreme Military Council last month (April 1967) is the of states as a basis for stability. This must be done first so as to remove the fear of domination.

Representations drawn from the new states will be more able to work out the future constitution for this country which can contain provisions to protect the powers of the states to the fullest extent desired by the Nigeria people....

While the present circumstances regrettably do not allow for consultations through plebiscites, I am satisfied that the creation of the new states as the only possible basis for stability and equality is the overwhelming desire of the vast majority of Nigerians. To ensure justice, these states are being created simultaneously." – (Gowon, ibid).

The 12 new states were officially announced on 27 May 1967 when Gowon proclaimed a state of emergency in his broadcast to the nation. But the creation of new states was also the spark that lit the fuse. The country was already sitting on a powder keg.

Exactly on the same day, Ojukwu received a regional mandate to declare independence for Eastern Nigeria as a sovereign nation.

One of the most important decisions made by the military governors together with Gowon at the Aburi meeting in Ghana, and which played a critical role in igniting the Nigerian civil war because it was not implemented, was that the regions should move further apart than they originally had been while trying to find a solution to the crisis.

Gowon not only reneged on that promise and divided the four regions – North, East, West, and Md-West – into 12 states without getting the approval of all the military governors; he infuriated Ojukwu and his compatriots in the Eastern Region by making such an arbitrary decision. That was the last straw.

On 27 May 1967, on the same day General Gowon announced the creation of 12 states breaking the Eastern Region into three states, Lieutenant-Colonel Odumegwu Ojukwu, in his official capacity as the military governor of Eastern Nigeria, was given the following mandate to declare independence for the region as the Republic of Biafra:

"We, the chiefs, elders, and representatives of all the 20 Provinces of Eastern Nigeria assembled in this joint meeting of the Advisory Committee of Chiefs and Elders, and the Consultative Assembly at Enugu this 27th day of May, 1967, do hereby solemnly mandate His Excellency Lieutenant-Colonel Chukwuemeka Odumegwu Ojukwu, the Military Governor of Eastern Nigeria, to declare at an early practicable date Eastern Nigeria as a free, sovereign, and independent State by the name and title of the Republic of Biafra...(and) recommend the adoption of a federal constitution based on the new provincial units."

The preamble to the Eastern Nigeria Consultative Assembly's mandate to Ojukwu to declare the region an independent state explained that, as a consequence of the injustices and atrocities committed against Eastern Nigeria, "we have shamefully realized that the Federation of Nigeria has failed and has given us no protection." It added that "the hopes which the Aburi agreements engendered have proved to be misplaced and have been destroyed by a series of acts of bad faith and distortion and finally by a refusal on the part of the Lagos Government to implement these and other agreements, notwithstanding the fact that they were freely and voluntarily entered into."– (*Africa Contemporary Record*, p. 649).

The preamble also stated that the Federation of Nigeria had "forfeited any claim to our allegiance by these acts and, by economic, political, and diplomatic sanctions imposed against us by the so-called Federal Government. Now, therefore, in consideration of these and of other facts and injustices, we, the chiefs, elders, and representatives of all the 20 Provinces of Eastern Nigeria assembled in this joint meeting of the Advisory Committee of Chiefs and Elders, and the Consultative Assembly at Enugu this 27th day of May, 1967, do hereby solemnly:

- Mandate His Excellency Lieutenant-Colonel Chukwuemeka Odumegwu Ojukwu, the Military Governor of Eastern Nigeria, to declare at an early practicable date Eastern Nigeria as a free, sovereign, and independent State by the name and title of the Republic of Biafra.

- Resolve that the new Republic of Biafra shall have the full and absolute powers of a sovereign State and shall establish commerce, levy war, conclude peace, enter into diplomatic relations, and carry out as a right other sovereign responsibilities.

- Direct that the Republic of Biafra may enter into arrangements with any sovereign unit or units in what remains of Nigeria or in any part of Africa desirous of association with us for the purpose of running common services organizations and for the establishment of economic ties.

- Recommend that the Republic of Biafra should become a member of the Commonwealth of Nations, the OAU, and the UN.

- Recommend the adoption of a federal constitution based on the new provincial units.

- Reaffirm His Excellency's assurance of protection for persons, properties, and business of foreign nationals in our territory.

- Declare our unqualified confidence in the Military Governor of Eastern Nigeria, Colonel Chukwuemeka Odumegwu Ojukwu, and assure him of our unreserved support for the way and manner he has handled the crisis in the country. So help us God." – (*Africa Contemporary Record*, ibid).

On 30 May 1967, Ojukwu, 33 years old, declared Biafra independent. Eastern Nigeria became the second region of an independent African country to secede.

The first was the province of Katanga, led by Moise Tshombe, which seceded from the former Belgian Congo on 11 July 1960 only a few days after the country won independence on the June 30th under the leadership of Prime Minister Patrice Lumumba.

But there was one fundamental difference between the two secessionist movements. While Katanga's secession was inspired and supported by foreign interests, especially Belgian and American as well as French, British, West German and South African, Biafra's was indigenous in response to the massacres against Eastern Nigerians in Northern Nigeria and the unwillingness of the northern authorities and the federal government to protect them.

Having been given the mandate to proclaim Eastern Nigeria a sovereign independent state, Ojukwu declared on 30 May 1967 that Eastern Nigeria would henceforth be named "The Republic of Biafra" and dissolved all ties with the Federal Republic of Nigeria. The new country was named after the Bight of Biafra in the Atlantic Ocean on the coast of Eastern Nigeria.

On the same day Ojukwu declared independence, Gowon denounced the secession and ordered full mobilisation of federal forces to end it. An official statement issued in his capacity as head of the federal military government declared "the ill-advised secession statement by Lieutenant-Colonel Ojukwu as an act of rebellion which will be crushed." All leave of military personnel was cancelled and officers on courses were recalled. Able-bodied ex-servicemen were being re-enlisted. The official statement went on to say:

"The Head of the Federal Military Government has emphasized that the three (newly created) Eastern States remain an integral part of the Federal Republic of Nigeria and the Government is taking adequate steps to deal with the rebellion.

The Federal Military Government has warned all countries and international organizations to respect the territorial integrity of the Federal Republic of Nigeria. He also appealed to them to avoid giving any support whatsoever to Ojukwu's rebel group.

The Federal Military Government has re-imposed all the economic measures recently lifted in the spirit of national reconciliation and added new ones on customs facilities in Port Harcourt and Calabar.

Shipping companies have been warned to keep off these ports till further notice in their own interest.

Appropriate instructions have been issued to the Nigerian Navy. The details of further economic measures and other sanctions will be announced from time to time." – (Gowon, ibid., p. 650).

On 3 June 1967, Ojukwu responded in kind. He declared Biafra a disturbed area and declared a state of emergency. He ordered total mobilisation of Biafran forces and empowered all police officers and men to arrest and detain any persons of non-Biafran origin engaged in or suspected of being engaged in any act of subversion.

The "Biafran Constitution Interim Provision Decree, 1967" was promulgated by the military governor on June 4th. Under this constitutional decree, the legislative powers of the Republic of Biafra were vested in the military governor and head of state. The legislative powers would be exercised by means of decrees signed by him. "The validity of this or any other decree shall not be questioned in any court." – (Ojukwu, *Africa Contemporary Record*, pp. 649 - 650).

On June 12th, Major-General Gowon, who was promoted from the rank of colonel during the state of emergency, told a meeting of the enlarged Federal Executive Council that his decision to crush Ojukwu's rebellion was "irrevocable." He said this was aimed at reuniting the Nigerians in the three Eastern states – East Central, South Eastern, and rivers – with "our brothers and sisters in other parts of the country as equal partners in progress." – (Gowon, *Africa Contemporary Record*, ibid., pp. 650 - 651).

On July 6th, fighting broke out between the two sides. The federal military government announced on July 7th that fighting broke out between the Nigerian army and the rebel forces in the three Eastern states. According to the statement, rebel troops opened fire on the Nigerian army positions on the border between Benue-Plateau state and East-Central state in the early hours of 6 July 1967:

"The Federal troops immediately returned fire. The Commander-in-Chief of Armed Forces has since issued orders for the Nigerian Army to penetrate into the East-Central state and capture Ojukwu and his rebel gang.

Already Federal troops have taken Obudu in Ogoja and Obolo near Nsukka and inflicted heavy casualties on the rebl forces. Orders have also been given for the Nigerian armed forces and the Nigerian Police to take adequate measures to safeguard the security of the citizens in the Rivers, South-Eastern, and the East-Central states.

The Federal Military Government recalls that on Friday, June 30th, Ojukwu boasted to the whole world that he will wage total war against the people of Nigeria. He immediately unleashed terrorist activities in Lagos and other parts of Nigeria.

The rebel regime in Enugu had earlier committed acts of provocation by blowing up the Igumale bridge in Idoma Division and attacking several villages on the northern side of the border. The villages terrorized included Ofante, Akpanya, Obale (and) Ogurugu in Igala Division. The rebel forces have since been cleared from these areas.

For the past six months, while Ojukuwu was planning secession, he and his collaborators carried out unprecedented acts of terrorism and intimidation against the innocent minority people of the Calabar, Ogoja, and Rivers areas for wanting their own States within the Federation of Nigeria. These acts included wholesale murders, pillage, arson, unlawful imprisonment, and seizure of personal properties and money.

The Federal Military Government appeals to the general public to remain calm and alert and give their full support to the civil defence organization in their areas. To keep Nigeria one is a task that must be done." – (Gowon, ibid.).

The war had officially begun.

When the first shots were fired in the early hours of July 6th, 1967, signalling the beginning of the Nigerian civil war, both sides were fully prepared for the conflict although in varying degrees of firepower.

The odds were heavily against the secessionists and in favour of the federal side. Yet the secessionist forces had the iron-will to fight, an indomitable spirit which sustained them against overwhelming odds.

They were fighting for what they sincerely believed to be a just cause in a war that had been forced upon them by the federal government which had shown such little regard for the lives of Eastern Nigerians when they were being massacred in Northern Nigeria.

That night, when the civil war began, was one of the darkest moments in African history. Yet, ironically, it was also one of the brightest for the secessionists.

It marked the dawn of a new era, of freedom and independence from their oppressors who also happened to be their fellow countrymen but who denied oppressing them.

Unfortunately, it was a conflict of perceptions and perspectives which was to be settled on the battlefield in a war both sides had been preparing for months. As Ojukwu stated on 6 May 1967 at the State House in Enugu, Eastern Nigeria, just three weeks before he declared independence for Biafra:

"I started off this struggle in July 1966 with 120 rifles to defend the entirety of the East. I took my stand knowing fully well that in doing so, whilst carving my name in history, I was signing also my death warrant. But I took it because I believe that this stand was vital to the survival of the South.

I appealed for settlement quietly because I understood that this was a naked struggle for power. Quietly I built. If you do not know, I am proud, and my officers are proud that here in the East we possess the biggest army in black

Africa. I am no longer speaking as an under-dog, I am speaking from a position of power." – (Ojukwu, *Africa Contemporary Record*, p. 687).

He seemed to demonstrate that on the battlefield when full-scale war started. From July to December 1967, Biafran forces pushed back the much superior Federal Army all the way to Western Nigeria and almost captured Ibadan, the capital of the former Western Region now divided into states like the rest of the former regions.

This dramatic advance into Federal territory – what was left of the Federation after the secession of Eastern Nigeria – was partly helped by a planned insurrection in the former Mid-West Region on 9 August 1967 in collusion with the secessionist forces.

Ojukwu hoped that if he captured Ibadan from the federal forces, he would find substantial support among the Yoruba in the war against Northern Nigerians who dominated the federation as well as the federal army. He hoped to get support not only from Ibadan but also throughout the Western Region.

His optimism was based on the fact that the majority of the Yorubas had, not too long ago in 1964 during the marred general election, formed a coalition with the Igbos which resulted in the formation of the United Progressive Group Alliance (UPGA) as a counter-force, or counter-weight, against Northern Nigerians and their Yoruba allies led by Chief Samuel Akintola who was being used by Northern Nigerian leaders to perpetuate northern domination of the federation.

The Biafran radio broadcasting from Enugu, the capital of the former Eastern Region and now of the Republic of Biafra, appealed to the Yorubas to "rise up in arms" and liberate themselves from "Hausa and Fulani domination" (Radio Enugu, Biafra, August 1967, *Africa Contemporary Record*, op. cit., p. 551).

The Nigerian federal military government imposed a

dusk-to-dawn curfew on Ibadan, and Chief Obafemi Awolowo, the leader of the largest political party in Western Nigeria, the Action Group, dampened Ojukwu's enthusiasm about getting Yoruba support when in a radio broadcast on 12 August 1967 he unequivocally stated that he fully supported the Nigerian federal government and its policy of keeping Nigeria one. The majority of the Yorubas agreed with him. Otherwise they would have seceded from the federation.

But in spite of the dramatic push into the western part of the country by Biafran troops, the federal forces were able to halt further westward advances beyond Benin, capital of the former Mid-West Region, and moved cautiously southwards towards the university town of Nsukka – which had been captured on 15 July 1967 – located in the northwestern part of Biafra. Nsukka lay in the path of the federal government's main objective, Enugu, Ojukwu's operational headquarters.

Even the Biafran hold on Benin, whose capture by Ojukwu's forces had been a great military victory, did not last long, following the "treachery (of) a few highly placed people in my army," as Ojukwu put it, who had betrayed African Biafran plans. On 20 September 1967, federal forces regained control of Benin without resistance.

Three days later, Brigadier Victor Banjo, the "Commander of the Biafran Liberation Army" who had masterminded the capture of Benin, and three other army officers, were executed in Enugu for "plotting the overthrow to overthrow the government of Biafra" (*Africa Contemporary Record*, pp. 551, and 553).

One of the officers executed was Emmanuel Ifeajuna, who was one of the main leaders of the January 1966 military coup.

After the federal forces regained control of Benin, they started moving eastwards towards Onitsha, a major city in Biafra. They had other targets as well in their multi-pronged attack which put millions of Igbos in a precarious

168

situation:

"The southern thrust at the port of Warri and Bonny in the oil-bearing regions of the Rivers State, and the slow but inexorable advance on Enugu, were the beginnings of an encircling movement by the Federal army which, during the course of some 12 months of sanguine warfare, was to squeeze the Biafran army and several million Ibo men, women and children, into an area of 100 miles by 70 miles, with all the consequences of famine." – (*Africa Contemporary Record*, p. 553).

It was a death trap. And as the fighting continued, it became almost impossible for the smaller and weaker Biafran army to break out of the encirclement, let alone push back the bigger and better-equipped federal forces and enlarge the small area in which millions of Igbos were trapped, only waiting to die.

They did not seem to have much choice left. Having suffered and sacrificed so much, surrender was unthinkable, especially at the hands of an army led by the very people – the Hausa and other northerners – who had massacred tens of thousands of their people in Northern Nigeria only a few months earlier. As Ojukwu stated in July 1999, almost 30 years after the war, in an interview with *USAfrica*:

"It was a Hobson's choice for Igbos and other Biafrans. What else could we have done? Line up, bare our necks, shave it if possible, and say 'come on' to the Hausas, Kanuris, Tivs, Fulanis and other members of the Nigerian army and civilians who were killing our people of Eastern Nigeria, later Biafra? No!....We never declared war on anybody....It was simply a choice between Biafra and enslavement."

Yet some of the people who inflicted some of the

heaviest casualties on the Biafrans during the war were not always Hausas or other northerners. There was, for example, the legendary "Black Scorpion," Colonel Benjamin Adenkule, whose father was a Yoruba and his mother a Bachama and who went down in history as a brilliant strategist and field commander and one of the best soldiers Africa has ever produced. He masterminded several attacks by the Nigerian federal forces which led to the defeat of the secessionist troops in many battles.

His brilliance on the battlefield was probably matched only by Ojukwu's who himself went into combat and was responsible for directing a number of Biafran advances which led to victory against the far superior Federal Army in some of the deadliest engagements of the war.

Biafra's struggle for independence or self-determination was, not in terms of aspiration but in terms of context, different from that of other African countries which had not yet attained sovereign status.

Eastern Nigerians were fighting to win freedom from the very same country they were an integral part of, and which won independence from an external colonial power just like all the other African countries did.

And although a number of African countries were still not independent by 1967, there was no country which won independence that year. But there was an important development taking place in terms of liberation. And that was the armed struggle in the countries of southern Africa still under white minority rule.

It was one of the most important developments in Africa in the late sixties as we will learn later when we look at what happened on the continent towards the end of the decade.

1968

PROBABLY more than in any other period during the Nigerian civil war, the year 1968 witnessed the fiercest and deadliest military engagements between the federal army and the secessionist forces. It was also a year of intense diplomatic efforts to end the conflict.

And probably no single group caused so much devastation as did the Egyptian pilots in their indiscriminate bombings of civilian centres in Biafra when they went on bombing missions on behalf of the federal forces. As William Norris, a British journalist who covered the war, reported in his eyewitness account in the *Sunday Times* of London, 28 April 1968:

"I have seen things in Biafra this week which no man should have to see. Sights to scorch the mind and sicken the conscience. I have seen children roasted alive, young girls torn in two by shrapnel, pregnant women eviscerated, and old men blown to fragments. I have seen these things and I have seen their cause: high-flying Russian Ilyushin jets operated by Federal Nigeria, dropping their bombs on civilian centres throughout Biafra." – (William Norris, "Nightmare in Biafra," *Sunday Times*,London, 28 April 1968, p.12).

All the main towns in the secessionist region were bombed by Egyptian pilots flying Nigerian war planes. They included Aba, Abakaliki, Afikpo, Arochuku, Awgu, Bonny, Brass, Degema, Ikot Ekpene, Itu, Okigwi, Onitsha, Opobo, Oron, Owerri, Port Harcourt, Umuahia, and Uyo. Schools and hospitals and other places where civilians sought refuge were also bombed; so were numerous villages across Biafra.

President Julius Nyerere of Tanzania was said to have asked President Gamal Abdel Nasser of Egypt to withdraw his pilots in order to stop the bombing of Biafra:

"The Biafrans hoped that President Nyerere's close friendship with President Nasser – whom he had visited in March (1968) – would influence him to withdraw Egyptian pilots flying MIGS. According to a Biafran radio announcement, such a request was in fact made by the Tanzanian Government." – (*Africa Contemporary Record*, p. 220. See also the Biafran paper, *The Mirror*, April-May 1968).

A few months earlier when federal troops took back Benin, the capital of the former Mid-West Region, from the Biafrans, the secessionist forces did not entirely lose out. It is true that with the loss of Benin, Ojukwu failed in a major strategic gamble to outmanoeuvre the federal army. But he was able to seize and carry away a substantial amount of money from the Mid-West when Biafran troops occupied the region from September to October 1967. The Biafrans took at least £2 million (2 million pounds) from the Benin branch of the Federal

Central Bank.

The money, together with an even bigger amount of £37 million which had been seized from branches of the same bank at Enugu and Port Harcourt, gave the Biafran government substantial foreign exchange resources which they used to help finance their war effort and put up stiff resistance against the federal forces although the Biafran troops were confined to a very small area with millions of people. And Ojukwu himself kept the spirits high among his besieged brethren:

"With the crucial assistance of a mobile transmitting station still using the signal of Radio Enugu, Biafra's charismatic leader welded the 8 million Ibos into a defiant and unyielding people of immense fortitude, sagacity nd resourcefulness." - (*Africa Contemporary Record*, p. 553).

Ojukwu's speeches had a tremendous emotional impact on his beleaguered compatriots. And cries of "genocide" and dire warnings about the extreme cruelty of the federal troops were some of the most powerful battle cries coming out of Radio Enugu to mobilise and sustain resistance among the Igbos against their enemies.

Ojukwu himself and others repeatedly invoked those themes and images, warning their people in no uncertain terms what would happen if Biafra lost the war: total extermination of the Igbo. Therefore fighting was the only alternative they had left, they were told. And the invocation of such apocalyptic themes worked:

"In the eyes of many of them, the 'Muslim hordes' – as the Biafran radio described the Federal forces – were bent on the elimination of the 'Christian Ibo,' encouraging the belief that there was more than a political issue at stake. 'Holy Archangel Michael' Colonel Ojukwu postulated in one midnight broadcast, 'defend us in battle.'" – (Ibid.).

The response from his people was overwhelming. They were solidly behind their leader. On 28 September 1967, General Gowon in a nationwide broadcast, appealed to the Igbo to overthrow Ojukwu "who is the only barrier between peace and the people of Nigeria," as he put it (Gowon, *Africa Contemporary Record*, p. 553).

But his appeal fell on deaf ears. And that strengthened Ojukwu's resolve to accept nothing less than full independence for Biafra during several but unsuccessful peace talks arranged by the Organization of African Unity (OAU) in different capitals: Addis Ababa, Ethiopia; Kinshasa, Congo Democratic Republic; Kampala, Uganda; and Niamey, Niger. The OAU summit held in Algiers, capital of Algeria, in September 1968 also made strenuous efforts to arrange peace talks between the two parties. But they kept on fighting.

In spite of the iron-will of the Igbos to resist and continue fighting, what happened on the battlefield was a different matter. They had a number of brilliant victories which defied the odds against them. But cumulatively, they were gradually losing the war, as one town after another under their control fell to federal troops.

Towards the end of 1967, the secessionist forces suffered a stunning defeat. In early October, the Biafran capital Enugu was captured by federal troops. Shortly thereafter, another major city, Calabar, also fell.

The battle for Onitsha, one of the major cities in the whole country, was one of the bloodiest. Federal troops made a sustained effort to try and capture it. But they were beaten back and suffered heavy casualties, inflicted on them by the much smaller Biafran army which had been underrated since the outbreak of the war. Finally, Onitsha fell on 22 May 1968 after months of bloody fighting on Biafran soil.

Port Harcourt, a major port city and oil terminal, was blockaded by federal forces, effectively denying Biafrans access to the sea; they had already lost Calabar, another important port city. But during the last two months of 1967, the push into Biafran territory by federal troops was halted when the secessionist forces fought them to a stalemate. It was a major setback for the superior federal forces, and the outcome of the war became unpredictable.

Earlier attempts to end the conflict failed because of the uncompromising positions taken by both sides. During the OAU summit in mid-September 1967 in Kinshasa, Congo Democratic Republic, when Biafran troops were still in control of the Mid-West, the African heads of state and government agreed to send the president of Cameroon, the Congo Democratic Republic, Ghana, Liberia, Niger and the Emperor of Ethiopia, Haile Selassie, to Lagos to confer with Gowon on ways of ending the war.

However, the OAU handicapped itself when in its resolution at the Kinshasa conference, it said it regarded "the situation as an internal affair." – (*Africa Contemporary ,Record*, p. 554).

If that was true, then what happened to the 6 million Jews in Nazi Germany was also "an internal affair" and Hitler was right; and the massacre of the Igbos in Northern Nigeria was also justified on grounds of ethnic cleansing.

When an entire segment of society faces extermination from war or other man-induced catastrophes such as starvation and famine, or is targeted for unjust treatment, the matter ceases to be an internal affair of any country; it becomes the concern for all mankind. That is the kind of principle the OAU employed in the case of apartheid South Africa.

There was no reason it could not apply the same principle in the case of Nigeria where Igbos faced annihilation, mainly from starvation, although the federal forces sometimes deliberately used hunger as a very effective weapon to starve the Igbos into submission.

The OAU also avoided direct involvement in the Nigerian conflict by invoking its charter in "adherence to the principle of respect for the sovereignty and territorial integrity of member-states," as the Kinshasa resolution also clearly stated.

The result of such non-interference was the near-extermination of the Igbos in the late sixties, the slaughter of 300,000 – 500,000 people by Idi Amin in Uganda during the seventies, and the massacre of about one million Tutsis and 130,000 moderate Hutus by Hutu extremists in Rwanda in 1994.

Had half a million – let alone a whole million – black people been massacred by whites in South Africa during the apartheid era, it is highly unlikely that the independent African countries would have simply dismissed that as South Africa's internal affair. They probably would have declared war on South Africa, come what may.

While the OAU unequivocally supported Gowon's policy of "one Nigeria," the Biafrans also articulated their position in explicit and equally uncompromising terms. According to the Biafran newspaper *The Mirror*, Enugu, Biafra, September 1967:

"Two conditions must be fulfilled before Biafra can submit to the peace talks. Firstly, all mercenaries now fighting for Gowon should be expelled; secondly, Biafra should be accorded the status of a Sovereign State."

In the eyes of many people, the Biafrans had earned their independence because of the enormous sacrifices they had made. Tens of thousands of their people were massacred in Northern Nigeria; more than 2 million of them were expelled from the same region and forced to leave other parts of Nigeria – or they would have faced more massacres and possible extermination if they insisted on staying; and now millions of them – almost the entire Igbo population – were facing annihilation, mostly from starvation, in the tiny area to which they were confined by the advancing federal forces.

Yet even all those massacres and mass expulsions of

Eastern Nigerians from Northern Nigeria did not attract international attention or win any sympathy for the victims of the atrocities. In fact, the exodus was hardly noticed at all. But it was heart-rending.

The London *Observer*, 16 October 1966, described the scene in Eastern Nigeria within two weeks of this mass return as "reminiscent of the in-gathering of exiles into Israel after the end of the last war. The parallel is not fanciful." And as Dr. Conor Cruise O'Brien who led the UN forces in Congo against the secessionists in Katanga Province only a few years earlier stated in *The New York Review of Books*, 21 December 1967:

"If this movement had taken place across international frontiers, it would have attracted world-wide attention. Because it was within the geographical unit called Nigeria, it drew no public comment and won no world sympathy."

When the conflict escalated into full-scale war after the expulsion of Eastern Nigerians from the Northern Region, it then started getting world-wide coverage in the print and in the electronic media; and the victims of the war won a lot of sympathy from around the world.

But that was not enough to induce the Nigerian government to stop the war. It was determined to crush the secessionists for a number of reasons – save the federation, punish them, make them suffer, set an example for others not to emulate them, and probably even more.

A Swiss correspondent, Dr. Edmond C. Schwarzenbach, interviewed one Nigerian commissioner in the federal government whom he descibed as "one of the most impressive in the present military regime in Lagos." He said it was an interview which provided him with a "significant insight into the political aims of the Federal Government." He went on to state in the *Swiss Review of Africa*, February 1968:

177

"The (Nigerian) war aim and 'solution'...of the entire problem was to 'discriminate against the Ibos in the future in their own interest.'

Such discrimination would include above all the detachment of those oil-rich territories in the Eastern Region which were not inhabited by them at the beginning of the colonial period, on the lines of the projected twelve-state plan.

In addition, the Ibos' movement would be restricted, to prevent their renewed penetration into other parts of the country. Leaving them any access to the sea, the Commissioner declared, was quite out of the question."

It was a deliberate policy of subjugation and exclusion of the Igbos. If implemented, it would have denied them equal rights under the law and would have turned them into second-class citizens.

Both parties to the conflict were diametrically opposed on the fundamental question of sovereignty for Biafra. The federal military government was determined to keep on fighting as long as the secessionists insisted that they had the right to have their own independent state. The Biafrans were equally determined; they wanted nothing short of independence.

As the war raged on, the Organization of African Unity was also running on a parallel track to pursue the peace process. The African heads of state who constituted the OAU Consultative Commission went on a peace mission to Lagos and met with Gowon on 23 November 1967. But Gowon offered no compromise.

He told the six heads of state that before a cease-fire could be declared by his government, the secessionists must lay down their arms; Ojukwu and his colleagues must be replaced by new leaders; and these leaders must accept the new structure of the federation based on the newly-created 12 states which replaced the four regions – North, East, West, and Mid-West. A communique issued after the meeting stated:

"The Consultative Mission agreed that, as a basis for return to peace and normal conditions in Nigeria, the secessionists should renounce secession and accept the present administrative structure of the Federation of Nigeria...." – (OAU Consultative Commission and the Nigerian Federal Military Government in a joint communique, Lagos, November 1967; quoted in *Africa Contemporary Record*, op.cit., p. 554).

The Ghanaian military head of state, Lieutenant-General Joseph Ankrah, was asked to deliver the text of the resolution to the Biafran leaders and report back to the OAU Consultative Commission; he first tried to contact Colonel Ojukwu by radio telephone but was unable to do so.

On 24 November 1967, the same day the communique was issued in Lagos by the OAU peace mission, the Biafran leaders issued a statement commenting adversely on the brevity of the consultations and on the fact that the six African heads of state who went to see Gowon had consulted with only one party to the conflict.

The Biafran statement went on to say that the OAU Consultative Commission had "condoned genocide and had proved itself a rubber stamp, merely endorsing Gowon's warning that their own countries would disintegrate if they did not rally to his support" – (*The Mirror*, Enugu, Biafra, 23 November 1967; *Africa Contemporary Record*, p. 554).

At the beginning of 1968, Gowon still believed that the civil war could be ended only if Ojukwu was out of the way and other Igbo leaders took his place. He was strongly convinced, for whatever reason, that these leaders would be receptive to his peace proposals than Ojukwu was. Yet, collectively, Gowon's proposals amounted only to one thing: an uncompromising demand for renunciation of

179

Biafra's claim to sovereign status, hence an unconditional surrender by the secessionists.

At a press conference in Lagos on 5 January 1968, Gowon named several Igbo leaders whom he said he believed he would be able to negotiate with and end the war. They included Nigeria's first president, Dr. Nnamdi Azikiwe, who also supported Biafra's secession.

Gowon said he believed that together with such leaders "who would discuss in good faith and keep agreements, effective arrangements could be negotiated to ensure that the territorial integrity of Nigeria is preserved while the safety and livelihood of all its citizens are guaranteed." – (Gowon, *Africa Contemporary Record*, p. 555).

He appealed to them to come forward and start negotiating with the federal government. But like his first appeal to the Igbos the year before on 28 September 1967 to overthrow Ojukwu, this one also fell on deaf ears.

However, some people noticed a slight change in Biafra's position following a broadcast by Ojukwu on 15 February 1968. The Commonwealth Secretariat in London saw this change, however slight, as an opportunity to renew peace talks. In his broadcast from Biafran territory, Ojukwu emphatically stated:

"Any peace plan which does not guarantee Biafrans security inside and outside our borders will clearly be unacceptable to Biafrans.

The challenge to those working on a peace plan is to find a formula which will enable Biafra to live peacefully, not in Nigeria, but with Nigeria." – (Ojukwu, ibid.).

The key component of what was called the "Commonwealth initiative" to end the war was a proposal to send a multinational peace-keeping force to oversee the transition from a cease-fire to a peaceful settlement under a new constitution. However, neither Biafra nor the Nigerian federal military government endorsed it.

Then at the end of March 1968, the World Council of Churches and the Roman Catholic Church sought ways to help end the conflict. The interest of the Roman Catholic Church was even greater for another reason: most of the Biafrans, hence the vast majority of the war victims, were Catholic.

In a joint statement, the two church organisations appealed to "the governments and international organizations that are able to act effectively in this field to act so as to bring about a denial of any outside military assistance to the two parties, and immediate cessation of hostilities, so that necessary guarantees be given to both sides in laying down their arms in order to open negotiations." – (*Africa Contemporary Record*, ibid).

The biggest supplier of weapons to Nigeria was Britain which, as the former colonial power, had been the traditional source of arms for that country.

The Soviet Union also played a big role in supporting the Nigerian federal government by supplying MIGs which wreaked havoc across Biafra when they were flowing by Egyptian pilots, dropping bombs on towns and many other places where the people had sought refuge.

Nigerian officials had their own interpretation of the statement from the World Council of Churches and the Roman Catholic Church. They saw it as an attempt by Christian churches to drive a wedge between Northern Nigerians, who were mostly Muslim, and their southern counterparts who were predominantly Christian.

In a nationwide broadcast on 31 March 1968, Gowon said he was disturbed that the Vatican and the World Council of Churches had called for a cease-fire and cessation of hostilities before Biafrans had accepted the new federal structure of 12 states as the basis for negotiations. Yet that was the very same condition which was totally unacceptable to the Biafrans; accepting it would have meant renunciation of their sovereignty.

Therefore, Gowon himself offered nothing new in

terms of peace proposals. He knew Biafrans would not accept renunciation of their sovereign status as a precondition for negotiations. His uncompromising stand meant only one thing: total war against Biafra until the secessionists capitulated to federal might.

Just two weeks later, after Gowon addressed the nation in a radio broadcast at the end of March, Tanzania recognised Biafra as an independent state. Tanzania's minister of state for foreign affairs, Chediel Mgonja, announced on 13 April 1968 that Tanzania had officially recognised the "State of Biafra."

He explained that Tanzania had done so because there was no longer any basis for unity between the 12 million Igbos as well as other easterners and the rest of the Nigerians. He went on to say that when an entire people are rejected by their fellow countrymen, they have the right to have their own country.

Mgonja's statement drew a sharp and swift response from the Nigerian federal government. Nigeria immediately broke diplomatic relations with Tanzania and issued this statement:

"The Nigerian Government regards this as a hostile act by a country it had sincerely treated as a friend. In Tanzania's hour of need in 1964 when the Tanzanian army mutinied against the Nyerere regime, Nigeria readily responded to President Nyerere's desperate appeal for Nigerian troops to save him, restore law and order and preserve the territorial integrity of Tanzania." – (Ibid., p. 556).

After Tanzania became the first country to recognise Biafra as an independent nation, there was some concern in Lagos that others would follow Nyerere's example and give full recognition to the secessionist region as a sovereign entity.

The Nigerian federal government tried to avert that by

exploring other possibilities for a peaceful settlement of the conflict.

Nigeria's commissioner for external affairs, Dr. Okoi Arikpo, told a press conference in Lagos on April 18th, five days after Tanzania recognized Biafra, that despite the military advantage federal forces had over Biafra, the federal government was still interested in holding peace talks "at any time and any venue acceptable to both sides." – (*Africa Contemporary Record*, ibid.).

Yet he at the same time precluded any possibility of such peaceful resolution of the conflict when he insisted that fighting would stop only when the rebels had renounced secession and accepted the new federal structure of 12 states.

That is something Biafrans would never do unless they were forced to do so by losing the war. Their unwillingness to do that was deeply rooted in fear for their safety and security; and that was the main reason Tanzania recognised Biafra to the consternation of the Nigerian federal authorities.

Towards the end of April 1968, not long after Tanzania recognized Biafra as an independent state, both sides – Nigeria dn Biafra – outlined their negotiating terms for peace talks scheduled before the end of the month. The talks were to be held on April 26th, coincidentally, on the fourth anniversary of the union of Tanganyika and Zanzibar which led to the formation of Tanzania; and it may not have been a coincidence.

If Nigerian officials are the ones who proposed the date (April 26th) for the peace talks, they may have intended to send a strong message to Tanzania as a country which recognised the secessionist region of Eastern Nigeria: the union of Tanganyika and Zanzibar could also face secessionist threats, especially from the former island nation of Zanzibar.

Whatever the case, the peace talks did not take place until May. A communique was issued by the

Commonwealth Secretariat stating that a peace conference would be held in Kampala, Uganda.

Tragically, while preliminary talks for the peace conference were going on, full-scale war between the two sides also continued unabated.

On 20 May 1968, federal troops captured Port Harcourt, a vital link to the outside world for Biafra and one of the major port cities in Nigeria. The government hoped that the capture of this important city on Biafran territory would demonstrate to the Biafran negotiators how vulnerable their secessionist forces were to federal military might; and that once they understood the precariousness of their military situation, they might soften their negotiating position and compromise on a number of vital issues. But exactly the opposite happened.

The Biafrans remained adamant, their spirits buoyed by Zambia's recognition of Biafra on the same day Port Harcourt was captured. Zambia's official recognition of the break-away region came only a few days after Gabon recognized it on May 8th and Ivory Coast on May 10th.

However, Zambia's recognition of Biafra just before the peace talks did not turn the Nigerian government against the peace process; it may in fact have helped to facilitate it, if Nigerian leaders thought more countries might recognise Biafra should the federal government decide not to seek a peaceful solution to the conflict.

The peace conference in Kampala opened on May 23rd just three days after Zambia became the fourth African country to recognise Biafra. At the opening session, the leader of the Nigerian delegation, Chief Anthony Enahoro, said he would later on put forward "concrete and sincere suggestions" which would satisfy both sides.

The proposals would include arrangements for restoring law and order, and guarantees for the security of lives and property for all Nigerians including the secessionists.

He went on to say that the federal government had

already formed committees, headed by Igbos, to secure properties left behind by Igbos who fled back to their home region from Northern Nigeria and other parts of the country before the war started.

Enahoro added that the properties had not been destroyed, an assurance that was not very convincing especially with regard to Northern Nigeria where there was large-scale violence against the Igbo and evidence that Igbo properties had been looted and destroyed while both the Northern Nigerian authorities and the federal government itself looked the other way; the same way they did when tens of thousands of Igbos were being massacred in that region, in many cases at the instigation of and in connivance with Northern Nigerian leaders.

However, Enahoro went on to say that in Lagos and its surrounding areas, 50,000 Igbos went on with their normal lives, working or just taking care of their families at home or going to school, without any problems from fellow Nigerians.

Proposals for a ceasefire offered by the Nigerian federal government were totally unacceptable to Biafran leaders. They included stipulations that federal authorities would administer the former Biafran areas and that law and order would be the responsibility of the federal government. They amounted to a demand for total renunciation of secession by Biafra.

It was an explicit demand federal officials had always insisted on from the beginning but which was out of the question as far as Biafrans were concerned.

To "soften" its hardline position, the federal government said instead of renouncing secession, Biafran leaders should simply say that they recognised the need for one Nigeria. That was only a semantic game. It amounted to the same thing: renunciation of secession which, to the Biafrans, was non-negotiable.

Sir Louis Mbanefo, the leader of the Biafran delegation to the Kampala peace talks, denounced Nigeria's terms for a ceasefire as no more than "a programme of arrangements for a Biafran surrender." – (*Africa Contemporary Record*, p.558).

After he made that statement, Sir Louis did not take part in any formal negotiations for the rest of the year; and the Kampala peace talks failed to resolve the conflict.

There was fear that the failure of the Kampala peace talks, and the capture of Port Harcourt only a few days earlier, would lead to more fierce fighting as federal troops continued to tighten the noose around millions of Igbos trapped in an area which had shrunk to an even smaller area than the 70-mile-by-100-mile area they were confined to by September 1967.

Their suffering was severe. It became even more intense with the advance of Nigerian troops on their tiny and barren territory. Also, malnutrition, starvation and disease continued to take their toll, claiming countless lives.

The British government also came under increasing pressure and criticism from the public because of its supply of weapons to the federal army which were being used to kill Igbos.

Concern in Lagos that such strong public criticism might force Britain to stop supplying Nigeria with weapons prompted Chief Anthony Enahoro to issue a warning on 12 June 1968 that if the British did that, they would accomplish exactly the opposite.

Cessation of arms supplies would only prolong the war, and the British would also jeopardise their interests in Nigeria. He went on to say that "a stoppage would also encourage rebel intransigents – they would be more reluctant to talk realistically about peace than they have been." – (*Africa Contemporary Record*, p. 559).

The British House of Commons held a debate on the Nigerian civil war on the same day Enahoro made his statement in Lagos. He spoke shortly before the debate started, obviously as a warning to the British not to stop supplying Nigeria with weapons.

The British Foreign Secretary, Michael Stewart, said during the debate that Britain would not cut off arms supplies because Nigeria only intended to use the weapons to preserve its territorial integrity, and not to slaughter or starve the Igbo; an argument that was not very convincing, if at all.

As fighting continued, the OAU Consultative Commission again tried to resolve the crisis. The six presidents who constituted the commission met in Niamey, capital of Niger, on 15 July 1968. They heard a statement from Gowon and then decided to invite Ojukwu to Niamey to continue exploring possibilities for a peaceful resolution of the conflict. In his statement, Gowon said:

"The rebel leaders and their foreign backers are playing politics with the whole question of human suffering in the war zones and trying to exploit the sufferings of our countrymen to their diplomatic and military advantage. Once the rebellion is ended by negotiations or otherwise, we will heal our wounds and care for the hungry and needy in the war zone.

If the rebel leaders persist in their contemptuous attitude to the conference table, the Federal Government will have no choice but to take over the remaining rebel-held areas....(In military terms, the rebellion) is virtually suppressed already....What the Federal Government is determined to prevent is any diplomatic manoeuvre which will enable the rebel leaders to sustain the rebellion and secession which they have lost in the battlefield." – (*Africa Contemporary Record*, ibid., p. 560).

On the secessionists' demand that a ceasefire must be accompanied by the withdrawal of federal troops from their territory, Gowon said accession to such a demand would be tantamount to recognition of Biafra as an independent state. That was totally out of the question.

The war continued, with the federal government using its military might to try to force the secessionists to surrender unconditionally.

The OAU also continued to pursue the peace process but did not make any progress because of the federal government's refusal to negotiate with the secessionists without preconditions, especially its insistence that Biafra must renounce its secession before serious negotiations could take place.

Prospects for a peaceful resolution of the conflict were almost destroyed when France "recognised" Biafra on 1 August 1968. It was *de facto* recognition. France supported Biafra's right to self-determination and provided the secessionist region with weapons to help it achieve its goal. For all practical purposes, such support amounted to virtual recognition of the new "nation" by France.

Israel also supported Biafra; so did apartheid South Africa, Rhodesia and Portugal. But it was France's support of the breakaway region which proved to be critical in terms military aid.

France was the sixth and the only non-black country which accorded the secessionist region recognition: the region's right to self-determination. The other five – Tanzania, Ivory Coast, Zambia, Gabon, and Haiti – formally recognised Biafra, unlike France.

In an official statement on France's "recognition" of Biafra as a sovereign entity, the French Minister of Information, Joel de Tatule, stated:

"The bloodshed and suffering that the Biafran people have endured for more than a year demonstrate their determination to affirm themselves as a people.

Loyal to its principles, the French Government considers, consequently, that the present conflict should be settled on the basis of the rights of peoples to self-determination and should comprise the setting in motion of the appropriate international procedures." – (Ibid., p.

188

562).

During the peace talks in Addis Ababa, Ethiopia, in August 1968, the leader of the Biafran delegation Dr. Eni Njoku promised that Biafra would accept a plebiscite in the "contested regions of Biafra" and Nigeria to determine whether or not the members of ethnic minorities wanted to be a part of Biafra. But the federal government, which had all along contended that the minority groups in the former Eastern Region had been forced by the Igbos to join Biafra, refused to hold the plebiscite.

Federal officials were probably worried about the outcome, since there was a high probability that the Biafrans would have beeen vindicated in their claim that the ethnic minorities, although not all of them, had willingly joined the Igbos to establish Biafra as an independent nation.

That seemed to have been the case, at least during the early part of the war up to 1968 and may be even beyond. That is why Ojukwu, confident of the outcome, asked for a plebiscite when he addressed the OAU conference on the Nigerian civil war in Addis Ababa on August 5th that year. Otherwise he would not have done that, risking his credibility, if he thought that the ethnic minorities would vote against Biafra.

The minority groups in the former Eastern Region which chose to join Biafra were probably aware that assurances by Nigerian leaders that the government would implement the principle of Nigerian federalism under which ethnic minorities would enjoy protection was no more than lip service, given their history in the past at the hands of the Hausa-Fulani who had dominated the federation since independence.

Had a plebiscite been conducted to determine the wishes of the minority groups in Eastern Nigeria, Biafra would have survived as a viable sovereign entity provided the federal government acknowledged the right of the

Biafrans to rule themselves in their own country; a concession which would have been a fulfillment of the demand made by the government itself that "if seven million Ibos are entitled to self-determination, equally so are five million Efiks, Ibibios, Ekois and Ijaws," as Chief Enahoro stated in his address to the OAU in Addis Ababa in August 1968. – (Chief Anthony Enahoro, *Africa Contemporary Record*, p. 684).

Yet, the federal government refused to conduct a plebiscite, denying the minority groups the very democratic right – to determine their own destiny – it claimed they were entitled to, which it also claimed was being denied to them by the Igbos, although many of them joined Biafra willingly. A plebiscite would conclusively have shown whether or not the minority groups in Biafra had indeed joined the Igbos willingly to establish the independent state of Biafra.

But since that option was rejected by the federal government, as much as it rejected Biafra's claim to sovereign status, continuation of the war was the only alternative left, short of unconditional surrender by the secessionist forces.

The Addis Ababa peace talks under the auspices of the OAU were adjourned indefinitely on 9 September 1968 without reaching any agreement on how to end the devastating conflict; and the odds were overwhelmingly against the Biafrans. Outnumbered and outgunned, their defeat seemed inevitable; and unable to win official recognition from most countries around the world, they had also lost the diplomatic contest in the international arena.

Worst of all, they got little support from their own continent where other African countries did not collectively bring enough pressure to bear upon Nigeria for her to unilaterally cease fire against a people who were already outgunned, and find a peaceful solution to the conflict even it meant forming a loose federation or a confederation and then gradually work towards establishing a strong central government with the consent of all the parties concerned, if that was the kind of government they wanted.

When it became obvious that the Addis Ababa peace talks were going nowhere, General Gowon ordered his field commanders to launch a "final offensive" on 24 August 1968. He felt that his assurance on June 6th that that the federal army and air force would not "drive into the heart of the East-Central state unless all appeals to end the Nigerian crisis fail," had been met. – (*Africa Contemporary Record*, p. 564).

The East-Central state was the Igbo heartland; it was almost entirely Igbo, unlike the other two states in the former Eastern Region which were not overwhelmingly Igbo but had substantial Igbo populations.

Gowon's ultimatum placed the blame for continuation of the war entirely in the hands of the secessionists. He took full advantage of Biafra's military weakness, and only unconditional surrender by the Igbos would save them from annihilation. But they were not willing to do that and faced the prospect of extermination from a combination of factors: starvation and disease, and attack by the federal forces.

By September 1968, the "final offensive" against Biafra had gained momentum. The Federal Second Division under Colonel I.B.M. Haruna had by then taken positions and linked up along the Onitsha-Enugu Road with the First Division operating from Enugu, the former Biafran capital which was captured by federal troops almost exactly a year earlier in early October 1967 just three months after the war started.

The Second Division, which also penetrated the east and captured Onitsha, Enugu and other parts of Biafra, was then led by Colonel Murtala Muhammad before he was succeeded by Colonel Haruna.

The joint operation by the two divisions led to an

escalation of the conflict which triggered an unexpected strong military response from the Biafran forces. After they seized the Onitsha-Enugu Road, federal military convoys were now able to move freely along this vital supply link so critical to logistical support for the federal troops advancing on Biafran-held territory.

But even with the capture of this main artery, the road was subjected to periodic and sometimes sustained attacks by Biafran troops.

On the southern front, the Third Division of Marine Commandos led by the legendary "Black Scorpion" Colonel Benjamin Adenkule had seized Aba, an important rail and road link located midway between Port Harcourt and Umuahia southeast of Onitsha. Aba became the new Biafran capital in October 1967 after Enugu fell to sustained federal bombardment during that month.

After Colonel Adenkule captured Aba, the Biafrans moved their capital further north on the same road to Umuahia, another important road and railway terminal south of Okigwi. Despite the loss of Aba, Biafrans scored one of their major victories in the war in the same month they lost their capital. Ojukwu himself went to the war front and led the offensive:

"Following an attack led personally by Colonel Ojukwu at the end of September (1968) on the strategic town of Oguta, which commands the Uli-Ihiala airstrip, the Biafrans pushed the frontier back some 13 miles to the Niger River. The airstrip, which was under constant Federal artillery fire at the end of September, was reported safe on 26 October.

During October the Biafran fire power changed significantly as a considerable increase of military supplies, allegedly from France, were flown in via Libreville, Gabon.

The Biafrans had succeeded in taking the northern suburbs of Owerri which fell to federal forces on 16

September. On the northern front the Biafrans maintained pressure on Onitsha, cutting the road from Umuahia – the Biafran headquarters – to Onitsha, and the road from Onitsha to Abagana, which was held by Federal forces. An international observer confirmed the Biafran claim to have regained Okigwi. No further substantial gains were made by either side by the end of 1968." – (*Africa Contemporary Record*, p. 564).

On 16 September 1968, Biafra suffered yet another blow when African heads of state and government passed a resolution at the OAU summit in Algiers, Algeria, which did not recognise its sovereign status but, instead, supported the Nigerian federal government's position on the conflict. Nigerian leaders said they would be willing to participate in peace talks with the Biafrans only if they were conducted in compliance with that resolution.

The resolution was supported by 33 countries. Rwanda and Botswana abstained from voting, and the four countries in the OAU which recognised Biafra – Tanzania, Zambia, Ivory Coast, and Gabon – voted against it.

The resolution was based on a draft prepared by Cameroon, Congo Democratic Republic (Kinshasa), Ghana, Liberia, Niger, and Ethiopia – the six members of the OAU Consultative Commission on the Nigerian conflict under the chairmanship of Emperor Haile Selassie.

It is also understandable why the Nigerian federal government was willing to participate in renewed peace talks – provided they were based on the Algerian resolution. Most of the African heads of state and government sided with Nigeria, a stand clearly reflected by the wording of the resolution:

"[The resolution] appeals to the secessionist leaders to co-operate with the Federal authorities in order to restore peace and unity in Nigeria...(and) calls upon all member States of the United Nations and the OAU to refrain from any action detrimental to the peace, unity and territorial integrity of Nigeria...." – (*Africa Contemporary Record*, p. 620).

At a plenary meeting, Tanzania, Zambia, Ivory Coast, and Gabon urged the OAU to demand an immediate ceasefire, followed by renewed peace talks to be attended by both parties to the conflict. The proposal was opposed by many speakers. Instead, they all supported the majority view that the war was Nigeria's internal affair and that Nigeria's territorial integrity must be maintained at all costs.

As 1968 came to an end, there was still no hope for a negotiated settlement of the conflict. Even an appeal by Emperor Haile Selassie to the Nigerian government to grant a seven-day truce during the Christmas season was rejected. Instead, Nigerian federal officials proposed a one-day truce on both – the Christian and Muslim annual festivals.

They were determined not to give Biafran forces any respite from the war. Even provision of relief supplies to the war victims was interrupted by the federal government. A visit to the newly independent Republic of Equatorial Guinea – which won independence from Spain on 12 October 1968 – by a Nigerian federal delegation brought all mercy flights from the island of Fernando Po (later renamed Bioko) to a halt on December 21st. There were hardliners in Lagos who didn't mind starving the Igbos.

However, following international protests and appeals to the Nigerian federal government, the embargo on these flights was lifted on December 23rd. Yet, the interruption provided a strong case for Biafrans who contended that the Nigerian government was indeed determined to starve them to death in pursuit of its policy of 'genocide" against the Igbos; and that it would have do so had it not been for the intervention by the international community on their behalf.

On 28 December 1968, the United States announced that it was assigning four C97-G Strato-Freighters to join the international airlift of relief supplies to the war victims in both Biafra and Nigeria. The planes were made available to the International Red Cross, and another four to American voluntary relief organisations.

The eight planes and others from other countries were to airlift food and medical supplies from Fernando Po in Equatorial Guinea, and from another island, São Tomé, which was then a part of the Portuguese African island colony of São Tomé and Principe located in the Atlantic Ocean southwest of Fernando Po and northwest of the coast of Gabon. The international relief effort was an enormous task without precedent in the history of the Red Cross:

"Red Cross statistics put the (number of) displaced persons in Biafra's non-combat areas at a minimum of 4.5 million. Since July (1968), the Red Cross had brought 4,633 tons of supplies into Biafra with up to 4,000 tons still stockpiled in Santa Isabel (capital of the island of Fernando Po). It was the greatest single action that the Red Cross had ever carried out in its one hundred years of existence." – (Ibid., p. 565).

The war dragged on. It was also a conflict which attracted strange bedfellows who were ideologically opposed to each other, yet united in their support for one side or the other. For example, Britain and the Soviet Union supported Nigeria.

France and the People's Republic of China supported Biafra.

Among the African countries, two ultra-conservative and capitalist-oriented states which were also some of the strongest French allies – Ivory Coast and Gabon –

195

supported Biafra. At the other end of the ideological spectrum were two socialist-oriented and militant states, Tanzania and Zambia, which supported Biafra. Tanzania also served as a conduit for weapons from China to Biafra and would have played an even bigger role had she shared a common border with Biafra.

The secret supply of arms to Biafra was also facilitated by Portugal and Spain whose intervention on Biafra's side made the alliance of Biafra's supporters look even more strange. For example, what did Tanzania have in common with Portugal and Spain?

In fact, Tanzania was at war with Portugal in Mozambique where she supported the guerrilla fighters of FRELIMO fighting for independence. All the other African countries were in a state of war with Portugal because of her colonial domination of Angola, Mozambique and Portuguese Guinea (renamed Guinea-Bissau by the freedom fighters in that colony).

As if that was not strange enough, here was another team of Biafran supporters who had nothing in common with Tanzania and Zambia, two of the four strong African supporters of Biafra: in the early stages of the war, some of the weapons going to Biafra came from white-ruled Rhodesia via Angola, a Portuguese colony, and then flown directly from there to the secessionist region. And "when, in desperation, Biafra began to recruit a mercenary force towards the latter part of 1967, it introduced into the conflict the white mercenaries who had for so long held the Congo to ransom." – (*Africa Contemporary Record*, p. 566).

Many of them were South African mercenaries led by the highly notorious "Mad" Mike Hoare who wreaked so much havoc in Congo during the turbulent sixties.

They all had different reasons for supporting Biafra or Federal Nigeria, a subject I have also addressed in one of my books, *Ethnic Politics in Kenya and Nigeria*, a comparative study, as others have elsewhere.

It is obvious why Biafrans were fighting. They wanted to have their own country where they could be safe and secure.

Another African country that was sympathetic towards the Biafran cause was Tunisia. However, the Arab North African country withheld recognition for the sake of African solidarity with Nigeria based on Africa's determination to maintain the territorial integrity of its countries no matter what the cost and even if it means exterminating an entire group of people.

But Tunisia's reservations about the inviolability of this principle and her sympathy for Biafra were clearly expressed in the official press – which reflected government thinking – in May 1968 that recognition of Biafra by four African countries was a "protest against massacre." – (*Africa Contemporary Record*, p. 114).

Uganda under Dr. Milton Obote came close to recognising Biafra but backtracked when Obote became actively involved in the peace talks between Nigerian and Biafran representatives held in Kampala, Uganda. But before then, "it was expected that Uganda would follow the example of Tanzania and Zambia in recognizing the breakaway Republic of Biafra." – (*Africa Contemporary Record*, pp. 236 - 237).

Therefore, support for Nigeria among other African countries was not automatic or unanimous and could not be taken for granted in all cases; annd it is very much possible that even some of the countries which – out of African solidarity – refused to recognise Biafra as an independent state sympathised with her cause because of the injustices which had been perpetrated against Eastern Nigerians especially in Northern Nigeria and the suffering they had endured throughout the ordeal. It was a horrendous tragedy.

Among the African countries which recognised Biafra as a sovereign entity, Tanzania set a precedent that was followed by others even if for their own reasons. But as the first country to recognise Biafra, and because of President Nyerere's stature on the continent and in the international arena, it came to play a central role in the debate over the Nigerian-Biafran conflict.

Nyerere also became the most prominent, and most articulate, spokesman for the Biafran cause among all the leaders whose countries recognised Biafra as a sovereign entity.

Tanzania's recognition of Biafra ignited considerable debate over the merits and demerits of the principles enunciated in the OAU Charter defending the sanctity of the borders inherited at independence; maintaining the territorial integrity of African countries ; and non-interference in the internal affairs of another state or other states.

But, as experience would show even in the following years after the Nigerian civil war, it was clear that Tanzania under Nyerere pursued an activist foreign policy and placed a high premium on moral principles even at the expense of the principles enshrined in the OAU Charter and to which the country subscribed. In fact, Tanganyika – before it became Tanzania after uniting with Zanzibar in April 1964 – was one of the 32 founding members of the Organisation of African Unity (OAU) in Addis Ababa, Ethiopia, in May 1963.

Tanzania under Nyerere was not only the first African country to recognise Biafra; it also became the first African country to capture the capital of another African country in a full-scale war. It was also the first African country to overthrow a government of another African country – of Idi Amini in April 1979 – which it saw as a threat to its security and an embarrassment to the rest of Africa.

Tanzania also intervened militarily in the Comoros and in the Seychelles in the seventies and eighties to restore constitutional government and law and order at the invitation of the leaders of the two island nations.

Tanzania also, under Nyerere, sent troops to fight in liberation wars in Mozambique, Zimbabwe, Angola, and Namibia; and fought alongside Cuban and Angolan troops and others from other African countries against apartheid South Africa when that country invaded Angola in the seventies.

So, Tanzania's recognition of Biafra was only among the first in a series of policy initiatives by Nyerere in a Pan-African context which he found to be necessary for different reasons, in different contexts, if Africans were to remain true to the ideals and principles they claimed to uphold; among them safety and security, and justice and equality for all the people; and the liberation of Africa from colonial rulers and white minority regimes on the continent.

Although some people differed with Nyerere when he recognised Biafra as an independent state, few questioned his moral arguments and his commitment to the ideals of African unity and to the principles collectively espoused by African leaders under the auspices of the Organisation of African Unity. He was so committed that even his fellow African heads of state and government and other leaders nicknamed him "Africa's minister of foreign affairs."

He was not only a staunch supporter of African unity but lived up to his commitment to this Pan-African ideal.

He was the first East African leader to call for federation and even offered to delay independence for Tanganyika in order for the three East African countries of Kenya, Uganda, and Tanganyika to attain sovereign status on the same day and form an East African federation.

He also engineered the first union of two independent states, Tanganyika and Zanzibar – and the only one on the entire continent – which led to the creation of Tanzania, one of the most united and most stable and peaceful countries in Africa.

Yet, under his leadership, Tanzania also was the first

199

African country to recognise a secessionist region as an independent state – Eastern Nigeria as the independent Republic of Biafra – a move his critics denounced as anti-Pan-African by one of the strongest advocates of African unity.

Yet, Nyerere's decision to recognise Biafra, which he himself admitted had been made with great reluctance, was based on moral principles. The people of Eastern Nigeria, especially the Igbos, no longer felt secure within the Nigerian federation after tens of thousands of them had been massacred by their fellow countrymen, especially in Northern Nigeria, while the authorities did nothing to stop the pogroms.

Therefore, to protect themselves, they decided to withdraw from the federation and establish their own independent state.

Unity is based on the willingness of the people to be part of the union, and on the willingness of the government to be fair to all its citizens. A government which refuses to protect some of its citizens cannot claim to be fair and has abdicated its responsibility.

Therefore, the people who have been rejected have the right to choose the type of government they want to live under, and in their own independent state where they can be guaranteed protection and feel secure.

That was the case for Biafra.

Critics of Biafra's secession tried to draw parallels between Biafra and Katanga. But there were fundamental differences between the two.

The secession of Eastern Nigeria was in response to the pogroms in Northern Nigeria and other parts of the federation, but mostly in the north, which claimed and estimated 30,000 – 50,000 lives in about three months in 1966. It was not foreign-inspired to break up Nigeria.

By contrast, Katanga's secession was engineered by Western powers to secure their political and economic interests by detaching the mineral-rich province from the rest of the country which they feared could be ruled by a staunchly pro-African nationalist government that would threaten their interests. Moise Tshombe, the leader of Katanga province and a Western puppet, was a traitor.

Colonel Chukwuemeka Odumegwu Ojukwu, the Biafran leader, was an African patriot trying to save his people from oppression and possible extermination by other Nigerians who hated the Igbo reminiscent of the plight of the Jews under Hitler in Nazi Germany. Not all Nigerians hated the Igbo but many of them did; and they hated them enough to massacre them, thus justifying the Igbos' imperative need to have their own country where they would be safe and secure and away from the people who did not want to live with them.

It is also important to remember that the anti-Igbo sentiments in the Northern Regional Assembly in February-March 1964 were expressed almost two years before the Igbo-led military coup of 15 January 1966 which triggered the massacre of tens of thousands of Igbos and other Eastern Nigerians in Northern Nigeria in the following months.

The anti-Igbo venom spewed in the Northern legislative chamber had also been preceded by the massacre of hundreds of Igbos in Jos in 1945 and in Kano in 1953.

Therefore, there was a history of anti-Igbo hysteria in Northern Nigeria, and even in other parts of the country, long before the 1966 military coup; a history which puts in proper perspective the secession of the Eastern Region as an inevitable response to the cumulative impact of Igbophobia on the people of Eastern Nigeria that had infected large segments of the federation.

It is also in this context that Tanzania's recognition of Biafra should be looked at, in order to understand why the government of Tanzania reached this momentous decision. As President Julius Nyerere stated when he explained why Tanzania recognised Biafra:

"The Declaration of Independence by Biafra on the 30th May, 1967 came after two military coups d'etat – January and July 1966 – and two pogroms against the Ibo people. These pogroms, which also took place in 1966, resulted in the death of about 30,000 men, women, and children, and made two million people flee from their homes in other parts of Nigeria to their tribal homeland in Eastern Nigeria.

These events have been interspersed and followed by official discussions about a new constitution for Nigeria, and also by continued personal attacks on individual Ibos who have remained outside the Eastern Region.

The basic case for Biafra's secession from the Nigerian Federation is that people from the Eastern Region can no longer feel safe in other parts of the Federation. They are not accepted as citizens of Nigeria by other citizens of Nigeria. Not only is it impossible for Ibos and people of related tribes to live in assurance of personal safety if they work outside Biafra; it would also be impossible for any representative of these people to move freely and without fear in any other part of the Federation of Nigeria.

These fears are genuine and deep-seated; nor can anyone say they are groundless. The rights and wrongs of the original coup d'etat, the rights and wrongs of the attitudes taken by different groups in the politics of pre- and post-coup Nigeria, are all irrelevant to the fear which the Ibo people feel.

And the people of Eastern Nigeria can point to too many bereaved homes, too many maimed people, for anyone to deny the reasonable grounds for their fears. It is these fears, which are the root cause both for the secession, and for the fanaticism with which the people of Eastern Nigeria have defended the country they declared to be independent.

Fears such as now exist among the Ibo people, do not disappear because someone says they are unjustified, or says that the rest of Nigeria does not want to exterminate Ibos. Such words have even less effect when the speakers have made no attempt to bring the perpetrators of crimes to justice, and when troops under the control of the Federal Nigerian authorities continue to ill-treat, or allow others to ill-treat, any Ibo who comes within their power.

The only way to remove the Easterners' fear is for the Nigerian authorities to accept its existence, to acknowledge the reason fir it, and then talk on terms of equality with those involved about the way forward.

When people have reason to be afraid you cannot reassure them through the barrel of a gun; your only hope is to talk as one man to another, or as one group to another. It is no use the Federal authorities demanding that the persecuted should come as a supplicant for mercy, by first renouncing their secession from the political unit. For the secession was declared because the Ibo people felt it to be there only defence against extermination.

In their minds, therefore, a demand that they should renounce secession before talks begin is equivalent to a demand that they should announce their willingness to be exterminated. If they are wrong in this belief, they have to be convinced. And they can only be convinced by talks leading to new institutional arrangements, which take account of their fears.

The people of Biafra have announced their willingness to talk to the Nigerian authorities without any conditions. They cannot renounce their secession before talks, but they do not demand that Nigerians should recognize it; they ask for talks without conditions.

But the Federal authorities have refused to talk except on the basis of Biafran surrender. And as the Biafrans believe they will be massacred if they surrender, the Federal authorities are really refusing to talk at all. For human beings do not voluntarily walk towards what they believe to be certain death.

The Federal Government argues that in demanding the

renunciation of secession before talks, and indeed in its entire 'police action,' it is defending the territorial integrity of Nigeria. On this ground it argues also that it has the right to demand support from all other governments, and especially other African governments. For every state, and every state authority, has a duty to defend the sovereignty and integrity of its nation; this is a central part of the function of a national government.

Africa accepts the validity of this point, for African states have more reason than most to fear the effects of disintegration. It is on these grounds that Africa has watched the massacre of tens of thousands of people, has watched millions being made into refugees, watched the employment of mercenaries by both sides in the current civil war, and has accepted repeated rebuffs of its offers to help by mediation or conciliation.

But for how long should this continue? Africa fought for freedom on the grounds of individual liberty and equality, and on the grounds that every people must have the right to determine for themselves the conditions under which they would be governed.

We accepted the boundaries we inherited from colonialism, and within them we each worked out for ourselves the constitutional and other arrangements, which we felt to be appropriate to the most essential function of a state - that is the safeguarding of life and liberty for its inhabitants.

When the Federation of Nigeria became independent in 1960, the same policy was adopted by all its peoples. They accepted the Federal structure which had been established under the colonial system, and declared their intention to work together. Indeed, the Southern States of the Federation - which include Biafra - delayed their own demands for independence until the North was ready to join them.

At the insistence of the North also, the original suggestion of the National Council of Nigeria and the

Cameroons (NCNC) that Nigeria should be broken up into many small states with a strong center, was abandoned. The South accepted a structure, which virtually allowed the more populous North to dominate the rest.

But the constitution of the Federation of Nigeria was broken in January, 1966, by the first military coup. All hope of its resuscitation was removed by the second coup, and even more by the pogroms of September and October, 1966. These events altered the whole basis of the society; after them it was impossible for political and economic relations between the different parts of the old Federation to be restored.

That meant that Nigerian unity could only be salvaged from the wreck of inter-tribal violence and fear by a constitution drawn up in the light of what happened, and which was generally acceptable to all the major elements of the society under the new circumstances. A completely new start had to be made, for the basis of the state had been dissolved in the complete breakdown of law and order, and the inter-tribal violence, which existed.

The necessity for a new start by agreement was accepted by a conference of military leaders from all parts of the Federation, in Aburi, Ghana, in January 1967.

There is a certain difference of opinion about some of the things, which were agreed upon at the conference. But there is no dispute about the fact that everyone joined in a declaration renouncing the use of force as a means of settling the crisis in Nigeria. Nor does anyone dispute that it was agreed that a new constitution was to be worked out by agreement, and that in the meantime there would be a repeal of all military decrees issued since January 1966, which reduced the power of the Regions.

There was also agreement about rehabilitation payments for those who had been forced to flee from their homes, and about members of the armed forces being stationed in their home Regions.

The Aburi Conference could have provided the new

start, which was necessary if the unity of Nigeria was to be maintained. But before the end of the same month, Gowon was restating his commitment to the creation of new states, and his determination to oppose any form of confederation. And on the last day of January, the Federal military authorities were already giving administrative reasons for the delay in the implementation of the Agreements reached at Aburi.

It was in the middle of March before a constitutional decree was issued which was supposed to regularize the position in accordance with the decisions taken there.

But unfortunately this Decree also included a new clause - which had not been agreed upon - and which gave the Federal authorities reserved powers over the Regions, and thus completely nullified the whole operation.

Nor had any payment been made by the Federal Government to back up the monetary commitment for rehabilitation, which it had accepted in the Ghana meeting. In short, the necessity for an arrangement, which would take account of the fears created during 1966 was accepted at Aburi, and renounced thereafter by the Federal authorities.

Yet they now claim to be defending the integrity of the country in which they failed to guarantee the most elementary safety of the twelve million people of Eastern Nigeria. These people had been massacred in other parts of Nigeria without the Federal authorities apparently having neither the will nor the power to protect them. When they retreated to their homeland they were expected to accept the domination of the same people who instigated, or allowed, their persecution in the country which they are being told is theirs - i.e., Nigeria.

Surely, when a whole people is rejected by the majority of the state in which they live, they must have the right to live under a different kind of arrangement which does secure their existence. States are made to serve people; governments are established to protect the citizens of a state against external enemies and internal wrongdoers.

It is on those grounds that people surrender their right and power of self-defence to the government of the state in which they live. But when the machinery of the state, and the powers of the government, are turned against a whole group of society on grounds of racial, tribal, or religious prejudice, then the victims have the right to take back the powers they have surrendered, and defend themselves.

For while people have a duty to defend the integrity of their state, and even to die in its defence, this duty stems from the fact that it is theirs, and that it is important to their well-being and to the future of their children. When the state ceases to stand for honour, the protection, and the well-being of all its citizens, then it is no longer the instrument of those it has rejected. In such a case the people have the right to create another instrument for their protection - in other words, to create another state.

This right cannot be abrogated by constitutions, or by outsiders. The basis of statehood, and of unity can only be general acceptance by the participants. When more than twelve million people have become convinced that they are rejected, and that there is no longer any basis for unity between them and other groups of people, then that unity has ceased to exist.

You cannot kill thousands of people, and keep on killing more, in the name of unity. There is no unity between the dead and those who killed them; and there is no unity in slavery or domination.

Africa needs unity. We need unity over the whole continent, and in the meantime we need unity within the existing states of Africa.

It is a tragedy when we experience a setback to our goal of unity. But the basis of our need for unity, and the reason for our desire for it, is the greater well-being, and the greater security, of the people of Africa.

Unity by conquest is impossible. It is not practicable; and even if military might could force the acceptance of a particular authority, the purpose of unity would have been destroyed.

For the purpose of unity, its justification is the service of all the people who are united together. The general consent of all the people involved is the only basis on which unity in Africa can be maintained or extended.

The fact that the Federation of Nigeria was created in 1960 with the consent of all the people does not alter that fact. That Federation, and the basis of consent, has since been destroyed. Nor is this the first time the world has seen a reduction in political unity.

We have seen the creation of the Mali Federation, the creation of a union between Egypt and Syria, and the establishment of the Federation of Rhodesia and Nyasaland. And we have also seen the dissolution of all these attempts at unity, and the consequent recognition of the separate nations, which were once involved.

The world has also seen the creation of India and Pakistan out of what was once the Indian Empire. We have all recognized both of these nation states and done our best to help them deal with the millions of people made homeless by the conflict and division.

None of these things mean that we like these examples of greater disunity. They mean that we recognize that in all these cases the people are unwilling to remain in one political unit.

Tanzania recognizes Senegal, Mali, Egypt, Syria, Malawi, Zambia, Pakistan and India. What right have we to refuse, in the name of unity, to recognize Biafra?

For years the people of that state struggled to maintain unity with the other people in the Federation of Nigeria; even after the pogroms of 1966 they tried to work out a new form of unity which would guarantee their safety; they have demonstrated by ten months of bitter fighting that they have decided upon a new political organization and are willing to defend it.

The world has taken it upon itself to utter many ill-informed criticisms of the Jews of Europe for going to their deaths without any concerted struggle. But out of sympathy for the suffering of these people, and in recognition of the world's failure to take action at the appropriate time, the United Nations established the state of Israel in a territory, which belonged to the Arabs for thousands of years.

It was felt that only by the establishment of a Jewish homeland, and a Jewish national state, could Jews be expected to live in the world under conditions of human equality.

Tanzania has recognized the state of Israel and will continue to do so because of its belief that every people must have some place in the world where they are not liable to be rejected by their fellow citizens.

But the Biafrans have now suffered the same kind of rejection within their state that the Jews of Germany experienced. Fortunately, they already had a homeland. They have retreated to it for their own protection, and for the same reason - after all other efforts had failed - they have declared it to be an independent state.

In the light of these circumstances, Tanzania feels obliged to recognize the setback to African unity, which has occurred.

We therefore recognize the state of Biafra as an independent sovereign entity, and as a member of the community of nations. Only by this act of recognition can we remain true to our conviction that the purpose of society, and of all political organization, is the service of man."

The preceding statement by President Julius Nyerere was issued by the government of Tanzania on 13 April 1968, the day Tanzania recognized Biafra. It was also published in the ruling-party's (TANU's) daily newspaper, *The Nationalist*, whose editor during that time was Benjamin Mkapa who later became president of Tanzania from 1995 – 2005. He was the country's third head of state since independence in 1961.

The statement was also published in another daily newspaper, the privately-owned *Standard*, whose editorial staff I joined in June 1969 when I was a 19-year-old student in Form V (Standard 13, what Americans would call grade 13) at Tambaza High School in Dar es Salaam.

The *Standard* and *The Nationalist* were also the country's two major newspapers and some of the largest and most influential in East Africa.

President Nyerere also explained Tanzania's position on Biafra in another statement, which was substantively the same as the preceding one, but with other nuances to his central argument.

The statement was published in a British newspaper in a country which was the biggest supplier of weapons to Nigeria during its war against Biafra and played a critical role in sustaining the conflict and in wreaking havoc across the secessionist region, as much as Soviet-supplied MIGs flown by Egyptian pilots – on behalf of the Nigerian military government – did. As Nyerere stated in "Why We Recognised Biafra," in *The Observer*, London, April 28, 1968:

"Leaders of Tanzania have probably talked more about the need for African unity than those of any other country. Giving formal recognition to even greater disunity in Africa was therefore a very difficult decision to make.

Our reluctance to do so was compounded by our understanding of the problems of unity - of which we have some experience - and of the problems of Nigeria. For we have had very good relations with the Federation of Nigeria, even to the extent that when we needed help from Africa we asked it of the Federation.

But unity can only be based on the general consent of the people involved. The people must feel that this state, or this nation, is theirs; and they must be willing to have their quarrels in that context. Once a large number of the people of any such political unit stop believing that the state is theirs, and that the government is their instrument, then the unit is no longer viable. It will not receive the loyalty of its citizens.

For the citizen's duty to serve, and if necessary to die for, his country stems from the fact that it is his and that its government is the instrument of himself and his fellow citizens.

The duty stems, in other words, from the common denominator of accepted statehood, and from the state government's responsibility to protect all the citizens and serve them all. For states, and governments, exist for men and for the service of man. They exist for the citizens' protection, their welfare, and the future well-being of their children. There is no other justification for states and governments except man.

In Nigeria this consciousness of a common citizenship was destroyed by the events of 1966, and in particular by the pogroms in which 30,000 Eastern Nigerians were murdered, many more injured, and about two million forced to flee from the North of their country. It is these pogroms, and the apparent inability or unwillingness of the authorities to protect the victims, which underlies the Easterners' conviction that they have been rejected by other Nigerians and abandoned by the Federal Government.

Whether the Easterners are correct in their belief that they have been rejected is a matter for argument. But they do have this belief. And if they are wrong, they have to be convinced that they are wrong. They will not convinced by being shot. Nor will their acceptance as part of the Federation be demonstrated by the use of Federal power to bomb schools and hospitals in the areas to which people have fled from persecution.

In Britain, in 1950, the Stone of Scone was stolen from Westminster Abbey by Scottish Nationalists while I was still a student at Edinburgh. That act did not represent a wish by the majority of the Scottish people to govern themselves.

But if, for some peculiar reason, that vast majority of the Scottish people decided that Scotland should secede from the United Kingdom, would the Government in London order the bombing of Edinburgh, and in pursuing the Scots into the Highlands, kill the civilians they overtook? Certainly the Union Government would not do this; it would argue with the Scots, and try to reach some compromise.

As President of Tanzania it is my duty to safeguard the integrity of the United Republic. But if the mass of the people of Zanzibar should, without external manipulation, and for some reason of their own, decide that the Union was prejudicial to their existence, I could not advocate bombing them into submission. To do so would not be to defend the Union. The Union would have ceased to exist when the consent of its constituent members was withdrawn.

I would certainly be one of those working hard to prevent secession, or to reduce its disintegrating effects. But I could not support a war on the people whom I have sworn to serve - especially not if the secession is preceded by a rejection of Zanzibaris by Tanganyikans.

Similarly, if we had succeeded in the 1963 attempt to form an East African Federation, or if we should do so in the future, Tanzania would be overjoyed. But if at some time thereafter the vast majority of the people of any one of the countries should decide - and persist in a decision - to withdraw from the Federation, the other two countries could not wage war against the people who wished to secede. Such a decision would mark a failure by the Federation. That would be tragic; but it would not justify mass killings.

The Biafrans now feel that they cannot live under conditions of personal security in the present Nigerian

Federation. As they were unable to achieve an agreement on a new form of association, they have therefore claimed the right to govern themselves.

The Biafrans are not claiming the right to govern anyone else. They have not said that they must govern the Federation as the only way of protecting themselves. They have simply withdrawn their consent to the system under which they used to be governed.

Biafra is not now operating under the control of a democratic government, any more than Nigeria is. But the mass support for the establishment and defence of Biafra is obvious. This is not a case of a few leaders declaring secession for their own private glory. Indeed, by the Aburi Agreement the leaders of Biafra showed a greater reluctance to give up hope of some form of unity with Nigeria than the masses possessed. But the agreement was not implemented.

Tanzania would still like to see some form of co-operation or unity between all the peoples of Nigeria and Biafra.

But whether this happens, to what extent, and in what fields, can only be decided by agreement among all the peoples involved. It is not for Tanzania to say.

We in this country believe that unity is vital for the future of Africa. But it must be a unity which serves the people, and which is freely determined upon by the people.

For 10 months we have accepted the Federal Government's legal right to our support in a 'police action to defend the integrity of the State.' On that basis we have watched a civil war result in the death of about 100,000 people, and the employment of mercenaries by both sides. We have watched the Federal Government reject the advice of Africa to talk instead of demanding surrender before talks could begin. Everything combined gradually to force us to the conclusion that Nigerian unity did not exist.

Tanzania deeply regrets that the will for unity in Nigeria has been destroyed over the past two years. But we are convinced that Nigerian unity cannot be maintained by force any more than unity in East Africa could be created by one state conquering another.

It seemed to us that by refusing to recognise the existence of Biafra we were tacitly supporting a war against the people of Eastern Nigeria - and a war conducted in the name of unity. We could not continue doing this any longer."

The secession of Eastern Nigeria should also be looked at in the context of Nigerian history. Secessionist sentiments are nothing new in Nigeria; nor are they in a number of other countries on the continent.

Northern Nigerians wanted to secede in 1950, then in 1953 and at different times throughout the fifties. They also tried to secede in 1966.

Western Nigerians also tried to secede in 1953, 1954 and even wanted the federation dissolved in 1966 when, during constitutional talks held that year, they proposed that Nigeria should be reconstituted as a commonwealth of sovereign entities.

Eastern Nigerians, victims of brutal massacres and traumatised by this experience, felt they had no alternative but to secede from the macro-nation of Nigeria composed of ethnic entities many of which were agitating for their own autonomous ethno-states even if they did not demand full independence; some of which were big and viable enough to constitute sovereign entities.

The declaration of independence by the Eastern Region should also be looked at in the African context as a whole where the countries are a product of European whims and caprice, created by the colonial powers when they drew arbitrary boundaries cutting across ethno-regional, cultural and linguistic groups, and lumping together groups which had never even known each other and some of which had

214

been enemies for years.

There were cases in which fundamental differences made national integration virtually impossible. Sudan is a typical example, north versus south, a dichotomy defined by race and religion; Nigeria is another case, characterised by the same divide, north versus south, but for historical, cultural, and religious reasons and not necessarily racial as in the case of Sudan or Chad. There are others in different parts of the continent.

That is where the concept of ethno-states comes into the picture, with all that it entails if fully implemented.

The idea of establishing independent ethno-states is probably very appealing to oppressed ethnic groups, but terrifying to African countries almost all of which are multi-ethnic societies. It may even be argued that they are multi-national states, if ethnic groups are considered to be nations, or micro-nations.

Yet, in spite of this complex configuration of African nations or ethno-polities – characterised by ethnic diversity – built into the very architecture of national identities, the continent has not experienced major secessionist movements in almost 50 years since independence, except Katanga and Biafra. That is because, despite the tenuous bonds of national unity among the different tribes or ethnic and racial groups in a given country, there still is some acceptance of the idea of a common national identity among the majority of the people, largely forged by a common history of colonial experience; the coercive power of the state to maintain national unity and territorial integrity at all costs; the capacity of the one-party system – the most dominant political institution across the continent for decades during the post-colonial era – to embrace all ethnic groups by eschewing divisive politics typical of multiparty democracy in the African context; and by the cultivation of a personality cult – Nkrumah, Sekou Toure, Kenyatta, Mobutu, Banda – or the existence of a popular charismatic leader such as Nyerere who serves as a rallying point for the masses and the entire nation to forge a common identity and achieve national unity.

That is why even in the Democratic Republic of Congo, a country which has virtually ceased to exist and function as a state and as a nation, the people across this vast expanse of territory still identify themselves as Congolese – thanks to the enduring legacy of Patrice Lumumba, and a common history of suffering probably more than anything else, infused with a dose of Pan-African solidarity. There has been no major secessionist threat since the sixties when Katanga, and then South Kasai led by Albert Kalonji, declared independence.

Even the different rebel groups which in the late 1990s and beyond virtually carved up the Congo into fiefdoms dominated by warlords, plundering the nation's resources, did not say they wanted to break up the country into independent states; although their control of at least the entire eastern half of Congo by the late nineties and during the following years amounted to *de facto* partition, hence secession – in the practical even if not in the legal sense – from the central government in Kinshasa.

Tragically, Congo is only one example of the collapse of institutional authority and erosion of political legitimacy in many parts of the continent.

What is needed in Africa, where – because of bad leadership – failed states are the norm rather than the exception, is an alternative configuration that will facilitate the establishment of institutional authority in many areas where the state is unable to function, or where it has abdicated responsibility.

In many parts of the continent, people rely on foreign-funded non-governmental organisations (NGOs) and civic institutions to provide them with goods and services – which they can't get on their own – more than they do on the government. But one thing these organisations and civic institutions have not been able to provide is security.

It is this lack of security, especially for entire groups some of which have been targeted for ethnic cleansing, that can be a very powerful motivation for secession in a number of African countries.

The Igbos of Nigeria could have had all the goods and services they wanted and needed. But without security, all those would have meant absolutely nothing to them in terms of survival as a people. Theirs may have been a case of self-determination based on ethnicity, but precisely because they were targeted as an ethnic group.

Yet, the independent Republic of Biafra they established also included other ethnic groups in the former Eastern Nigeria. The ethnicity of these other groups was also grounds for secession from the Nigerian federation after they were also targeted for elimination in the pogroms directed against all easterners by their fellow countrymen in Northern Nigeria.

In response to the charge by the federal government that Igbos had forced minority groups to become an integral part of Biafra, Biafran leader Odumegwu Ojukwu asked the federal authorities to conduct an internationally-supervised plebiscite if they sincerely believed that the minorities had been coerced into joining Biafra. But the Nigerian federal government refused to do so, thus losing its credibility. As he stated in his speech to the OAU summit on the Nigerian civil war in Addis Ababa, Ethiopia, on 5 August 1968:

"The Nigerian Army has occupied some non-Igbo areas of Biafra. But this cannot be regarded as a settlement of the 'minority question.' This is why we have suggested a plebiscite.

Under adequate international supervision, the people of these areas should be given a chance to choose whether they want to belong to Nigeria or to Biafra.

Plebiscites have been used in the Southern Cameroons, in Togo, in Mid-Western Nigeria – and by the British recently in Gibraltar – to determine what grouping is most acceptable to the people of disputed areas. If Nigeria believes that she is really defending the true wishes of the minorities, she should accept our proposal for a plebiscite in the disputed areas of Nigeria and Biafra." – (Ojukwu, *Africa Contemporary Record*, p. 668).

By refusing to hold a plebiscite, the Nigerian federal government not only lost credibility on the disputed issue of minority rights but strengthened Biafra's case for self-determination.

Ironically, the federal authorities tried to play the same ethnic card they claimed the Igbos were using in their attempt to establish an independent state. Yet they only ended up causing embarrassment for themselves.

Ethnicity has always been an integral part of life in Africa. It will always be with us. But, besides its tragic aspect where ethnicity is seen as a liability and is used by some people to discriminate against some groups and even target them for extermination, ethnicity also has positive attributes which cannot be overlooked and must be acknowledged as an enduring feature of the African political landscape, and not the ugly phenomenon it is portrayed to be. As Professor Christopher Clepham states in his essay, "Rethinking the African State," in *Africa Security Review*:

"Ethnicity, quite regardless of arcane academic debates over its 'primordial' or 'constructed' character, has likewise developed into an enduring feature of African life, and provides a ready basis for the consolidation of political identities....

Critical to the relationship between ethnicity and statehood is not just the existence of an ethnic identity as such, but more importantly the substantive *content* of this identity in terms of shared attitudes toward issues of political authority and control that it embodies.... The decay of viable and effective states has created massive political violence." – (Christopher Clapham, "Rethinking African States," in *Africa Security Review*, Vol. 10, No. 3, 2001. See also Sam G. Amoo, "The Challenge of Ethnicity and Conflicts in Africa: The Need for A New Paradigm," United Nations Development Programme (UNDP), New York, January 1997).

Although the Nigerian federal state was not weak when the Igbos were being massacred in Northern Nigeria and other parts of the country, it was an accomplice to their persecution because of its unwillingness to stop the massacres and provide security to the victims.

It was this total disregard for their lives by federal and Northern Nigerian authorities which forced them to withdraw from the federation. They felt that the only way they could be safe and secure was by establishing their own independent state, in their home region, under their own government.

It is in this overall context that the secession of Eastern Nigeria must be looked at, in order to understand why Tanzania recognised Biafra, a decision President Nyerere admitted was a painful one to make, yet necessary if we were to remain true to our conviction that "there is no other justification for states and governments except man."

The secession of Biafra and subsequent civil war was a horrendous tragedy. But it also had an important lesson for Africa, especially for countries facing major secessionist threats; for example, the Oromo Liberation Front in Ethiopia, fighting to establish its own autonomous or independent state whose jurisdictional boundaries coincide with the ethnic identity of the people who seek self-determination or want to secede.

The Oromo, like other Ethiopians, live in a country, which, at least in theory, has acknowledged the imperative need for ethnic confederalism as the basis for national unity.

Yet, true unity cannot be achieved by force, and Africa may have to concede the legitimacy of major secessionist movements as one of the ways to resolve conflicts on the continent and guarantee equality and justice for oppressed and neglected groups.

Such a concession is a first step towards conflict resolution which entails: conflict management, containment, reduction, and finally, resolution. One of the best ways to resolve conflict is to address the grievances of the people who want to secede, and therefore prevent secession.

Trying to force them to remain in a country from which they want to secede will only exacerbate and perpetuate conflict and lead to national instability.

Secessionist movements can be robbed of momentum if the regions which want to secede are granted extensive autonomy enabling them to rule themselves while remaining an integral part of the nation from which they want to break away. Such extensive devolution of power can be achieved under federation or confederation far better than it can under a unitary state whose very nature is to centralise power, while assigning a peripheral role to its constituent units.

However, the right to self-determination, hence secession, must also be enshrined in the constitution of every African country as a bargaining tool for oppressed groups to extract genuine concessions from the central government, short of secession.

Therefore the intent here is *not* to encourage secession but to discourage secession in African countries. Paradoxically, the right to secede serves to neutralise the very tendency it seems to encourage.

More often than not, people want to secede, not just because they want to separate; they want to secede because they are ignored, oppressed, exploited, and even rejected by their government and by their fellow countrymen. Usually, there is a long record of historical

220

injustices which serves as a catalyst for secessionist movements, fuelled by contemporary oppression.

In Nigeria, had the grievances of the Igbo – who had been the victims of earlier massacres in Jos in 1945 and in Kano in 1953 – been addressed during those critical months in 1966 when their people were being systematically slaughtered in Northern Nigeria, and even in some parts of Western Nigeria, it is highly probable that they would not have seceded; especially if the federal government had agreed to extensive devolution of power to the regions under genuine federalism or even confederalism, as it did in the Aburi agreement. Unfortunately, those grievances were never addressed, forcing Eastern Nigerians to secede.

The Nigerian military head of state, General Yakubu Gowon, even reneged on his promise to implement the Aburi accords which had been agreed upon by all the military governors, and by Gowon himself, at a meeting in Aburi, Ghana, in January 1967, which could have prevented Biafra's secession and the subsequent civil war, had they been fulfilled.

The Biafran leader, Colonel Ojukwu, was explicit in his condemnation of Gowon for refusing to implement the Aburi agreements which granted more autonomy to the regions and rescinded any decrees which curtailed the power of regional governments and other institutions of authority to manage their affairs.

It was a betrayal of trust on the part of Gowon, and nothing was done through the years after the civil war to seriously address the grievances of the Igbos. As Ojukwu said in an interview with BBC, 13 January 2000, nothing had really changed since the war. The cause of the war was never addressed:

"None of the problems that led to the war have been solved yet. They are still there. We have a situation creeping towards the type of situation that saw the beginning of the war....

At 33 I reacted as a brilliant 33-year-old. At 66 it is my hope that if I had to face this I should also confront it as a brilliant 66-year-old.

Responsibility for what went on – how can I feel responsible in a situation in which I put myself out and saved the people from genocide? No, I don't feel responsible at all. I did the best I could."

He articulated a sentiment shared by many Igbos and even by members of other groups who feel marginalised in a federation still dominated by northerners.

Ojukwu's candour on this incendiary subject on a number of occasions prompted a sharp response from President Obasanjo who accused the former Biafran leader of again fomenting trouble and threatening secession. He warned that secessionists would pay dearly as they did in the last war.

In fact, it was Obsanjo himself, then a colonel in the federal offensive against Biafra, who accepted the surrender of the Biafran forces after they capitulated to federal might on 15 January 1970.

Although the Igbos suffered tremendously during the war, the majority of them continued to support Ojukwu because they believed that they had no other choice besides continued domination and oppression at the hands of the Hausa-Fulani, their nemesis, who were determined to control the federation perpetually.

Even today, hatred of the Igbos is an enduring obsession among a large number of them, and with it potential for ethnic cleansing, not only of the Igbos but other groups as well, in different parts of the giant federation.

The war itself remains a contentious issue in Nigeria and elsewhere, especially in other African countries where secession is a potential threat that could galvanise some groups to demand their own independent states, as happened in Casamance Province in Senegal, Cabinda in Angola, Caprivi Strip in Namibia, Anjouan and Moheli islands in the Comoros, Bioko island in Equatorial guinea, and in Nigeria itself, especially in the Niger Delta, in Yorubaland in the west as well as in the former short-lived independent Republic of Biafra in the east.

Although Biafrans lost the war because they were outgunned, they are still fighting another war on a different front, for inclusion in the Nigerian polity as equal members of society instead of being treated as traitors and outcasts because they fought for an independent homeland.

They are also fighting against distortion of history about what really happened and what the war was all about. As Ojukwu said about the conflict and the distortion of historical facts about the war in an interview with Paul Odili of the *Vanguard*, Lagos, Nigeria, 4 November 2001, entitled "Ojukwu at 68 on State of the Nation: Why We Can't Have Peace Now":

"It is clear to me that many things are going on particularly in the recent interventions, by some of the ex-military officers, that Nigeria is not yet ready for the truth....They know that the distortions are deliberate....

Let me ask you, who mounted the coup of 1966? Clearly, it was Ifeajuna, but for their own reasons, some northern officers are insisting that it was Chukwuma Nzeogwu; against all the facts. Let me ask you again, who was the rebel in the crisis that befell Nigeria in 1966? Everybody knows actually that the rebel was Gowon. But no, they prefer to say that it was Ojukwu. How could it be me? I was a loyalist serving the army in Kano.

On the radio, I heard my name (that I had been) appointed governor of the East, by somebody who was legitimately appointed head of state. By the way, if Ironsi was not legitimately appointed head of state, then Gowon's appointment under Ironsi would have been illegal too. But I continued the task assigned to me legitimately.

The fact that Gowon decided to assume the position of head of state was a major departure from both military discipline and accepted norm. Now, everybody knows that. Gowon knows that, Danjuma knows that, Obasanjo knows that. So, why keep pretending?

I rejected the coup; that is an honourable act. And it is for that reason that I keep telling people that Gowon will go down in the *Guinness Book of Records* as the man who perhaps mounted the longest coup ever. In that actually, the war could be looked at as Gowon consolidating the coup, which he mishandled.

You see, Gowon mounted a counter-coup...and never got complete control of Nigeria. He then proceeded to force the entirety of Nigeria to go under his command. I refused, and my refusal got to a point that he thought he should now fight me. And he never got control of Nigeria until he won that war. So it was a continuation of his coup actually."

In the same interview, Ojukwu was also asked: "When Gowon maintained his position, you initiated the Mid-West invasion?" To which he responded:

"Absolute lie. I was in Enugu and it is on record that Gowon ordered the troops into the East. They had a two-prong entry. One from Nsukka and one from Afikpo axis. The war had been (going) on for months, before I mounted an attempt at capturing Lagos or destablising Lagos through the Mid-West.

How can that be that I took the initiative? I suppose your answer should be that I should stay in the East and do nothing. Again that is part of the lie.

Everywhere you go, they say Ojukwu waged, mounted, declared war against Nigeria. But it is a lie. I had the opportunity of declaring war. I had the opportunities of doing so many things, check.... Gowon is a liar....

He had already prior to that (declaration of independence by Biafra) committed certain acts that were tantamount to acts of war. How do you stay in Nigeria, if you were under a total blockade? Tell me....

There is no way Nigeria can move forward in peace and harmony, without some restructuring. There is no way we can all feel part of Nigeria, if we do not go through a quasi re-negotiation of Nigeria, and our Nigerianness.

In saying this, I want to make it clear, because I am the most misunderstood Nigerian. Nigeria itself, there is nothing wrong with it, nothing. It is our position in Nigeria that we do not like. There is nothing wrong with Nigeria; it is what we suffer in Nigeria that we can't accept. There is nothing wrong with Nigeria; there is nothing wrong with West Africa.

What we continue to oppose is the oppression in Nigeria of Ndigbo, that's all. So, as far as I am concerned, a national conference is to make us feel better in Nigeria. Restructuring is to make Ndigbo feel part of Nigeria. That is how Ndigbo look at it....

I cannot help being sentimental about a Nigeria that has done me no good."

That probably sums up the way many Igbos feel, although one cannot be sure exactly how many. But it is a collective sentiment shared by many of them as demonstrated by their continued support of the ideals which inspired the emergence of Biafra on the international scene. they even had an office in Washington D.C. in the 1990s and beyond which some people erroneously called "an embassy," as if Biafra were a legal sovereign entity recognised by the United States and other countries.

However, this collective sentiment of Igbo nationhood and marginalisation in the Nigerian context is a sentiment articulated by a man – Ojukwu – who was one of the most

225

influential Igbo leaders in modern times and who continued to command allegiance among his people across the spectrum decades after the war when emerged on the international scene as their saviour, leading his troops against the federal army.

It was David against Goliath.

Besides the differences in the interpretation of what actually happened, what Ojkwu said clearly shows that bitter memories of the war continue to poison relations between many Igbos and the rest of the Nigerians because of the injustices that were never corrected and which continue to be perpetrated against them as one of the most marginalised groups in the country; in spite of their high qualifications in many fields and their status as an integral part of the nation like the rest of their fellow countrymen.

Had the cause of the war been addressed, and had the grievances of the secessionists been redressed through the years since the end of the war, the Igbos would not be marginalized as they are today; and the Nigerian federation would be much stronger than it is now, even more so if all the other groups shunted to the periphery of the mainstream were treated fairly.

Ironically, the situation is analogous to that of Tanzania – the first country to recognise Biafra – where secessionist sentiments in the former island nation of Zanzibar have grown strong through the years because of what many Zanzibaris consider to be their marginalised status in the union. Whether Zanzibar really plays a marginal role in the conduct of union affairs, as a junior and not as an equal partner as a former independent nation, is highly debatable. But many Zanzibaris, rightly or wrongly, believe that.

They have other complaints. Their basic demand is restoration of their sovereign status that ended when the union was consummated in April 1964. If this demand is met, that will be the end of the union. One solution to the crisis is to form a confederation of Tanganyika and

Zanzibar to replace the current unitary state.

There is no question that if their grievances are not addressed, the union of Tanzania will face very serious problems in the future even if it does not break up.

Should Zanzibar be allowed to secede? It depends on what the people want; a point also underscored by President Nyerere, the architect of the union, when he explained why Tanzania recognised Biafra, as we learned earlier:

"As President of Tanzania it is my duty to safeguard the integrity of the United Republic. But if the mass of the people of Zanzibar should, without external manipulation, and for some reason of their own, decide that the Union was prejudicial to their existence, I could not advocate bombing them into submission. To do so would not be to defend the Union. The Union would have ceased to exist when the consent of its constituent members was withdrawn."

If a referendum were held in the former island nation and the majority of the people in Zanzibar voted to dissolve ties with Tanganyika and return to the status quo ante, that would be the end not only of the union but of any hope of even forming a confederation under which members enjoy far greater autonomy than they do under federation.

As a Tanzanian myself and strong believer in African unity, I don't want to see the union dissolved anymore than I would like to see any other African country break up. But there are cases when such dissolution of ties may be necessary.

If people are abused, oppressed, and discriminated against by their fellow countrymen, that's grounds for secession, unless the injustices are stopped. Otherwise there is no reason why they should not be allowed to secede and establish their own independent state – if that is the only way they can live in peace and security in their own country.

If you don't want them to secede, stop oppressing them and denying them equal rights; and if the right to self-determination has to be enshrined in the constitution of every African country as one of the best ways to guarantee equal treatment of oppressed groups, by threatening secession, so be it: "Treat us fairly. Otherwise we are gone."

Therefore, in a paradoxical way, the right to secession may not only prevent secession. It can also help maintain and strengthen unity by using the threat of secession to demand and get justice and equal treatment from the government which has failed or refuses to protect oppressed groups who have also been rejected by their fellow citizens. It will also enable all citizens to hold their leaders accountable for their actions. Otherwise they will have nobody left to lead.

Yet, unlike Biafra, the case of Zanzibar presents a unique problem for Tanzania because there are many people in the former island nation who want to maintain the union.

The secessionists on the islands of Pemba and Zanzibar, especially Pemba, are not motivated by any genuine desire to correct whatever injustices exist. They want to restore historical ties with the Gulf States, especially Oman, reminiscent of the era when the islands were an integral part of the Arab world and Zanzibar the seat of the sultan of Oman.

Also, Islamic fundamentalists want to turn Zanzibar into a theocratic state and use it as an operational base from which they will be able to export their radical ideology to the mainland in a country which is constitutionally a secular state.

There is another reality that is sometimes overlooked. Contrary to what the agitators say, the majority of Zanzibaris are not Islamic fundamentalists. They do not support the agenda for a theocratic state based on a radical interpretation of the Koran.

Yet, secessionist sentiments may continue to grow on the isles if the islanders are not granted far greater autonomy than they now enjoy.

Tanzania may have to learn a lesson from one of the neighboring countries, the island nation of the Comoros, which also has had historical ties with Zanzibar for a long time. In fact, many Zanzibaris are of Comorian origin, as are many Tanzanians on the mainland; and Kiswahili, Tanzania's national language, is also spoken in the Comoros where the overwhelming majority of the people are Muslim just like those in Zanzibar are.

Two islands, Anjouan and Moheli, seceded from the Comoros in 1997. Federal troops failed to suppress the insurgency. The Comoros, a federation of three islands, was left with one island, Grande Comoro, which is also the largest and the seat of the federal capital.

In 2001, the federal government and the secessionist islands agreed to hold a referendum on a new constitution which would give extensive autonomy to all the islands in the federation. An overwhelming majority of the people, at least 75 percent, approved the constitution, and the secessionists rejoined the union.

Extensive devolution of power saved the federation, although in some cases, it can be recipe for disaster, fuelling secessionist movements if not carefully managed within prescribed limits. But such extensive autonomy, short of sovereign status, may also dampen and neutralise secessionist sentiments and tendencies in Zanzibar and strengthen the union of Tanzania.

It also could have saved Nigeria from exploding into civil war, thus preventing the secession of Biafra and its aftermath including loss of at least one million lives, had the federal authorities implemented the Aburi accords to transform the highly centralised Nigerian federation into a confederation; a transformation that would have assured

229

Igbos and other easterners that they would be guaranteed security in their own autonomous region, under their own jurisdiction, but without attaining full sovereign status.

It is a tragic irony that 50 years after independence, African countries have not yet adequately addressed the question of ethnicity in a continent whose very traditional societies, the building blocks of African nations, are ethnic entities.

Ethnic differences and loyalties will always be exploited by unscrupulous politicians to promote their own partisan interests. Yet, ethnic groups have an enormous potential to serve as a solid foundation for stable nations, provided all the tribes and other groups in every African country, including racial minorities of Arab, Asian, and European origin in countries such as Kenya and Tanzania, are treated equally and have equal access to power and the nation's resources.

It is the denial of such equality, and exclusion of some groups from participation in the political and economic arena, that has served as a lightning rod in many conflicts ignited across the continent. As Dr. Sam Amoo, a Ghanaian scholar and United Nations specialist in conflict resolution, states in "The Challenges of Ethnicity and Conflict in Africa: The Need for a New Paradigm":

"Conflicts arise from dysfunctional governance or socio-political systems that deny or suppress the satisfaction of a group's ontological needs, such as the universal needs for identity, recognition, security, dignity and participation.

This denial generates conflict, which can only be resolved through alterations in norms, structures, institutions and policies. The causes and remedies of conflicts in Africa therefore essentially relate to the socio-political structures of the particular state....

Sources of conflicts in Africa are located in basic human needs for group – ethnic – identity, security, recognition, participation and autonomy, as well as in the circumstances, policies and institutions of political and economic systems that attempt to deny or suppress such basic needs."

The significance of ethnicity in African life across the spectrum cannot be ignored or underestimated. Attempts to ignore it, or gloss over it, have only exacerbated conflicts where they already exist, and generated new ones where there weren't any.

Like the English, the Scots, the Irish and the Welsh in the United Kingdom, African ethnic groups are not going to disappear, and would be a tragic loss if they did. That is because they are Africa itself.

They constitute the African organic entity and the spirit that animates its very being. They are natural entities, not artificial constructs like the countries across the continent created by the colonialists.

The Kikuyu, the Luo, the Kamba and others existed before Kenya was created; the Ewe and the Ashanti before the Gold Coast, now Ghana; the Igbo, the Yoruba, the Hausa, the Fulani, the Ijaw, the Tiv and the rest of the ethnic groups in Nigeria and other African countries – they all existed, at different levels of social and political organisation, long before Europeans came and created the countries we have in Africa today. Europeans did not teach us our customs and traditions; nor did they teach us or invent or create our languages. Instead, they tried to destroy all that, one way or another, and exploited ethnic differences to consolidate their hegemonic control over Africa.

The question is how all these groups can be harmonised as corporate entities, functioning smoothly as interlocking units that constitute an interdependent whole, without tearing African countries and the continent apart. And this requires a new – yet old, traditional – approach to nation-building and conflict resolution in Africa.

Therefore, there is a need for a paradigm shift in Africa; one that incorporates into its analytical framework the salience and primacy of ethnicity as an organising concept, but one that does not nullify the legitimacy of the nation-state; one that also sees ethnicity as a basis for nation-building, and for power and resource allocation where it has generated and has the potential to generate conflict; and as a mechanism for conflict resolution through consensus building within a specific ethno-polity and across ethnic lines, with primary emphasis on the use of traditional institutions of authority as the key players in resolving conflicts.

If Africa takes this approach, she may be on her way towards reducing and ending civil wars and other conflicts which have devastated the continent for years, as hundreds of millions of her people continue to suffer, and look helpless, in a world which couldn't care less if they vanished today from the face of the earth.

In the Nigerian civil war, the Igbos would have suffered even more casualties – far more than the 1 to 2 million who had already died, mostly from starvation – had they not capitulated to federal might after fighting a brutal war for almost three years to sustain their short-lived independent Republic of Biafra. It was an unnecessary war, which could have been avoided. But after it started and kept on going, recognition of Biafra by Tanzania became a moral imperative; and President Nyerere made that clear.

Denying Biafra recognition would have been tantamount to sanctioning genocide against a people whose only crime was their desire, and right, to be safe and free in their own homeland.

In a very tragic way, most African leaders sanctioned the massacre of the Igbos and other easterners – but mostly Igbos – when they refused to take a firm stand against the Nigerian federal authorities who continued to wage war against Biafra even after the "contested" minority areas of non-Igbo ethnic groups (which the federal government erroneously claimed had been forcibly incorporated into Biafra), and the oil fields, had been "liberated" from the secessionist forces; and after they had captured most of the Biafran territory in a brutal military campaign which verged on genocide.

Even from the beginning of the war, most African countries supported the Nigerian federal government when they contended that this was an internal affairs that should be resolved by the Nigerians themselves – which was tantamount to sanctioning a war of genocide against the Igbos; and when they invoked two of the most sacred principles of the Organization of African Unity (OAU), but in a perverted way.

Those principles were non-interference in the internal affairs of another state – no matter what the cost even if it meant extermination of an entire group of people; and maintaining the territorial integrity of a member state, again at whatever cost and by any means possible: the end justifies the means.

Had African leaders taken an uncompromising stand on the war and told the Nigerian federal government that there would be a price to pay if it continued to wage war against a large segment of its own population, instead of negotiating an end to the conflict and seriously taking into account the fears and concerns of the Igbos; this catastrophe would have been averted.

The Nigerian federal government should have been told in no uncertain terms by other African leaders that they would recognise Biafra if the federal authorities did not stop trying to bomb and starve the Biafrans into submission.

Threats of recognition of Biafra as a sovereign entity would have been a powerful bargaining tool to extract meaningful concessions from the Nigerian federal government which could have been accepted by the secessionists on the basis of mutual compromise; provided the Biafrans were guaranteed security in their own homeland under a different political system, probably a confederation.

President Nyerere took his fellow African leaders to task for not being honest and for refusing to confront the issue and putting the secession of Biafra in its proper context. As he stated in his pamphlet, *The Nigeria-Biafra Crisis*, which was labelled "For Private Circulation Only" – later declassified – published on 4 September 1969, and circulated among African heads of state and government just before the OAU summit on the Nigerian civil war was held in Addis Ababa, Ethiopia, from 6 – 10 September the same year:

"In arguments about the Nigeria/Biafra conflict, there has been a great deal of talk about the principles of national integrity and of self-determination; many analogies have been drawn with other conflicts in the world, and particularly in Africa; and finally, there has been a considerable amount of discussion about the role of the OAU and other international organizations in relation to the present conflict.

It is my purpose to discuss some of these problems and to examine the lessons which are, and which I believe should be, drawn from the analogies.

Let me look first at the analogies and their relevance to the principles which are under discussion.

Gibraltar

The British give three reasons for their opposition to the demand for the incorporation of Gibraltar into the Spanish State. First is the Treaty of Utrecht 1713 - to which the Gibraltarians were not a party; second is the opposition of the Gibraltarians; and third is the dictatorship in Spain.

It is the second reason which Britain mostly uses to

justify her position, and indeed it is the more important one. For if the Gibraltarians wished, they could say: 'To hell with the Treaty of Utrecht: we were not a party to it anyway.' If, after that, the territory were incorporated, Britain would not be able to do anything about it, unless she was to come out openly in favour of imperialism.

Yet I believe that Britain is simply using the fact of the Gibraltarians' opposition to incorporation, just as she is using the legalities of the Treaty. When Britain feels that it is in her interests to come to terms with Spain, I doubt that either the Treaty or the Gibraltarians' feelings will prevail - indeed this doubt is buttressed by the fact that Britain will not accept the 'integration with Britain' policy.

But this is not the point I want to argue. My point is that two quite separate arguments are used by Britain in this dispute: one, an imperialist Treaty between several powers, including Britain and Spain; and two, the feelings of a group of people who were the object of that Treaty.

In the political climate of the modern world, the opposition of the Gibraltarians is the more important matter for winning world support for Britain's cause. But the Treaty argument also has an importance.

Look now at the analogy with the Nigeria/Biafra issue.

Britain appears to be arguing that she is helping Nigeria to stop the Ibos from unilaterally breaking the "Treaty" under which all the peoples of Nigeria agreed to accept independence as a single Federation. In this case, in other words, she is leaving out the question of self-determination, although it is the main plank of her argument on the Gibraltar question.

But in the case of Nigeria and Biafra, the issue is not some minor, technical issue about the legalities or morality of a Treaty. It is an issue of life and death, involving a massacre by one party to that Treaty of more people among another party to the Treaty than all the inhabitants of Gibraltar.

After the failure of several serious attempts to secure

reassurance for the resultant fears, the People who had been the victims decided to break away to form their own State. If the principle of self-determination is relevant in the case of Gibraltar - as it is - then surely it is relevant under these circumstances? But the rest of Nigeria objects, and says: 'These Ibos must remain part of Nigeria.' Surely we should be saying to Nigeria: 'Get their consent.' Instead, what we are saying is: 'Shoot and starve them into submission.'

It may be argued that all those involved in a Treaty should be consulted about any change in it, and that therefore in this case the Nigerians should be consulted as well as the Biafrans. That is not actually my argument, but let us look at it in these two cases.

Consult the People of Spain about the incorporation of Gibraltar: I do not know what their verdict would be. Consult the People of Britain: they will vote against Spain - not because of the Treaty of Utrecht but because the Gibraltarians do not want to be part of Spain. They would vote, I hope - indeed I am sure - in support of the self-determination of the people of Gibraltar as it has been so freely expressed, not for Spain's claims.

Then ask the Nigerians about the forcible incorporation of the Ibos. At worst their answer would be equivalent to that of the Spanish Government, and of their own Government now: 'Keep them part of Nigeria, even against their will.' Ask the people of Britain about this issue: in this case I am not sure what their verdict might be, in spite of the clear determination of the 8 million Biafrans to be left alone.

But neither is (British Prime Minister Harold) Wilson sure, so we shall never know. What we do know is that the 29,000 Gibraltarians have been asked their opinion about the dispute in which they are involved, and they have given their answer. The 8 million Biafrans have not been asked, and will not be asked their opinion on their conflict; but they have given their answer nevertheless - with their blood.

Britain invokes the principle of self-determination in the case of Gibraltar, because it serves her interests to do so. She must justify her stand on some acceptable principle - international law, plus self-determination - because she still wants the Rock.

Nevertheless, the principles she advances are valid. I am not going to say that they are not valid because they are advanced by Britain. In the case of Nigeria, Britain invokes a different principle - the principle of territorial integrity - because it suits her own interests to do so.

The choice of principle is the result of a decision taken on the basis of British interests, not because one principle is more valid than another. If British interests had been different, we would have self-determination being advanced as a reason for supporting Biafra.

If the dictatorship of General Franco is an additional reason for supporting the Gibraltarians, one may rightly ask for similar consideration to be given to the people of Biafra. They object to incorporation because before secession 30,000 Easterners were massacred without anyone being punished; and the same regime threatens them with complete extermination through starvation unless they surrender.

Are not such actions, and the attitudes they reveal, at least as good a reason as Franco's dictatorship for the Biafrans' opposition to being incorporated into Nigeria? Have the Gibraltarians so much reason to fear General Franco?

The American Civil War

What, then, about the analogy which is sometimes drawn to the American Civil War?

Like the Nigerian Civil War, it was about secession. Like that in Nigeria it caused very dreadful suffering.

But we do justify wars, or condemn them, because of

what they are about. And in America, the South was not trying to break away because Southerners had been rejected in the North, and had been massacred in their thousands with the connivance or the assistance of the forces of law and order. The Southern States were not swarming with millions of refugees who had fled from the North, leaving their property behind, in order to save their skins.

Of course it is true that Lincoln fought to save the Union. But he believed, even before the war, that the Union could not last half free, half slave. He was concerned to make it what it had proclaimed itself to be - a society of free and equal men.

Had there been a Lincoln in Nigeria, he would have fought the prejudices which led to that inordinate and almost pathological hatred of the Ibos which made secession inevitable and justifiable.

Katanga as a Comparison

A politically more serious comparison, however, is made between the secession of Biafra and that of Katanga. Tanzania, in particular, is accused of the most blatant inconsistency because it opposed Katanga and recognizes Biafra.

I know that there are similarities between Katanga and Biafra. But these similarities can be grouped into those which are superficial and irrelevant and those which are real and crucial.

An examination of the real and crucial similarities reveals some apparently unnoticed facts.

First, let me acknowledge the similarities which are advanced by the opponents of Biafra, but which I believe to be superficial and irrelevant to the main issue.

Katanga was part of a United Congo; Katanga decided to secede; the Centre objected; a war then broke out between secessionist Katanga and the Centre. (Notice that

I am not trying to say 'why' Katanga decided to secede; I am merely stating the fact of secession). Similarly, Biafra - or the Eastern Region of Nigeria - was part of a federated Nigeria; Biafra decided to secede; the Centre objected; (this is not quite correct, but I must admit a few similarities); a war broke out between secessionist Biafra and the Centre.

Now, for a different and more fundamental group of similarities. Katanga had vast copper resources; the former colonial power was very much interested in this vast amount of wealth; her economic interests were threatened by Lumumba at the Centre; when war broke out between Katanga and the Centre, Belgium supported one side in an effort to safeguard her economic interests; she joined *the side supported by the copper companies*. No need to go further.

Now, for the conflict in Nigeria. Biafra had vital oil resources; the former colonial power was vitally interested in this vast amount of oil; her interests were threatened in the conflict; (the really vital matter was the threat, not whether the threat came from the Centre or the periphery; this is only important in deciding who is going to be ally and who enemy); but in this case, due to relations between the British and the Ibos, the threat came from the secessionists. When war broke out between Biafra and the Centre, Britain, like Belgium, *was on the same side as the Foreign Companies* - in this case the Oil Companies.

Let those who love the superficial similarities of secession have the courage and honesty to accept this unpleasant fact also. In Katanga, Belgium and the Copper Companies were on one side; in Nigeria, Britain and the Oil Companies are on one side. This is the one constant and crucial factor in both cases, around which everything else can be variable.

In both cases, the former colonial power and the vested economic interests are on one side. Tshombe was a stooge of the Copper Interests. They filled his coffers with their

239

vast financial resources. Ojukwu is not a stooge of these interests; they refuse to pay him a penny from the wealth they derive from Biafran oil.

This vital contrast is the corollary to the decision to support the Centre instead of secession. In the one case it was the Centre under Lumumba which was the threat to the economic interests if the Congo remained united; and therefore it was the Centre which had to be starved of Revenue. In the other case it was a separate Ibo state which was the threat, and it was Biafra, therefore, which had to be strangled.

Is this really so difficult to see? Only great simplicity - or even extreme naivety - could lead anyone to accept that Britain is defending the unity of Nigeria, or African Unity in general. She is defending her own economic interests. That may be natural and even understandable, but it is as well that it should be understood and not camouflaged by talk of a particular principle.

The Netherlands decision to stop the supply of arms to Nigeria after the capture of Port Harcourt and its oil-rich surrounding areas is a reflection of her assessment that the oil supplies were then assured. But the British wish to be more certain. I am told that Britain expects to get 25 per cent of her oil supply from Nigeria by 1972. With her traditional Middle East suppliers being (in her view) unreliable, this is a very serious matter indeed for industrial Britain.

From Britain's point of view, what is vital is her oil interests; as she decides on her own policy, this is what the war is about. The Biafrans are fighting a most unequal war, and if they go on fighting, God alone knows what their end will be. Completely blockaded as they are, Nigeria no longer needs to shoot them into submission. Starvation and disease can fight for Nigeria, and Britain can go on explaining to the world that this is inevitable and justifiable because it is part of warfare.

Those who want peace before the Biafrans are wiped

out must convince the British of one of two things. They have to be convinced that, in their present helpless position, the Biafrans are no longer a threat to British interests. And truly, the Biafrans know how weak they are; they are less interested in the oil than in their lives. This is the relatively easier thing to try and convince the British.

The more difficult one is to try and convince Britain that her oil interests would be safe in an independent Biafra.

But how could they know that Russia would not help Federal Nigeria to win total victory against the Biafrans? And if that happened, where would Britain be?

These are the vital issues, and those who are saying that the OAU can solve this problem are being fooled, or are conveniently fooling themselves.

Britain is the vital force in this conflict; more important even than Federal Nigeria.

The Biafrans believe they are fighting for their very survival; they are fighting to live in freedom and security. The Nigerian people are not quite sure what they are fighting for. Some of their leaders hate the Ibos; some may have ambitions of being Lincolns; some may even believe that they can force others into a United Nigeria and still have a meaningful nation. But that is all.

Without Britain's military and - in particular - her diplomatic support, the Nigerians would have no hope of winning against the Biafrans. The Soviet Union would not have been able to help them secure victory.

Indeed, without Britain, the Soviet Union would have become a huge diplomatic embarrassment to the Nigerians; (and Nigeria would have become a wee embarrassment to Russia). For if Russia had supported Lagos and Britain did not, most of the Western world would have been anti-Lagos; and since there is so much popular sympathy for Biafra in many Western countries, it is hard to think of a reason which would have prevented Western Governments from supporting Biafra. After all,

241

they would be fighting against communism.

Under these circumstances it would not have mattered whether African Heads of Government had continued to fear the effect of an example of successful secession; the Western powers, the only ones who have real power in Africa, would be fearing a different example, and one more vital to their own interests.

But if this argument is not convincing, those who believe that there is a direct and valid comparison between Katanga and Biafra must be able to answer some few questions.

Which tribe in Katanga is the equivalent of the Ibos? Azikiwe, an Ibo at the Centre, was trying hard, under very difficult circumstances, to co-operate with the dominant North to build a United Nigeria: who was his equivalent in the Congo? The Ibos, because of their education, industry, enterprise (and consequent arrogance?) were almost universally hated in Nigeria. Who in Katanga represented this educated, industrous, enterprising, arrogant and almost universally hated People?

Who in the Congo represented the 30,000 massacred Easterners? Who in Katanga represented the 1.5 or 2 million refugees? What in the Congo represented the National Council of Nigeria and the Cameroons (NCNC), a party led mainly by Ibos it is true, but one which was nevertheless truly aimed at Nigerian Unity?

Who in the Congo was the equivalent of the Sardauna of Sokoto, so powerful that he did not even bother to go to the Centre but governed the Federation through lieutenants while he himself governed the vital North? What in Katanga was the equivalent of the Northern People's Congress (NPC)?

Or again, who is Biafra's Tshombe? Who in Biafra represents the Copper Companies? Africa appealed to the United Nations to support Patrice Lumumba; why are we not appealing to the United Nations to support General Gowon, who in this analogy would be Nigeria's

Lumumba?

Perhaps the true answer is that it is not necessary; he already has strong support. But why is not necessary? Because the Ibos are simply fighting for their own survival and therefore have no strong supporter. That is their strength and weakness: it is the major difference between Katanga and Biafra.

In the one case, foreign economic interest was on the side of the secessionists and that made them very strong; in the other case, foreign economic interest is on the side of the Federalists, and makes them too very strong. They can even quote the OAU Charter on non-interference in the internal affairs of a member state. The devil can quote Scripture - when it suits him.

In the one case, a despicable African stooge allowed himself to be used as a tool of foreign economic interests; in the other case, a brave African people are fighting against immense odds purely and simply for their own survival and their own self-respect and dignity. How does this analogy stand up to examination?

The break-up of Nigeria is a terrible thing. But it is less terrible than that cruel war.

Thousands of people are being shot, bombed, or seeing their homes and livelihood destroyed; millions, including the children of Africa, are starving to death. (It is estimated that possibly more people have died in this war in the last two years (since 1967) than in Vietnam in the last ten years). We are told that nothing can be done about this. It is said that the sufferings of the Biafrans in the war are regrettable, but that starvation is a legitimate war weapon against an enemy.

Yet by this statement you have said that these people, the Nigerians and the Biafrans, are enemies, just as Britons and Germans in Hitler's war were enemies. If that is the case, is it rational to imagine that, once a Federal victory is obtained, they can immediately be equal members of one society, working together without fear? Or is the logic of being enemies not a logic which leads to conquest and domination when one side is victorious?

We are told that Ojukwu should end the terrible sufferings of his people by surrender. We are told that he should reason thus: 'The Nigerians are stronger than we are and they have stronger friends than we could ever hope to get. If we go on resisting, a combination of bombing, starvation and the inevitable epidemics, would exterminate us.' Perhaps he should add, kindly: 'Even if the Nigerians never intended to exterminate us.'

He should then convince the Biafran people about the wisdom of surrendering and then duly send the appropriate notice to the Nigerians. When the Federal Government gets this note, they presumably say: 'At last you have come to your senses. As you rightly say, we never intended to exterminate you; but had you gone on resisting we would have continued the bombing and the blockade and the result would have been exactly the same as if we had intended to exterminate you.'

Perhaps they would add, kindly: 'But, of course, the fault would have been yours.' Then the Biafrans surrender and all is well.

Historically and logically, however, surrender on such terms as these – with the alternative being extermination – is for the purpose of creating empires.

Surrender to an implacable enemy on his own terms, with the only condition being that you should not be killed, cannot lead to any kind of friendship, or even toleration. If it is a battalion which surrenders, the soldiers become prisoners-of-war; if it is a People, they become a colony, or an occupied territory, or something like that. Those who surrender cannot become an integral part of the conqueror's territory because they did not do so of their own free will; they did so as the only alternative to death.

The Internal Domino Theory

The argument is being advanced that if Biafra is allowed to exist, Nigeria cannot exist. Nigerian leaders themselves have advanced this argument. If the Ibos are allowed to go, so the argument runs, Nigeria will break up completely, for the others will also go.

To deal with this argument seriously, let us assume the worst: let us assume that, if the Biafrans leave the Federation, all the others will also secede and set themselves up as separate States. What this argument amounts to is that only two things bind the Hausa and the Yorubas (these being the major elements) together. These two facts are, firstly, the recent historical accident that all (plus the Ibos) were conquered by, and then governed by, the British; and secondly, the more recent historical fact that, when the British left, they left these Peoples as one Nation.

If these accidents of history were in fact the only reason for Nigeria, and if there is no feeling of mutual benefit arising from the political unity, then the secession of the Biafrans would certainly and inevitably lead to the break-up of the Federation as the Yorubas – and the Hausas? – secede.

In using this argument, therefore, we are in effect saying: 'The Yorubas, the Hausas (and the others) cannot remain together without the Ibos; we want the Yorubas and the Hausas to remain together; therefore we must forcibly prevent the Ibos from breaking away - even if this attempt to prevent them, together with their stubborn resistance, may lead to their extermination.'

This is an extremely logical and nice argument. But it must be directed to people other than the Biafrans. They cannot be asked to sacrifice their freedom in order that two Peoples, who are not otherwise willing to attempt the building of a nation together, may carry on a precarious united existence.

It is bad enough to force the Biafrans to make immense sacrifices for their own freedom; it would be worse than absurd to expect them to surrender the freedom for which they are dying in order to maintain a precarious unity among other Peoples – whose own commitment to that unity must be very slight if this argument has any validity at all.

In fact, the argument 'If you allow the Ibos to go, the others will also go,' inevitably provokes the question: 'Who are these others, and where will they go?' For properly considered, this argument is an Imperialist argument. I can well imagine Winston Churchill saying: 'If I allow India to go, the others will go, and I was not appointed the King's First Minister in order to preside over the liquidation of the British Empire.'

But how can this kind of thing be said of Nigeria – most all by Nigerians? Who in the Nigerian issue represents Churchill? And who represents the 'Others' who would break away if the Ibos are allowed to go? And who is the imperialist metropolitan power in Nigeria?

Those who advance this argument assume the Hausas to be the Churchill and the 'Others' to be the Yorubas in particular, and also the smaller groups. They assume that the Hausas would like to complete their conquest of the South, which was interrupted by the British, and are saying that the only way the Hausas will be able to continue to dominate the Yorubas and the smaller ethnic groups is if they succeed in dominating the Ibos.

If this is the basis of the argument, and if it stated the actual position, I would be amazed at Africa's reaction to an African Imperialism abetted and supported by British Imperialism. Indeed, it would be very shameful if Africa, which is still groaning from the yoke of European Imperialism, was to make a cynical distinction between that and an internal African Imperialism.

Such an argument must be rejected by the whole of

Africa. Not only would it make nonsense of the principles we have been proclaiming; it is also an insult to the people of Nigeria - the Hausas, the Yorubas, and the others.

Let us reject the Internal Domino Theory in relation to the Nigerian question. For it assumes that the people now in the Federation of Nigeria are, and wish to be, imperialists. I cannot believe that.

I still believe that they are capable of recognizing the tragedy which has caused one part of the Federation to break away, and of acknowledging that very different tactics are necessary if the old Nigeria is ever to re-created. For surely they could decide to leave the Biafrans to go their own way and, by the kind of Nigeria which they create, to show the Biafrans what they are losing by remaining separated from their brethren. For if the other peoples of Nigeria decide to work together, they will continue to be a strong and powerful force in Africa; they really have the opportunity to build a good nation of which every Nigerian - indeed every African - can be proud.

Then it may be that at some time in the future the Biafrans will wish to rejoin the peoples from whom they now wish to part; if this happens, it will be the accession of a free people to a large and free political unit. For if the secession of Biafra is a setback to African Unity - as of course it is - no one is suggesting that we should consequently stop working for African Unity on the basis of willing commitment.

Why then are we suggesting that our Nigerian brethren have a different conception of unity, and that they want a unity of conquest only? I am not making such an argument: I am saying that, although our Nigerian brothers want to maintain one Nigeria, including Biafra, on the basis of equality of citizenship, they are wrong in thinking that this can be done now. I refuse to impute bad motives to General Gowon; I believe he is mistaken in his judgment and that Africa must not make the same mistake.

The African Domino Theory

There is another Domino Theory which relates to the rest of Africa. We are told that, if we allow 'tribalism' to break up Nigeria, no African country would be safe; for every African nation consists of tribes which find themselves in the same country by an accident of history and by the grace of the Imperialists.

I fully accept the danger of tribalism in Africa. When we started TANU (Tanganyika African National Union) in 1954, the first of the objectives of our Party was preparation for independence, and the second was 'to fight against tribalism.' We have not completely succeeded in eradicating tribalism from our society; indeed I was recently forced to remind our people of this objective, and to warn them about certain tendencies.

But the dangers of tribalism are so well-known that, although I would never wish to minimize them, I do not think it is now necessary to expound them afresh.

There is, however, a different fact which can be equally dangerous. Sometimes, indeed very often, the spectre of tribalism is raised by the enemies of Africa against Africa. It is dangerous for Africa to accept the argument of tribalism without examining its relevance in every given case. Indeed to the extent that we need to learn from Nigeria's "tribalism,' I have a feeling that Africa is being bamboozled or mesmerized into learning the wrong lesson.

But first, what is a Tribe? And how comparable is Nigeria's position to that which exists elsewhere in Africa? Are the Hausas a tribe? Are the Yorubas a tribe? Are the Ibos a tribe? It may be said that they are not "Nations"; but are they Tribes?

There are Scottish clans, but the Scots are not a Tribe simply because of the fact that they are not a Nation. The Welsh: are they a Tribe? Are the Protestants of Northern

248

Ireland a tribe?

The Hausas, the Ibos, and the Yorubas, are not Nations in the legal sense; but they are not Tribes either. Each one of them is a "People" which could easily become a very coherent Nation. Each one of these "Peoples" of Nigeria has a better chance of forming a really viable and stable Nation than many of the legal Nations of Africa and other parts of the world.

Indeed, those who glibly compare Nigeria with other African countries show that they did not begin to understand the immense significance for the rest of Africa of the Nigerian experiment. Nigeria was trying (and if they do not allow themselves to be convinced by the internal Nigerian Domino Theory, they may continue trying) to build a Nation which incorporates several Peoples who could have become Nations on their own.

Had Nigeria succeeded (and Nigeria can still succeed if she rejects the argument of all or none), Africa would have a great example before it. We would be able to say: 'Within Nigeria there are several Peoples, each conscious of itself and conscious of its ability to be a Nation on its own. If they have nevertheless succeeded in submerging their natural unity into a larger artificial unity, for the greater benefit of them all, then the rest of Africa can submerge its smaller artificial units into that greater artificiality (indeed that more natural unit of all Africa) which holds greater promise for all the peoples of Africa.'

In other words, any success in Nigeria - even if partial - is a demonstration of the practicability of our declared aim of African Unity - even though a Nigerian failure would not make this aim impossible of achievement. This, I repeat, is Nigeria's real significance to Africa.

No other political unit in our continent has the same significance for Africa; not even the Sudan, although the two cases are similar in one respect.

Both have a basic problem of 'Peoples' in the sense that the North of Sudan is different from the South, racially, religiously, culturally, and socially – although the one "People" of the South are divided into several different tribes. The Sudan's problem, therefore, is very serious – just as Nigeria's problem is.

But fortunately for Sudan, and for Africa, Southern Sudan is not blessed (or cursed) with immense mineral wealth. As a result, foreign economic interests are not involved in this conflict (until years later when oil was discovered in significant quantities in the South after Nyerere wrote this pamphlet).

However agonising the problem may be for the authorities in Khartoum - and for the people of the country - the former Colonial Power is most unlikely to pour arms into the Sudan to help maintain Sudanese unity. It is also unlikely to intervene in support of any attempt at secession. This situation will continue irrespective of the ideological leanings of the Government in Khartoum, and irrespective of what Russia does.

In this case Sudanese leaders, and African leaders, have a real chance of solving the problem provided we do not make the same mistake as we made in Nigeria and act as if there is no genuine problem to be solved.

The solution, as the present Government in the Sudan has rightly foreseen, lies in a constitution which recognizes both the unity of the Sudan, and the legitimate interests of the South. This is what Eastern Nigeria was asking for before it seceded; this is what the Aburi Agreement was all about.

It was the refusal, by Lagos, to accept this necessity that finally led to secession and the present situation.

The fact is that the Peoples of Nigeria have less in common, historically, linguistically, culturally, and as regards religion, than the Peoples of Scandinavia. The only thing that the Peoples of Nigeria have in common is that they are all Africans and all have been under British rule for a few decades - and Britain governed them virtually separately.

It would be infinitely easier for the Peoples of Scandinavia to form one nation than for the Peoples of Nigeria. Those who do not see this do not understand Nigeria's significance for Africa.

One final point must be made about this tragedy. In spite of attempts on both sides of the quarrel to bring in religion, the conflict between Nigeria and Biafra is not a religious one. Yet if it were, that would be simply an additional complication: it would not justify the war. In fact, however, there are Christians and Muslims on both sides: religion cuts across the divisions between the Peoples.

The True Lesson for Africa

I said earlier that Africa is learning the wrong lesson from the Nigerian tragedy. We are saying that if Biafra is allowed to secede, every country in Africa is going to have its own Biafra. But what we are doing is looking at results without looking at the cause of those results, and then saying that the same results will happen elsewhere without there having been any causes. That is nonsense.

But there is a very serious lesson to be learned from the present tragedy. We should learn that where in any African state there is a dominant group, whether that group is ethnic, religious or otherwise, it must wield its power and influence on behalf of all the elements which go to form that country. In particular, it should be very solicitous of the interests of the minorities, because they are the ones which need the protection of the State. If a dominant group does not act in this protective manner, then civil strife and consequent Biafras become inevitable. That is the lesson Africa should learn from the Nigerian tragedy.

We African leaders had a golden opportunity at the OAU Summit Conference in Kinshasa (in September 1967), but we missed it because we were confused by the tribal domino theory. At that time the whole of Africa, including those countries which now recognize Biafra, supported the territorial integrity of Nigeria. Yet I believe that all States had some sympathy for the Easterners, who had already experienced a massacre of some 30,000 of their brethren, and who were trying to absorb nearly 2 million refugees in the Eastern Region.

Previous to secession the Ibos were simply asking for a loosening of the constitutional structure so as to maintain the Unity of Nigeria and still meet the understandable fears of the Peoples from that Region. Africa should have accepted the legitimacy of this demand. Since we were all supporting Nigeria in its main objective of maintaining national unity, we should have used our moral strength to urge Nigeria to listen to those demands.

We should have pointed out that under the circumstances of the two coups and the massacres, what they were asking for was not only understandable but was also justifiable.

Since we were supporting the Nigerian authorities in their efforts to keep Nigeria one, and since by that support we were rejecting any claim by the East to secede, we were in a very strong position.

We did not have to worry about Domino Theories and the Charter of the OAU. But we were so obsessed, bewitched and terrified by the Domino Theory that we did not dare raise a voice for the Ibos even when we all supported the Federal Authority.

That opportunity was lost. But we must not therefore even appear to acquiesce in the present situation of war and suffering. The least we can do is now ask our brethren in both Nigeria and Biafra to stop fighting and to begin talking about their future relations.

It is being said that the situation has changed from what it was two years ago, and that Biafrans need no longer fear for their future. If that is the case, we should ask Nigeria to convince the Biafrans of it at a conference table. You cannot convince people that they are safe while you are shooting and starving them.

The OAU was established by the Heads of African States. But it is intended to serve the Peoples of Africa. The OAU is not a trade union of African Heads of State. Therefore, if it is to retain the respect and support of the People of Africa, it must be concerned about the lives of the People of Africa.

We must not just concern ourselves with our own survival as Heads of State; we must even be more concerned about peace and justice in Africa than we are about the sanctity of the boundaries we inherited. For the importance of these lies in the fact that their acceptance is the basis for peace and justice in our continent, and we all have a responsibility to the whole people of Africa in this regard.

Many African Governments, some of them very good governments, have been overthrown through coups. Some countries have had more than one coup; but none of them has broken up. Only the Nigerian Federation is in danger, and this from the effects of a failure to meet the legitimate interests of the Easterners, not directly because of the coups. And the fall of African Governments, however regrettable, is not the same thing as the disintegration of African countries.

We must not be like the French monarch who said: *L'etat c'est Moi* – 'I am the State.' The OAU must *sometimes* raise a voice against those regimes in Africa, including independent Africa, who oppress the Peoples of Africa. In some countries in Africa it might be the only voice that can speak on behalf of the people. If we dare not do that, even in private, we shall deserve the scorn of those who accuse us of double standards.

In this connection we could learn a good lesson from our former masters. For European Governments are not often very polite to European regimes which fail to show respect for basic human rights within their own countries.

Europeans do care about what happens to Europeans.

253

(Sometimes, as in the case of Stanleyville, we are reminded of that fact rather unpleasantly). I think that is a lesson worth learning.

Thus, for example, European Governments do not invade Greece, for they respect the territorial integrity of fellow European States; but they have not left, and will not leave, the Greek regime in any doubt at all about what they think of it. Yet what have the Greek Colonels done? They have carried out a military coup against a constitutionally established government, and are detaining and persecuting the supporters of the constitution - an occurrence so familiar in young Africa that is hardly considered wrong anymore.

If we do not learn to criticise injustice within our continent, we will soon be tolerating fascism in Africa, as long as it is practised by African Governments against African Peoples.

Consider what our reaction would have been if the 30,000 Ibos had been massacred by whites in Rhodesia or South Africa. One can imagine the outcry from Africa. Yet these people are still dead; the colour of those who killed them is irrelevant. We must ask Nigeria to stop more killing now, and to deal with the problem by argument, not death.

Justice is indivisible. Africa, the OAU, must act accordingly."

Nyerere became the most eloquent spokesman for the Biafran cause besides the Biafrans themselves.

Even more tragic is the fact that the Nigerian civil war was not the last major conflict in Africa. It was only one in a series of catastrophes that have befallen the continent since independence in the sixties, mainly because of the unwillingness of African leaders to address the grievances of some groups and treat them as equal members of society; and because of their failure to institute

254

mechanisms of conflict management and resolution within their borders and on regional basis. Africa has paid a heavy price for that, blood-soaked through the decades in conflicts which could have been avoided.

The Biafrans were ignored and lost about 2 million people within three years since the war began. But they were also vindicated by history, best summed up in the words of Emperor Haile Selassie when Italy invaded Ethiopia, in his plea to the League of Nations:

"It is us today. It will be you tomorrow."

Wars and other conflicts through the decades have almost destroyed Africa as if nothing was learned from the Nigerian civil war, one of the bloodiest conflicts in modern world history.

While Nigeria, was going through that tragedy, the rest of the continent was not spared the agony. It was a traumatic experience for all Africans, and the year 1968 saw no end to the conflict.

The year 1968 also became a historic landmark in the struggle for independence. It was the last year, in the sixties, in which some countries won independence. None won independence in 1969.

It will also always be remembered for another reason in the history of African liberation: most countries on the continent had won independence by 1968.

The last countries to win independence in that decade were: Mauritius which won independence from Britain on 12 March 1968; Swaziland, also from Britain, on 6 September 1968; and Spanish Guinea on 12 October 1968. Spanish Guinea was the only Spanish colony in black Africa. It changed its name to Equatorial Guinea after it won independence.

The sixties will also be remembered for independence celebrations across the continent. But the liberation struggle was far from being over. As the sixties came to an end, the struggle gained momentum especially in the countries of southern Africa.

1969

IN AFRICA, the year 1969 was dominated by the Nigerian civil war probably more than anything else as much as 1968 was, and attempts to end the deadly conflict continued in many circles but with few tangible results.

Although the war was still going on in 1969, much of the fighting was almost over in most areas of the former secessionist region. The secessionist forces and their people were squeezed into a very small area in the northern part of Biafra, which was also agriculturally poor. It was only a matter of time before they would surrender.

The last major victory for the secessionist forces was in December 1968 when they fought the federal army to a stalemate after an infusion of arms from France and other sources, and the outcome of the war became uncertain. But that was it. After that, it was no longer a war of attrition but simply of survival for the Biafrans.

The war lasted for two-and-a-half years since fighting broke out in July 1967. Biafra finally surrendered and, on 15 January 1970, the war was officially over.

It is estimated that up to 2 million Eastern Nigerians,

mostly Igbo, perished in the war. Most died from starvation which the federal military government used as a legitimate instrument of war to force the secessionist forces to surrender. Some critics said it was a war of genocide against the Igbo.

It was, up to that time, the deadliest conflict in Africa's post-colonial era.

I remember those days after Tanzania became the first country to recognise Biafra as an independent state in April 1968. I was a student at a boys' boarding school, Songea Secondary School in Songea, Ruvuma Region in southern Tanzania. I was in Standard 12 then, my final year.

After I passed my final exams – they were the same for all Standard 12 students in the three East African countries of Kenya, Uganda and Tanzania – I was selected to go to Tambaza High School, formerly H.H. The Aga Khan High School, in the nation's capital Dar es Salaam for further education in Form V (Standard 13) and Form VI (Standard 14).

Our high school education lasted for two years after which you went to university for three years to earn your bachelor's degree – B.A., B.Sc., LL.B., or whatever – at one of the three East African universities: the University of Dar es Salaam in Tanzania, Makerere University in Uganda or Nairobi University in Kenya.

It was when I was a student at Tambaza High School in Form V (Standard 13) in 1969 that I had a "personal" encounter with the victims of the Biafran war. Some Eastern Nigerians, especially Igbos, came to live in Tanzania during that period; I don't know how many but there were a number of them in Dar es Salaam including professionals such as lawyers, judges and professors.

The Biafran representative to Tanzania, whose rank was equivalent to that of ambassador, was Dr. Austine Okwu who later became a professor in the United States; so did his wife, Dr. Beatrice Okwu, who got some of her education at the University of Dar es Salaam where she studied linguistics when her husband was the official representative of the Republic of Biafra in our country.

I also remember seeing Austine Okwu in Dar es Salaam. He used to driver the car himself, a white Mercedez Benz, but without the Biafran flag flying in front of the car. He was not recognised as an ambassador because Biafra had not won international recognition as a legal sovereign entity. But his car had the Biafran flag on the licence plate at the rear of the vehicle.

There was one sub-editor I worked with at our newspaper, the *Standard* later renamed *Daily News*, who came from Eastern Nigeria, what was then Biafra. He was an Igbo. There were other Biafrans, besides professionals, living in Tanzania in those days. But that is not the "personal" encounter I'm talking about – with my colleague on our editorial staff at the *Standard* and the *Daily News*. The experience I'm talking about has to do with what I saw about the war.

When I was at Tambaza High School, the plight of the Biafran war victims was a subject of a lot of discussion by the students, a few of whom were opposed to the secession of Biafra mainly for the wrong reasons, accusing the Igbos of "arrogance" without trying to find out what really happened in Nigeria and why Eastern Nigerians decided to withdraw from the federation.

We also got the chance to see a documentary film about the war. Students from other schools and other people also went to see it when it was shown in Dar es Salaam – not at our school – but somewhere in the city within walking distance from our residence, H.H. The Aga Khan Hostel in Upanga.

It was disturbing, to say the least. It featured graphic images of the Biafran war victims, men, women and children with emaciated bodies. The children we saw were terribly malnourished, mere skeletons with protruding bellies. It was enough to bother the conscience of even the most hardened souls. It was gut-wrenching.

Also featured in the documentary film was Colonel Ojukwu, in sombre mood, his face drooping with weariness, explaining to the world the plight of his people. He was in such mental and emotional anguish that the pain and suffering of his people was written all over his face.

The documentary was specially relevant to us because our country had recognised Biafra as a sovereign nation just the year before, and many students who saw the graphic images of starving and wounded Biafrans were overcome with emotion. It was the most graphic film about war I had ever seen in my short life of 19 years, and it left an indelible mark on my mind and probably on the minds others who saw it.

At that point, the Nigerian federal forces did not even have to wage war against the Biafrans. Hunger was already fighting the war for them. They used it effectively as a weapon against the Biafrans to force them to surrender. Nobody, of course, knew for sure back then in 1969 that the war would be over in a few months, in January 1970, considering the resilience and determination of the Igbos to be left alone since the fighting started.

Yet, to the war victims, those months must have been years. It is a tragedy that could have been avoided had the Nigerian federal government taken into account the fears and concerns of the Biafrans who felt that they were no longer safe in the federation.

As the sixties were coming to an end, another phenomenal event was taking place on the continent. It was a movement. It gained momentum in the last years of the decade far more than it did in any other period. It was the liberation movement.

So, while the war was still going on Nigeria in 1969, another war was also going on in another part of Africa. It was a different kind of war but not quite in terms of fighting for freedom just as the Biafrans did.

The other war was in southern Africa where the

freedom fighters were waging guerrilla war against the white minority regimes in one of the most protracted conflicts in the history of the continent since the advent of colonial rule. The end of the sixties turned out to be some of the most critical years in the conflict, especially in terms of escalation.

It was mainly horizontal escalation covering a war front of more than 2,000 miles stretching from the east cost of southern Africa to the western part of the continent in Portuguese Guinea, now Guinea-Bissau. But there was also vertical escalation in this conflict in terms of weaponry and intensity of warfare as the freedom fighters gained more experience and got more weapons from their allies especially countries in the Eastern bloc.

The Soviet Union, the People's Republic of China and other Eastern countries were willing to supply them with whatever weapons they needed to fight the white minority regimes which were being armed by the West. It was an ideological war between the two ideological camps – East versus West – but one of freedom and survival for Africans who accepted weapons from anyone who was willing to help them.

In 1968, President Kenneth Kaunda of Zambia warned the world of an impending war between Black Africa and White Africa along the banks of the Zambezi River which served as a demarcation line between the two in a large area of southern Africa.

Other African leaders had issued similar warnings around the same time and even before then in the case of President Julius Nyerere of Tanzania. One of Nyerere's warnings was in an article he wrote, "Rhodesia in the Context of Southern Africa," published in *Foreign Affairs* in April 1966 not long after the white minority regime in Rhodesia unilaterally declared independence on 11 November 1965.

By the late 1960s, especially by 1969, the danger these leaders had warned about had not only materialised but got worse. The fighting was already taking place in the form of guerrilla warfare; and it was escalating. The confrontation was costing hundreds of lives and millions of pounds (£) or dollars every year; and the war was being fought not just along the Zambezi. As John Parker stated in "Expanding Guerilla Warfare":

"Africans are fighting white men along a 'front' that stretches more than 2,000 miles from the Atlantic to the Indian Ocean.

The battle has been going on for nearly seven years, ever since African nationalists took up arms against the Portuguese authorities in Angola; but in 1968, for the first time, a 'grand purpose' began to emerge and the issues started to crystallize into recognizable shape.

The 'battle areas' are fairly clearly defined....Active fighting is going on in Angola, Mozambique and Portuguese Guinea (in West Africa). Periodic battles are occurring along the northern border of Rhodesia. And on both ocean flanks persistent...attempts are being made to infiltrate armed insurgents into South and South-West Africa.

So far, the 'purified white tip' of Africa has not yet announced a defence treaty between South Africa, Rhodesia and the Portuguese territories in Africa. Such a treaty has been urged by Afrikaner and Portuguese strategists from time to time, and there is no doubt that the South African Government has gone a good part of the way to taking the practical steps necessary to turn the idea into reality.

The reason for this reluctance is certainly political. While South Africa can maintain reasonable relations with her African neighbours she will do so, and there is no doubt that a 'White Defence Pact' would immediately focus strongly adverse world attention onto a situation which South Africa prefers brushed under the carpet.

But the military to-ing and fro-ing between Pretoria,

Salisbury, Lourenco Marques and Luanda is hard to keep secret; and only recently South Africa admitted for the first time that 300 'police' are now on regular duty in Rhodesia.

There can be no doubt that a co-ordinated policy exists for the defence of South Africa; even if it exists only in the minds of the South Africans who...are pragmatically willing to use the territories to the north of her as buffer zones toward off any form of attack – military, political, economic and ideological.

South Africa is currently spending £147m. a year on her defence forces and a further £42m.on the para-military police force. Her armaments are the most sophisticated on the continent of Africa, and her forces the most highly trained.

Portugal maintains 115,000 troops in Africa - 55,000 in Angola, 40,000 in Mozambique and 20,000 in Guinea-Bissau according to the Institute of Strategic Studies in London. Military expenditure in Portugal absorbs nearly half the entire budget.

In Rhodesia, expenditure has just increased by 10 per cent on both defence and police forces to a total of nearly £14m. a year – a very heavy strain on a budget already stretched tight by sanctions.

On the African side, details of expenditure are very hazy and deliberately obscured by the Organization of African Unity (OAU). But there is increasing evidence now that the African liberation effort, more and more co-ordinated by the African Liberation Committee of the OAU, is finding direction, purpose, training - and funds.

Already the Organization itself is voting an annual sum - undisclosed, but running into several millions of pounds - for the support of the various liberation movements. This figure is probably doubled by the communist sources of arms and training, both of which seem to be provided without cost to the guerilla movements which avail themselves freely of the services offered to them.

Although the struggle has been going on for some

years in the Portuguese territories, it is the sudden sharpening up of guerilla activities in Rhodesia which has brought the future into focus during 1968. Because of Mr. Ian Smith's Unilateral Declaration of Independence (UDI) in 1965, the eyes and ears of the world press have been trained on Rhodesia, and in spite of every effort to minimize 'adverse' publicity, details of the battles fought along the Zambesi escarpment have managed to filter out.

The casualty figures speak for themselves. The Rhodesians claim to have killed 20 guerillas in 1966, 25 in 1967; and so far in 1968 more than 100 have been killed and nearly as many captured. Hardly a day passes without another African being tried and sentenced in Salisbury for subversion and terrorism.

With one lull for the rains in 1967 and another for the downpours in 1968, fighting has been going on sporadically for more than 18 months. It shows no sign of diminishing.

By early December (1968), news came from Rhodesia that the Salisbury authorities have word of up to 1,000 insurgents preparing to cross the Zambesi Valley from base camps in Zambia.

There is no knowing how correct the figures issued by the Rhodesians are; and indeed the rival African nationalist movements in Rhodesia – n the Zimbabwe African National Union (ZANU) and the Zimbabwe African People's Union (ZAPU) - have from time to time claimed to have killed scores of white Rhodesians and South Africans. In some cases, they have 'substantiated' their claims by quoting names and service numbers (of the soldiers killed).

At first, the little bands of men who tried to take on the trained professionals of the Rhodesian army and the para-military police forces were badly armed, ill-equipped and inexperienced.

Some were killed, some were captured and some escaped to Botswana. More still died of thirst and starvation in the bush, and others just gave themselves up.

But now things have changed. The rivals ZANU and ZAPU are reported to be considering coming together as the Zimbabwe African Liberation Army, financed by the African Liberation Committee of the OAU. The men who now cross the Zambesi by boat have had months - and sometimes years - of training in bush fighting, endurance and personal survival in China, Cuba, Russia, Algeria and even North Korea.

They are well-armed with weapons they know how to use, including the highly efficient Chinese Kalashinkov A.K. 47 automatic rifles. They carry 100-lb. packs of grenades, land mines, first aid kits and iron rations, and use short-wave radios to communicate with each other and their bases. Headquarters is in Dar es Salaam, where the former Rhodesian lawyer, Herber Chitepo - who was also Tanzania's first Solicitor-General - is responsible for much of the co-ordination work.

There are two main routes of entry across the Zambesi from the base camps (in Zambia)....

The first is to the West of Lake Kariba – in some cases using the smooth waters of the head of the lake itself. This is the route used by ZAPU, in conjunction with the African National Congress (ANC) men from South Africa. ZAPU and ANC have struck up a useful collaboration.

The second route, used mainly by ZANU forces, strikes across the river more than 250 miles to the east – below the Kariba Dam itself in the Chirundu area and as far east as Tete.

On the western front, the guerillas fan out west and south into the Wankie area – where Rhodesia's coal is mined - and towards the Kalahari and South West Africa. So intensive has been the fighting here that there are stories that the game has started to move from the Wankie National Park because it is continually disturbed by the firing and the air strikes.

On the Chirundu front, the guerillas form a potential

threat to the rich farming areas of Karoi and Sinoia, while at the same time pointing a warning spearhead at Salisbury itself. Some of the farmers in the area have moved their families to Salisbury for safety....

The overall objective of the African nationalists is long term....Their achievements in the face of a well-armed, sophisticated army and police force should not be underestimated. As one senior ZANU official told me: 'For two years we have kept the Rhodesian army and police at full stretch. They've had to send for help to South Africa, and their losses are far higher that they admit (including helicopters shot down by the guerilla fighters).'

He agreed that guerilla losses had been heavy, and with Rhodesian claims that the security forces have captured large quantities of weapons and ammunition. 'There's plenty more where that came from,' he said. 'And it doesn't cost us anything.'" – (John Parker, *Africa Contemporary Record*, op. cit., .pp. 53, 55 - 56).

The guerrilla strategy employed by the freedom fighters enabled them to mingle with the local population in the rural areas without being detected by the Rhodesian security forces. They also won sympathy and support from the people in the villages, many of whom provided them with food and shelter and even joined the liberation movement. When some of the guerrilla fighters were killed by the members of the Rhodesian army and the para-military police, the freedom fighters got even more support from the local population.

Also, the freedom fighters showed not only courage but competence on the battlefield when they fought the enemy. Before then, they had been dismissed as inept and inexperienced; no more than a ragtag army of rebels incapable of engaging even raw recruits of the white Rhodesian army. But that was no longer the case by the end of the sixties. They had become a credible fighting force.

266

The backbone of their support was the local population, in addition to the help they were getting from their supporters and allies in other African countries such as Tanzania, Zambia, Uganda, Nigeria, Algeria, Ethiopia, Ghana, Egypt, Guinea, Congo-Brazzaville, and others elsewhere, especially in the Eastern bloc:

"The (ZANU) official claimed significant advances in winning support from the local population. The Rhodesians claim their security is among the best in the world, and they are adept and experienced in the use of informers in the kraals in the bush....

The Rhodesian Air Force has become expert in winkling out guerilla strongholds. Their obsolescent Hunters, Vampires and Canberras, plus the Alouette helicopters they have acquired from France, are ideally suited to this type of 'search and destroy' operation, although at least one Alouette has been shot down by the guerillas....

But 'even the loss of our men has helped us,' said the ZANU official. 'Relatives and friends soon get to know about someone being killed or captured. And their attitude changes from apathy to military overnight.'

As the bushcraft of the security forces has improved along with that of the invaders, so the white troops and police have reluctantly grown to respect the African guerillas for their fighting qualities. True, the pictures fed to the Press by the Rhodesian authorities show tough, Afrika-Korps-type whites interrogating at gunpoint a grovelling captive who, they say, has 'spilled the beans.'

But the image is not borne out by facts. When they have met the white troops on an equal footing the guerillas have stood their ground and fought bravely; and their spirit of defiance has shone through even in the courts where they have faced mandatory death sentences." – (Ibid., pp. 57, and 56).

By the late sixties, the battle lines had not only been drawn but sometimes shifted because of the intensity of warfare and the increasing ability of the freedom fighters to win battles and hold the territory they had captured or reclaimed from the whites.

In southern Africa, Mozambique and Angola provided the best examples of this kind of success by the guerrillas. The freedom fighters in Zimbabwe were headed in the same direction; it would be only a matter of time before they also would claim major victories.

African journalists and others from elsewhere were some of the people who witnessed the major advances made by the freedom fighters in Mozambique and in Angola by the late sixties.

By 1969, large parts of Angola and Mozambique were liberated zones, protected and administered by the liberation movements in both countries – the MPLA (Popular Movement for the Liberation of Angola), and FRELIMO (Front for the Liberation of Mozambique).

The liberation wars had not yet been won by 1968 or 1969, and it would be a few more years before those countries would be finally free. But by the end of the sixties, there was no question that the guerrillas were not only competent fighters; they were also capable of defending the territories they had captured even when they were faced with massive attacks by the colonial forces which had been forced to depend on reinforcements from the mother country, Portugal, to continue fighting effectively.

Yet, even these reinforcements were not enough to neutralise let along dislodge the guerrilla fighters from the liberated zones. Even in Zimbabwe, the guerrillas were more than just a nuisance, in spite of the help the Rhodesian security forces got from apartheid South Africa, the country with the strongest army on the continent:

"The Zimbabwe freedom fighters have not yet matched

the exploits of their brothers-in-arms in Mozambique and Angola, who claim effective control over large tracts of their respective countries in spite of the huge forces ranged against them. Recent accounts by journalists who have made hazardous and often uncomfortable trips into the territories confirm the claims.

One journalist, Basil Davidson, went with Frelimo (the Mozambique Liberation Front) across the Ruvuma River which is technically the border between Tanzania and Mozambique and marched in daylight without any hindrance from Portuguese troops, to an astonishing congress in the bush. He wrote:

'At a place where newly-built huts stood within the cover of a wood, about 150 political and military leaders were assembled. They had come from all parts of a colony that is one-and-a-half times as big as France.

They began fighting the Portuguese in 1964. Since then they have cleared the Portuguese out of most of the rural country of Cabo Delgado and Niassa, a region not much smaller than the British isles. In this liberated zone they have set up schools and clinics and introduced their own economic system.

The congress I attended was the first since the fighting started. It was called to discuss how they could push farther to the south and extend the war. Present were the whole central committee of the Liberation Front, including its president 48-year-old Eduardo Mondhlane, once a Doctor of Sociology at Syracuse University, New York State....'

Just as astonishing is an account of a young Zambian journalist Tommy Chibaye, who only recently returned from six weeks spent with the African nationalist forces in Angola.

He attended a similar congress, headed by the poet, Dr. Agostinho Neto (he was a medical doctor by training), of the MPLA. He reports that the Africans claim considerable control in at least 10 of Angola's 15 provinces, with continuous fighting over the past seven years (since 1961):

'We passed many wrecked shops and villages razed to the ground by the Portuguese soldiers. Despite their having had their homes burned, the villagers had happily settled down in temporary camps under the supervision of the guerillas.

There they have established co-operative gardens to feed themselves and the guerilla forces, growing cassava, rice, tomatoes, onions and other vegetables.'

Not once in his six weeks, although he lived rough, did Tommy Chibaye go hungry. He found the MPLA providing schooling and instruction to Angolan Africans of all ages in a three-pronged drive. They set up a Post Command for military instruction, a Medical Assistance Service to look after health, particularly of war victims, and a Revolutionary Instruction Centre, where academic and political instruction is given.

From the centres, trained activists moved throughout the country raising more volunteers for the guerilla forces; in giving effect to a new policy for some time now all guerilla volunteers have been trained within Angola. Chibaye reports that the Portuguese have now taken to travelling everywhere in convoys of not less than 50 vehicles in the Moxico Province, covered by helicopters the whole time.

With the evidence at his fingertips, it is not surprising that Dr. Kaunda is apprehensive about the future. His country is already at the heart of the guerilla activity....

He has already complained that Zambian villages have been the subject of attack by Angolan Air Forces and commando raids; and he is worried by the constant threat the strong South African and Rhodesian Air Forces pose from the south." – (Ibid., pp. 57 - 58).

Although Zambia was highly vulnerable to attack from two fronts – the Angolan-Zambian and the Rhodesian-Zambian borders – the longest attack came from Angola because the war in that Portuguese colony had been going on for a number of years, thus for a longer period than the conflict in Rhodesia.

The liberation war in Angola started in 1961. In January of that year, there was a revolt on the cotton plantations in Malange. In February police stations and prisons in Luanda were attacked by the MPLA, and in March full-scale war broke out in the northern part of the country.

The MPLA was formed in December 1956 from a number of clandestine groups which first began to emerge in the capital, Luanda, in 1953. It underwent a series of initial crises between 1961 and 1965 when it began to consolidate itself under the leadership of Dr. Agostinho Neto.

Although a number of Angolan nationalist organisations were based in neighbouring countries and had offices elsewhere, one of them stood out. That was the MPLA. It was the best organised and most nationalist-oriented, transcending racial and ethnic differences.

When the MPLA was first formed and launched guerrilla attacks, it operated mainly from Congo-Brazzaville and Zambia. Shortly thereafter, it also had an office and training facilities in Tanzania which, in 1963, was chosen by the OAU as the headquarters of all the African liberation movements. The MPLA launched guerrilla operations in Cabinda, the Dembo region, and southeast Angola.

Another group was the UPA which was later renamed the FNLA (National Front for the Liberation of Angola). The UPA was formed in 1954 mainly with the support of the Bakongo and other ethnic groups in Northern Angola. It initially provided the main challenge to the Portuguese

271

colonial rulers at the beginning of the insurrection in 1961 and was even recognised by the OAU. Under the leadership of Dr. Holden Roberto, the UPA and its affiliated groups formed the Government-in-Exile of Angola (GRAE) in 1963 with the blessings of the OAU but later lost its legitimacy.

In February 1968, OAU Secretary-General Diallo Telli announced that a recommendation by the OAU Liberation Committee based in Dar es Salaam, Tanzania, had advised OAU member-states to re-examine and change their attitude towards GRAE. The report said investigations had shown that GRAE was more concerned with intrigue and personality conflicts than it was with the liberation struggle in Angola. GRAE, like its successor the FNLA under the same leadership of Roberto Holden, was also severely compromised by its ethnic base and bias.

Although other ethnic groups were involved in the formation of the FNLA as they were in GRAE's, the FNLA was still mainly Bakongo and was based in the Congo Democratic Republic (renamed Zaire); and its limited operations also had a strong ethnic base mainly in northern and northwestern Angola.

In 1964, another group emerged on the scene. It was UNITA (National Union for the Total Liberation of Angola) led by Dr. Jonas Savimbi. It was based in eastern Angola. UNITA was formed as a breakaway from UPA. Until 1967, UNITA had its headquarters in Lusaka, Zambia, but Savimbi was expelled by President Kaunda. After spending some time in Egypt and Guinea, Savimbi and his cadres moved to eastern Angola.

But like the UPA and later the FNLA, UNITA was also limited in its membership and support because of ethnicity. It drew its strongest support from the Ovimbundu in eastern and central Angola. Savimbi himself was a member of this ethnic group.

There were a number of smaller groups based mainly in the Congo Democratic Republic, pursuing a nationalist agenda in varying degrees. But none equalled the MPLA, the FNLA or UNITA – especially the MPLA – in stature, influence and support.

They were the largest Angolan nationalist organisations and even fought among themselves just before and after independence until the MPLA emerged victorious.

In fact, by the late sixties, the MPLA was the most effective nationalist organisation in Angola and fought the most, enabling it to capture most of the territory before the decade came to an end.

Even the bastion of white minority rule on the continent, apartheid South Africa, was apprehensive about its future as it came under increasing threat from the African nationalist forces supported by the independent African countries and other allies. The leaders of the apartheid regime made it clear that they took the threat seriously. As South African Defence Minister P.W. Botha, who later became one of the last two presidents of apartheid South Africa, warned in November 1968:

"We must realise once and for all that we will live in danger for many years to come, and we must realise that not only our soldiers, but all our people must be prepared to fight for all we hold dear." – (P.W. Botha, *Africa Contemporary Record*, p. 287).

He was definitely addressing whites, not blacks and other non-whites. As victims of officially-sanctioned racial oppression and exploitation, apartheid was not something they cherished or were prepared to die for.

Also, apartheid was not supported by all whites in South Africa. There were those who were strongly opposed to all other forms of racial discrimination, oppression and exploitation. Some of them were members and leaders of the largest anti-apartheid organisation, the African National Congress (ANC).

Yet, the clock was ticking, and time was running out

for the architects and supporters of that abominable institution. Racial confrontation and violence was looming on the horizon and prospects for guerrilla warfare in South Africa itself were real.

There was mounting concern among all sectors of the white society about the country's security which had never been expressed before since apartheid was instituted in 1948.

The sixties, especially the late sixties, were years of reckoning for many whites. Their future was uncertain. As one leading Afrikaner industrialist, Dr. Anton Rupert, told the Public Relations Institute in April 1968:

"Do we all realise that we nearly had a potential Cuba in our midst in Lesotho?

I have been studying the possible reply to this insidious revolutionary warfare for some years now. In the course of my travels I have spoken to many famous generals about this problem.

One of the most knowledgeable of them all warned me three years ago that within a decade at the utmost we would be faced with an Algerian-type situation in Southern Africa.

Yet, a revolutionary war is mainly a political action, for the final outcome depends on the support of the masses. It is, therefore, important to offer the masses hope for the future. It is essential that our own people of various races know that they are better off than the masses of Africa and Asia, and that this condition will improve even further.

It is essential that we work with our own and neighbouring peoples, who believe with us that terrorising, rioting and revolution is no way to improve the estate of man." – (Anton Rupert, ibid., p. 290).

The general who warned Dr. Rupert in 1965 that southern African would be faced with a situation similar to what happened in Algeria against the French in the fifties was right in his prediction. Within ten years, virtually the entire region of southern Africa was engulfed in guerrilla warfare.

All the countries bordering apartheid South Africa were at war. The freedom fighters were busy fighting the colonialist forces. Even Botswana, which became independent in 1966, was involved because it supported the freedom fighters. Its territory became a sanctuary for the freedom fighters including those from South Africa who posed an increasing threat to the apartheid regime.

In fact, within that ten-year period from 1965 to 1975, two colonies, Mozambique and Angola, won independence after 500 years of Portuguese colonial rule in the oldest colonies on the continent together with Portuguese Guinea in West Africa which won independence as Guinea-Bissau in 1974. And within five years after Mozambique and Angola became independent, Rhodesia also became independent. It won independence in April 1980 and was renamed Zimbabwe.

Only South Africa and South West Africa, both ruled by the same apartheid regime, remained under white minority rule.

The dagger was now pointed at the apartheid regime itself, the bastion of white supremacy on the African continent. In fact, the situation in South Africa had been deteriorating for quite some time.

The biggest change was caused by the regime itself as a repressive apparatus when it refused to negotiate with the African nationalist leaders and instead cracked down on them, forcing them to abandon non-violence and go underground and into exile to seek support for a violent confrontation with their oppressors. But the transformation came slowly. It was not until the Sharpeville massacre in March 1960 that African leaders and their supporters finally decided to embrace armed struggle as a complementary strategy in their quest for freedom and racial equality. They did not give up negotiations if the apartheid regime was willing to talk to them seriously

Still, it was a turning point in the liberation struggle and in the history of South Africa when leaders such as Nelson Mandela, Robert Mangaliso Sobukwe, Oliver Tambo and Walter Sisulu decided to use violence to end apartheid.

Their decision formally marked the end of an era; an era of conciliatory politics dominated by stalwarts of the freedom struggle such as Chief Albert Luthuli who was the national chairman of the African National Congress (ANC) during that time. As Oliver Tambo stated in the official publication of the African National Congress in exile, *Sechaba*, in 1968:

"For a long time the ANC has been conducting militant struggle relying on non-violent methods. This became particularly intense during the '50s and gradually led to a stage at which the Movement switched over from nonviolence to the phase of armed struggle.

During 1967 the first armed clashes occurred between, on the one hand, the combined forces of the Smith and Vorster regimes, and on the other, the united guerillas of the ANC (African National Congress) and ZAPU (Zimbabwe African People's Union).

It can be said that for the ANC this is the beginning of the armed struggle for which we have been preparing since the early '60s.

It is a phase in which we can rightly claim to have scored victories by virtue of the superiority which our fighters demonstrated over the racist forces sending a wave of panic throughout the area dominated by the racist regimes and arousing the masses to a new revolutionary mood.

This is, however, only a small beginning in terms of the bitterness and magnitude of the revolution which is unfolding and which embraces the whole of Southern Africa. But it is an impressive and effective beginning providing what I consider a guarantee for the success of our armed struggle." – (Oliver Tambo, *Africa Contemporary Record*, ibid.).

The freedom fighters first surfaced on South Africa's horizon in 1966. That was when they entered South West Africa which was virtually an integral part – a province – of South Africa.

It was also in the same year, in October 1966, that the United Nations passed a resolution to revoke South Africa's mandate over South West Africa (Namibia). But the apartheid regime remained defiant until 1988.

The guerrillas who entered South West Africa were members of the South West African People's Organisation (SWAPO) led by Sam Nujoma. They entered from Zambia and Botswana through Caprivi Strip which is a part of South West Africa.

Another guerrilla threat so close to South Africa came in 1967 from the guerrillas of the African National Congress (ANC) who forged links with the forces of the Zimbabwe African People's Union (ZAPU) in Rhodesia. They were right across the border and ready to enter South Africa itself.

The citadel of white power on the continent was not as secure as it seemed to be. As Colin Legum, writing during that period, stated:

"By 1968 the potential threat of escalating guerilla attacks became elevated to a top priority of the South African regime, in stark contrast to its claims in 1948 that its policies would increase the country's state of security.

Late in 1967 the Government appointed an expert in counter-insurgency, Lieutenant-General C.A. Fraser, as General Officer Commanding Joint Combat Forces.

This threat was taken a stage further on April 24 (1968) by Commandant-General S.A. Melville, former head of the South African Defence Force, who said that South

Africa already had sufficient justification and provocation for retaliation against countries which 'harboured' and encouraged terrorists whose only intention was to penetrate South Africa or South West Africa.

He supported the Minister of Defence's (P.W.Botha's) view that such countries should receive a 'sudden hard knock.'" – (Colin Legum, ibid., p. 291).

It was clear which countries they had in mind: Tanzania and Zambia. They were the only countries, together with Botswana, which were independent during that period in the region and close to South Africa. They were also the only ones in the region which offered sanctuary to the people who fled from oppression and persecution under the apartheid regime and the colonial governments in Angola and Mozambique.

Unlike Botswana, Tanzania and Zambia also provided military training for the freedom fighters from South Africa, South West Africa, and Rhodesia; and in 1968, Tanzania also built a powerful radio transmitter for the external service of Radio Tanzania, Dar es Salaam (RTD), to help the freedom fighters broadcast their message worldwide.

The two countries were clearly seen as enemies of South Africa. The threat by South Africa's Defence Minister P.W. Botha that countries which harbour and support terrorists – freedom fighters in the lexicon of Africans – should receive a "sudden hard knock" was, without question, a pointed reference to Tanzania and Zambia.

I remember some of the first "sudden hard knocks" Tanzania received in the late sixties when I was a student at Songea Secondary School in Ruvuma Region in the southern part of the country. They came from the Portuguese forces across the border in Mozambique who were getting a lot of help from the South African Defence Force.

The apartheid regime also had agents who infiltrated Tanzania and Zambia. Many of them went to those countries ostensibly as political refugees or freedom fighters to undergo military training in guerrilla camps.

They were engaged in subversive activities and did everything they could to weaken and undermine the liberation movements. The infiltrators were also a strain on the Tanzanian and Zambian intelligence services which had to track them down. The liberation movements themselves did a very good job identifying those enemies.

All that was a part of a grand strategy by the apartheid regime to neutralise the freedom fighters.

Although the Portuguese may have been capable of penetrating our air space during those years, the aerial bombing of southern Tanzania, especially Mtwara Region, including the use of napalm was facilitated by the assistance the colonial forces got from South Africa, the United States and other Western allies of Portugal. In fact, some of the weapons including bombs which were used by the Portuguese in Mozambique came from the United States; so did the ones used in Angola.

The United States collaborated with the South African apartheid regime, the white minority government in Rhodesia and with the Portuguese authorities in Angola and Mozambique to contain and neutralise what they perceived to be a threat to white and Western interests in Africa.

They had a number of people, including some leaders in the liberation movements, on the CIA payroll. For example, in the case of Angola, the Americans felt that the leader of the FNLA, Dr. Holden Roberto, was someone they could easily buy and manipulate at will and went on to put him on the CIA payroll around 1961 or 1962. Yet, at the same time, they continued to support the colonial regime while pretending to be sympathetic towards the freedom fighters, especially Holden Roberto his colleagues in the FNLA.

Even some of Africa's eminent leaders, Jomo Kenyatta and Emperor Haile Selassie, were on the CIA payroll. The CIA also had a large staff in Nairobi including a number of Kenyan government officials besides Kenyatta himself who worked for the spy agency. In fact Nairobi has always been one of the CIA's main stations in Africa. In neighbouring Ethiopia, the United States had a large secret military base in the southern part of the country since the early sixties. But the largest CIA station in Africa was in Kinshasa when Mobutu was in power.

Therefore it was not just Holden Roberto and Joseph Mobutu (as Mobutu Sese Seko was then known before he changed his name) who were on the CIA payroll since the sixties among Africa's political figures. But they were among the most prominent together with Kenyatta and Haile Selassie.

In the following years after the early sixties when Dr. Holden Roberto was put on the CIA payroll, the United States provided weapons and ammunition, and counter-insurgency training the Portuguese colonial rulers needed to contain and if possible neutralise the nationalist forces of the MPLA and the FNLA.

The devastation caused by American-supplied weapons used by the Portuguese against Africans including innocent civilians – women and children being among the biggest victims – was extensive. As John Marcum, an American scholar who walked 800 miles through Angola and visited FNLA training camps in the early sixties, wrote:

"By January 1962 outside observers could watch Portuguese planes bomb and strafe African villages, visit the charred remains of towns like Mbanza M'Pangu and M'Pangala, and copy the data from 750-point napalm bomb casings from which the Portuguese had not removed the labels marked 'Property U.S. Air Force.'" – (John Marcum, quoted by William Blum, "Angola 1975 to

1980s: The Great Powers Poker Game," in W. Blum, *Killing Hope: U.S. Military and CIA Interventions since World War II* (London: Zed Books Ltd., 2003, p. 250).

It was the same case in Mozambique. American assistance to the colonial forces in Mozambique was just as critical in their war against the freedom fighters; so was the assistance they got from South Africa.

The apartheid regime was also using the Portuguese colonies of Angola and Mozambique and the British colony of Rhodesia as buffer zones. But that was not enough to insulate white South Africa from the nationalist forces; a concession made by the government itself:

"On April 25 (1968), the Deputy Minister of Police, Mr. S.L. Muller, informed parliament on information about fresh groups of 'terrorists' gathering in Zambia.

The Prime Minister said in the same debate that while conditions were quiet inside the Republic he did not want to give an assurance that everything would always be like that. The ANC, he added, was still active (although it had been outlawed in 1960); but the Pan-Africanist Congress (PAC) was finding things more difficult.

The figures he gave of ANC casualties in Rhodesia were: in 1967, 29 killed, 17 wounded and 34 fled to Botswana; in 1968, of 30 ANC guerillas who entered Rhodesia, 'a number' was killed. He added: 'The combating of terrorism had advanced as well as could be expected under the circumstances.'

On May 17, Mr. Vorster, speaking at the National Party's 'twenty years of Nationalist rule festival,' said that slowly but surely an army would be built up in certain Central African States for an eventual 'now or never' attack on South Africa." – (Colin Legum, *Africa Contemporary Record*, op. cit., p. 291).

He was not far from the truth, as the independent

African countries and other allies especially in the Eastern bloc as well as the People's Republic of China, Cuba and North Korea, kept on supporting the freedom fighters, providing them with military assistance in their struggle against the apartheid regime.

Two days before Prime Minister Vorster issued that warning, a summit meeting of 14 East and Central African leaders was held in Dar es Salaam, Tanzania, on 15 May 1968. The leaders promised full support to the freedom fighters in all the countries in southern Africa still under white minority rule.

A number of African countries, not just those in East and Central Africa, were ready to mobilise forces to help the freedom fighters.

The independent countries close to white-ruled southern Africa – not just South Africa – were the frontline states in the struggle against white minority rule in the region; the exception was Malawi under Dr. Hastings Kamuzu Banda who had cordial relations with the apartheid regime and the Portuguese colonial rulers in Mozambique. And they were ready to support the freedom fighters. When Nyerere was asked in interview on an American television programme ABC's "Issues and Answers" in July 1977 if he would commit troops to help the freedom fighters if they went to war against apartheid South Africa, he answered: "Yes, I will commit troops. We would rather hang together than hang separately."

The apartheid regime introduced several measures in the late sixties to counter the "terrorist" threat, as the freedom fighters continued to mobilise forces in their struggle against white minority rule. On 2 June 1968, the South African minister of justice, P.C. Pelser, introduced the Terrorism Bill and announced that there was every reason to believe that South Africa had not "seen the last of the terrorists."

The bill sought extensive powers to detain indefinitely anybody suspected of being engaged in subversive activities or of withholding information about terrorist threats or activities. It also demanded the death penalty for the crime of terrorism. As he stated in parliament in Cape Town:

"The Bill should be judged against the whole background of internal onslaughts on the legal order since 1960.

The terrorists who are now returning are largely the harvest of the subversive activities of the ANC, PAC, SWAPO and the Communists.

It is largely their trained, so-called freedom fighters who are now returning." – (P.C. Pelser, *Africa Contemporary Record*, p. 292).

Nothing the apartheid regime did was able to deter the freedom fighters from pursuing their goal.

On 11 June 1968, the Portuguese colonial authorities in Mozambique announced that they had foiled an attempt by the Pan-Africanist Congress (PAC) to establish a new route to South Africa through that country. They claimed that four guerrillas were killed in a fight with the Portuguese forces near Vila Pery, 50 miles from the border with Rhodesia.

In July the same year, SWAPO claimed to have inflicted heavy damage on strategic places maintained by the apartheid regime in South West Africa. They included the airfield at Katima Mulilo in Caprivi Strip along the Botswana-South West African (Namibian) border. The guerrilla fighters claimed the South Africans lost some lives in the fiery exchange. At first, the South African authorities denied reports of any guerrilla activities in Caprivi Strip but later confirmed the existence of considerable activity by the freedom fighters in that area.

It was obvious that the threat to the apartheid regime was real; a point underscored by the Commandant-General of the South African Defence Force, General Hiemstra, on

8 August 1968 when he was answering a question about increasing guerrilla activity – whether or not he thought guerrilla fighting in neighbouring Rhodesia could one day develop into a full-scale war as in Vietnam. He said:

"Most certainly yes. This is the technique the communists used in Vietnam. This technique involves the gradual building up of terrorism until it eventually becomes conventional warfare." – (Hiemstra, *Africa Contemporary Record*, Ibid.).

Towards the end of the year in October 1968, South Africa's Commissioner of Police, Major-General J.P. Gouws, also admitted that there was increasing guerrilla activity in South West Africa in Caprivi Strip by the SWAPO freedom fighters whom he also called "terrorists," a term in the lexicon of the white minority rulers used to tarnish the image of the freedom fighters.

He said after the guerrillas fighters failed to penetrate by using force, they were now concentrating on slipping into South West Africa to recruit people from the local population for the insurgency. He knew the freedom fighters had adopted the right strategy since local support was critical to the success of any guerrilla warfare; and that worried the apartheid regime.

He went on to say that "terrorists" were moving from village to village in an attempt to recruit chiefs who would in turn mobilise local support for the liberation struggle, and conceded that they had had some success in this effort. He said five chiefs had recently been arrested in Caprivi Strip for supporting the guerrillas. Other people were also arrested in connection with the campaign to help SWAPO and recruit fighters. Although he said some arrests had been made, he still admitted that it was impossible to fully secure a border stretching 5,000 miles to protect South Africa:

"Some terrorists may have avoided security forces and be working much further inland. We have much more than 50,000 illegal immigrants in this country, and some of them could well be Communist-trained guerillas." – (J.P. Gouws, ibid., p. 293).

The Minister of the Interior, Mr. L. Muller, denied SWAPO reports that 63 Africans were "publicly slaughtered" after attacks in Caprivi Strip on 13 October 1968. However, South African intelligence officers admitted that there were signs of fresh attacks from "across the Rhodesian frontier soon." They claimed that the guerrilla offensive would be launched by 2,000 Africans who had left South Africa "under the pretence of studying abroad."

There was every indication that the end of the sixties, especially 1968 and 1969, was a time of intensified guerrilla activity in southern Africa, with the apartheid regime being one of the primary targets, unlike before when the South African authorities felt more secure.

The warning of an impending attack by the African nationalist forces in the form of a guerrilla insurgency was also issued by the Minister of Police and Interior, Mr. Muller, on October 13th who said, far from having receded, the danger of guerrilla attacks had become much more serious. As he put it:

"In actual fact the forces against South Africa are now stronger than ever before." – (L. Muller, *Africa Contemporary Record*, p. 293).

He also admitted that in some of the areas where guerrillas had been successful in getting support, not all Africans were well-disposed towards whites. That is something that should not have been difficult for him to understand. But, instead, he attributed that to illiteracy and poverty; implying that had those Africans not been poor, and had they been educated, they would not have been hostile towards or suspicious of whites – as if they did not suffer from racial oppression under apartheid.

The deteriorating situation in southern Africa also came into sharp focus when the apartheid regime sent its forces into Rhodesia to help neutralise guerrilla fighters who – as white rulers and their supporters felt – threatened the entire region and the well-being of white minorities. In November 1968, the United Nations discussed a resolution condemning the presence of South Africa's military forces in Rhodesia.

The UN also said South Africa's military involvement in Rhodesia aggravated the situation and constituted a threat to the sovereignty and territorial integrity of the independent African states. The South African delegate to the UN, Carl von Hirschberg, was defiant and had this to say in response to that:

"The South African police are in Rhodesia exclusively for the purpose of dealing with terrorists en route to South Africa for the purpose of committing acts of terrorism and subversion, and they will remain there for as long as this threat to the security of South Africa persists, for it is the duty of the South African government, no less than any other government, to resist with all means at their disposal, any and every attempt to endanger the safety and security of South Africa and her peoples.

Thus, those States which object to the presence of South African Police in Rhodesia and who, at the same time, train, equip or harbour these terrorists, need only to stop these unjustified and illegitimate practices and the need to have South African Police in Rhodesia will fall away." - (Carl von Hirschberg, ibid., pp. 293 - 294).

By the end of the sixties, the apartheid regime had more than enough warning about the perils it faced once sucked into guerrilla warfare, fighting virtually an invisible enemy hardly distinguishable from the local population. It was an outcome the white minority government and its supporters wanted to avoid, but chose the wrong approach, confrontation, when they refused to make meaningful concessions to the black African majority and other non-whites.

Yet, in spite of such defiance, the white rulers of South Africa conceded that they were facing a new enemy they had never fought before in terms of strategy and tactics.

At the end of August 1968, in the same month Defence Minister Pieter W. Botha made a threat against Tanzania and Zambia that the two countries should received a "sudden hard knock" for harbouring and training "terrorists," the South African General Officer Commanding Joint Combat Forces, General C.A. Fraser, gave a military appraisal of the nature of the guerrilla threat to South Africa at a symposium held in Potchefstrom and, in an ominous warning, had this to say:

"For 50 years, the world has seen widespread and virtually continuous political revolution. Probably more governments have come into being, passed through drastic change, or ceased to exist, than in any comparable period of history.

These changes in regime have been brought about, in the main, by a new kind of warfare, now widely termed revolutionary warfare. It has crystalised rapidly since the end of the Second World War. It differs fundamentally from the wars of the past in that victory does not come from the clash of two armies on a field of battle. Revolutionary wars are conducted as a carefully co-ordinated system of actions, political, economic, administrative, psychological, police and military.

The insurgent will use any means to overthrow the established regime, including ruthless force. His primary task is to gain support of the population. Without the consent and active aid of the people, the guerilla would be merely a bandit and could not long survive.

From the point of view of the insurgents, perhaps the basic ingredients of successful revolution are a popular cause, trained, efficient and dedicated leadership, support of the population, outside support and a firm base or sanctuary. It has been said that a revolutionary war is 20 per cent military action and 80 per cent political. The failure to recognise this is bound to lead ultimately to failure in countering and defeating the insurgency.

The basic tenet of the exercise of political power is that there is always an active minority for the cause, an uncommitted majority and an active minority against the cause. For ultimate victory it is necessary to gain support of the neutral majority. The objective for both sides in a revolutionary war is thus the population itself.

The operations designed to win the population, either by the insurgents or by the government, are essentially of a political nature. It is important to realise that adequate support for a guerilla movement does not necessarily mean the enthusiastic, voluntary backing of a large majority of the population. The active participation of a small number of people, or the general apathy of the majority, often provide all the popular support necessary to make a successful revolution.

The support of the population for a government is gained through the favourable minority. Every operation, whether in the military field or in the political, social economic or psychological fields, must be geared to this end.

Staying power is an attribute that is vital for eventual government success. Operations in Malaya took 12 years, and in Algeria eight years to be concluded. Mao-Tse-tung took 35 years to get China. The communists think they have a monopoly on patience.

We made a study of all this. We know what to do. May I assure that we will win." – (C.A. Fraser, ibid., p. 294).

History proved him wrong, although it was not until 26 years later – a time span almost equal to the number of years Nelson Mandela spent in prison – that the walls of that abominable institution, the edifice of apartheid, finally came tumbling down when the first multiracial democratic elections in the nation's history were held in 1994 and Mandela was elected president.

But even as far back as 1968 and 1969, as the sixties were coming to an end, it was clear to some people that mounting opposition to apartheid would finally prevail over racial oppression, ushering in a dawn of a new era when everybody would be free. The apartheid regime showed every sign of being under siege or felt that it was in imminent danger of attack, as it dramatically increased defence expenditure. The government was preoccupied with security more than anything else.

Procurement of weapons for armed forces went up; expenditure on police forces and on the intelligence services also went up as never before. For example, expenditure on secret services was increased by R640,000 to R2,342,000 for 1968/69. Fortunately for the regime, the rand was still very strong during those critical years.

South Africa also improved its capability to manufacture its own weapons to complement purchases from other countries such as Britain, France, the United States and Germany which were the biggest sources of arms for the apartheid regime; and in October 1968, the apartheid regime established its first missile base on the east coast of Natal Province. The first guided missile was launched from the site in December the same year.

The country was already building its own submarines, aircraft, and a number of war ships; making rifles, mortars, ammunition, grenades, bombs including napalm, mines and other weapons.

Its armaments industry was under the management of the Armaments Development and Production Corporation (ARMSCOR) whose first chairman was Professor H.J.

Samuels. But all those weapons were useless against guerrilla warfare and the strategy employed by the liberation movements to make the country ungovernable until apartheid was abolished.

Compounding the problem was the deteriorating situation in Rhodesia, a more vulnerable outpost of white tyranny over blacks where the freedom fighters from South Africa and Rhodesia itself coordinated their activities.

On 30 July – 31 July 1967, the Luthuli Combat Detachment – named in honour of Chief Albert Luthuli who was the president of the ANC – comprising ZAPU and ANC guerrillas, crossed the Zambezi River into Rhodesia. That was the beginning of guerrilla warfare in Rhodesia, South Africa's neighbour. And on 18 August 1967, ANC and ZAPU formally announced that they had formed a military alliance.

They clashed with Rhodesian and South African forces in Wankie and Sipolilo in Rhodesia and demonstrated their fighting ability in a way their enemies never expected. The conflict lasted until late 1968, sending a strong warning to the white minority government in Rhodesia and the apartheid regime in South Africa that guerrilla warfare would soon engulf the region.

The apartheid regime was fully aware of the danger although it claimed it would be able to contain it. But to show that it took the danger seriously, it increased its military preparedness and passed a law to achieve that goal.

On 4 August 1967, the Defence Amendment Act came into force. Every young white male would be liable for military service.

The amendments were also intended to make all medically fit citizens liable for military training – except those who join the permanent force, the South African police, and the railways or prison services.

Expenditure on citizen forces and commando training

was increased by almost R1m in 1968 to an estimated R30m.

In fact, many ordinary whites felt they were under siege. They already had a fortress mentality, further fortified by their fear of what they perceived to be an impending guerrilla war waged by freedom fighters trained in Tanzania and Zambia and other countries.

On 8 September 1967, it was officially disclosed by the apartheid regime that South African police were in Rhodesia actively helping Rhodesian armed forces in their fight against nationalist guerrillas. The South African government claimed it had been forced to intervene in Rhodesia because of an attempt by several hundred guerrillas to invade South Africa and South West Africa from Zambia at the urging of the OAU Liberation Committee.

It was also during the same time that Prime Minister B.J. Vorster announced the arrest of what he said was a fully trained KGB agent, Yuri N. Loginov, in Johannesburg, while on a special mission to South Africa. His arrest aroused widespread interest among Western intelligence services.

The arrest was deliberately timed to coincide with the announcement that African guerrillas were getting ready to invade South Africa and South West Africa (Namibia) from Zambia. And since one of their biggest supporters was the Soviet Union, providing them with arms, the implication of Loginov's presence in South Africa around the same time was obvious: He was sent there not only to spy on the apartheid regime but to coordinate guerrilla activities and collect information that would help the freedom fighters and their supporters in the Soviet Union.

That may have been the interpretation of the apartheid regime; if it was, it did not resonate well in African nationalist circles.

Tensions between South Africa and the independent African countries were heightened just a few months later on 5 April 1968, when Defence Minister P. W. Botha issued his first warning to them when he told the House of Assembly (Parliament) that countries aiding and inciting terrorism and guerrilla warfare against South Africa could provoke retaliation against them. It was interpreted as a warning to Zambia and Tanzania that guerrilla bases in those two countries could be attacked by South Africa. He issued the same warning again later in August the same year. But the two countries and the rest except Malawi and a few others continued to support the freedom fighters in spite of the threats by the apartheid regime that it would launch retaliatory strikes and engage in hot pursuit of the guerrilla fighters – chase them all the way back to where they were trained.

What this showed, however, was that in spite of the threats by the apartheid regime and its ability to defend South Africa, the situation was not getting any better; it was getting worse and neither side was willing to compromise.

Their differences were irreconcilable and inexorably led to conflict involving guerrilla warfare and other forms of confrontation including sustained strikes and total non-cooperation with the authorities to force the racist regime to capitulate and help pave the way for multiracial democracy. But the apartheid regime was still defiant even when the guerrilla threat got worse towards the end of the sixties.

Some of the South African freedom fighters formed a new nationalist party in Dar-es-Salaam, Tanzania, on 9 September 1968 to direct the freedom struggle inside South Africa. The party was named the National Liberation Front of South Africa (NALFSA) and applied for recognition by the OAU Liberation Committee.

As the apartheid regime continued to defy international opinion and the wishes of the non-white majority in its own country, Prime Minister Vorster announced in April 1969 that members of the South African Police Force would remain in Rhodesia as long as it was necessary to protect South Africa from "terrorist" attacks. In the following month, the African National Congress (ANC) at its conference in Morogoro, Tanzania, called for a full-scale offensive against apartheid using a multi-pronged approach.

It also said both armed struggle and mass political struggle must be used to defeat the enemy. But the ANC also emphasised that the armed struggle and the involvement of the masses in the liberation struggle depended on building ANC underground structures within South Africa to mobilise the people and ultimately weaken and end apartheid. It was a complementary strategy that was bound to succeed.

The Morogoro conference focused on bringing about a qualitative change in the organisational structure of the liberation movement in keeping with the new situation to launch a revolutionary people's war. It was one of the most successful conferences in the history of the ANC.

As the year 1969 came to an end, marking the end of the decade, guerrilla activity had intensified in southern Africa; and the apartheid regime was deeply involved in the neighbouring countries of Rhodesia, Angola and Mozambique where it had sent its armed forces and intelligence agents to help thwart guerrilla advances.

On 21 November 1969, the UN General Assembly condemned South Africa for its apartheid policies and for its collaboration with Portugal and Rhodesia; and also for intervening in Angola and Mozambique to help the colonial forces suppress Africans in their quest for freedom. But all that fell on deaf ears, as the regime defiantly continued to enforce apartheid and help the governments of Rhodesia, Angola and Mozambique fight the guerrillas.

In Rhodesia, the end of the sixties were some of the most critical years in the country's history. It was the first time that the Rhodesian army and security forces came face to face with the enemy on the battlefield. It was also the first time South Africans entered Rhodesia to launch preemptive strikes against the guerrillas in an attempt to stop them from moving south across the border into South Africa.

It was also the first time that the white settlers in Rhodesia became aware of the danger they faced from guerrilla war. It was also during that period that the Organisation of African Unity (OAU) launched a concerted effort to support the freedom fighters in their military campaign against the white minority regime in Salisbury.

The Rhodesian government was fully aware of the danger it faced. It was fighting a new war: guerrilla war. And it was fighting a new enemy who was as elusive as he was resilient, with an indispensable operational base in the local population of which he was an integral part. But without external support in the form of military training and provision of weapons and other necessities, he would not have been as effective as he was.

Underscoring the importance of such support, the rebel prime minister of Rhodesia, Ian Smith, described President Julius Nyerere of Tanzania, whose country was the headquarters of all the African liberation movements, as "the evil genius on the Rhodesian scene" who was also behind all the guerrilla wars in southern Africa.

As the decade came to an end, Rhodesia witnessed its first major conflict in March 1968 when guerrilla fighters who entered the British colony from Zambia clashed with the security forces. Clashes on this scale were unheard of before the white minorities unilaterally declared independence from Britain in November 1965.

Before the March 1968 military engagement, there had been other clashes on a smaller scale. One of those clashes took place in April 1966 in which seven seven guerrilla fighters who were members of the Zimbabwe African National Union (ZANU) crossed the Zambezi River from

Zambia and entered Rhodesia. They were shot in running battles with the security forces in the Sinoia area 85 miles north of the capital Salisbury.

By 1967, the guerrilla fighters were better organised, mainly because of the cooperation between the forces of ZAPU and the ANC. In the first military engagement with the security forces in August that year in Matebeleland in southwestern Rhodesia, 31 guerrilla fighters were killed and the security forces lost seven members. So serious was this incursion that the Rhodesian government immediately sought help from South Africa. The apartheid regime responded favourably and sent troops, so-called police, early in September.

But it was the fighting in March 1968 that marked a turning point in the history of armed conflict between the freedom fighters and the security forces in Rhodesia:

"The fighting in March continued intermittently for over a month; it was reported by Security Force headquarters in Salisbury on 25 April (1968) that the number of guerillas killed had reached 55.

Two members of the Security Forces were also reported killed, and quantities of arms, ammunitions and equipment captured.

A view of the seriousness of the unrest can be formed from the fact that additional Territorial Force personnel had to be called up at the end of March for 'base duties'; while the South African Minister of Defence, Mr. P.W. Botha, warned on 5 April that countries aiding and inciting terrorism and guerilla warfare against South Africa could eventually provoke South Africa into 'hitting back hard.'"
– (*Africa Contemporary Record*, pp. 373 - 374).

Another clash occurred in July 1968 when Rhodesia's minister of law and order, Lardner Burke, announced that "terrorist" groups had crossed into Rhodesia from Zambia.

It was also during the same time that it was announced

that the first South African "policeman" had been killed when a South African-Rhodesian patrol was ambushed by the freedom fighters near the Zambezi River.

Three other South Africans and two Rhodesians were wounded in the same incident; and 10 guerrilla fighters were reported killed.

Fighting continued for another week during which, according to Radio Salisbury, at least two members of the Security Forces and 18 more guerrillas were killed. The fighting was intense enough to force the Rhodesians to resort to other means to contain the guerrillas. Fighter jets of the Rhodesian Air Force were brought in to support the ground forces.

A joint communique issued by ZAPU and the ANC in Lusaka, Zambia, on 25 July 1968, claimed that 33 members of the Rhodesian Security Forces were killed in the conflict in the Zambezi Valley. Confirmation of the improved capacity of the guerrilla fighters came from the annual report of the Rhodesian Commissioner of Police published in July in which he said:

"It would be wrong to minimise the dangers which Rhodesia faces from terrorist infiltrators; these are now employing more sophisticated tactics and are well armed."

Rhodesia had been in a state of emergency for quite some time because of increasing guerrilla activity and the government was compelled to extend it to cope with the crisis and assure the white minority that they would be protected by the security forces.

There was also apprehension in official circles in Salisbury that the assistance the guerrilla fighters were getting from other countries such as Tanzania and Zambia was a critical factor in the conflict and could even tip scales in their favour, even if not necessarily on long-term basis. But it was a problem the white minority government had to contend with; a concession that was made by the minister of law and order in the rebel colony:

"The Rhodesia rebel Minister of Law and Order, Mr. Lardner Burke, extending the state of emergency at the beginning of 1968, said that the number of 'terrorists' waiting in Zambia and Tanzania to cross the Rhodesian border continued to mount.

The South African Deputy-Minister of Police, Mr. S.L. Muller, said Tanzania posed 'the greatest potential threat to the Republic.' He claimed there were '40 camps in Tanzania for the training of terrorists and all the offices of subversive organisations.' In Zambia, he said, there were '19 training and transit camps.'

A new external service of Radio Tanzania was inaugurated in 1968 to assist in 'propagating the ideological principles of the liberation movements in Tanzania.'" – (Ibid., p. 220).

The guerrilla camps in Tanzania and Zambia were not only for the freedom fighters from South Africa and Rhodesia but also for those from Mozambique, Angola, and South West Africa.

Among all the white minority regimes in southern Africa, the Portuguese were the most vulnerable and came under sustained attack. As President Nyerere said at the OAU summit in Cairo on 20 July 1964, African countries were strong enough to expel Portugal from Africa. He was right. The problem was the powers behind her. As he stated at the conference:

"I am convinced that the finer the words the greater the harm they do to the prestige of Africa if they are not followed by action …

Africa is strong enough to drive Portugal from our continent. Let us resolve at this conference to take the necessary action." – (Nyerere, quoted by Ali A. Mazrui in his lecture "Nkrumahism and The Triple Heritage: Out of the Shadows" at the University of Ghana-Legon in 2002).

By 1969, the Portuguese had 130,000 troops tied down mostly in Angola and Mozambique, with a smaller number in Guinea-Bissau. But they were fighting a losing battle. Portugal was the poorest and weakest country in Western Europe. It could not have been able to maintain her colonies without support from other Western countries which was critical in fighting the guerillas. As Dr. Eduardo Mondlane, the leader of FRELIMO, said about the armed struggle in Mozambique – which started on 25 September 1964 – in an interview with the Tanzanian daily newspaper, *The Nationalist*, on 30 July 1968:

"The meaning of the protracted struggle is more clear now and the combatants have redoubled their determination to fight to the bitter end until they destroy the enemy.

The situation of the war now inside Mozambique is more favourable to us as the Portuguese are in a stalemate and the only active force of the enemy is the Air Force.

We have now moved from the phase of ambushes and we are concentrating on attacking the enemy in his own territory, that is in garrisons, bases, posts and isolating the towns where he is hiding.

The enemy is completely isolated and the revolutionary enthusiasm of the masses is very high. We have actually more people ready in technical warfare training than we can provide the arms for fighting. All ages are involved and now we have formed the women's fighting detachment.

The prospects of crossing the Zambezi River and carrying the struggle farther south are very bright and no matter what the Portuguese do the war rages on and it is a fierce one.

We know that they are increasing their forces of white soldiers and they have intensified in Mozambique the forced conscription of Africans. They get a lot of technical aid from NATO countries, and the apartheid regime of South Africa is deeply involved – it has many of its military officers fighting in Mozambique.

Countries like West Germany, it is well-known to us, are training white Portuguese soldiers in Portugal in counter-insurgence techniques. In short, we are fighting Portugal and all her NATO allies."

Six months later, they killed him. But Mondlane's assassination on 2 February 1969 in Dar es Salaam, Tanzania, did not stop the people of Mozambique from fighting for their independence. In fact, they expected such setbacks as a part of the struggle.

So, the struggle continued even after Mondlane was killed. His assassination was a big tragedy as the sixties came to an end. But it was also a moment of reflection on the liberation struggle and the problems that lay ahead, as the war became more intense. For example, on 25 September 1968, which was the fourth anniversary of the armed conflict, FRELIMO said that during the past year (1967), its forces had killed more than 1,000 Portuguese soldiers, shot down 20 aircraft, and destroyed more than a hundred military vehicles; a claim that was later confirmed by some journalists and other observers; and by September 1968, more than 100 Portuguese soldiers were killed and hundreds injured within that year alone.

The sixties ended with the death toll mounting in all the liberation wars throughout southern Africa, as the freedom fighters intensified the struggle and scored bigger victories they never had won before. It was the dawn of a new era.

Thus, while the early and mid-sixties were years of celebration, as one African country after another won independence from colonial rule, the late sixties witnessed another phenomenon in the liberation struggle. And it had an equally profound impact on the destiny of the continent.

Africa entered a new phase. It was the phase of the armed struggle. And it proved to be the most difficult phase in the history of African liberation until the rest of the continent was finally free many years later.

The end of the sixties, or the year 1969 in particular, was also significant in another important respect. The bleeding heart of Africa, Congo, had finally stopped bleeding; at least not as profusely as it did in the first years of the decade and even as late as 1965 and 1966, although the pro-Lumumbist nationalist forces never gave up until Mobutu was finally ousted from power about 30 years later in May 1997. But as the decade came to an end, so did the life of one man who wreaked so much havoc across the Congo during the turbulent sixties. The man was Moise Tshombe.

In June 1967, his plane flying from Spain en route to Congo where he intended to cause more mischief was hijacked and forced to land in Algiers, Algeria. After it landed, Tshombe was arrested and kept under house arrest. He died in the same month, reportedly of heart failure. He was 49, a few months before his 50th birthday on November 10th.

His death also marked the end of an era.

Not long after Tshombe died, another personality emerged on the African political scene. That was Colonel Muammar Qadhafi. On 1 September 1969, he overthrew 79-year-old King Idris of Libya in a bloodless military coup. He was 28 and became one of the youngest heads of state in the world. He instituted a controversial regime which became one of the most prominent in Africa and the rest of the Third World for decades.

So much for Africa, as the sixties came to an end. It is, indeed, a decade to remember.

Africa in The Sixties

THE SIXTIES changed the destiny of the African continent and its people in many fundamental respects.

It was a period marked by the end of colonial rule as one country after another won independence. Coincidentally, it was during the same period that the civil rights movement in the United States gained momentum and reached its peak.

The victory of Africans in their struggle for independence in most countries on the African continent also inspired black Americans in their struggle for racial equality. They not only drew inspiration from this victory but felt proud because of the common African heritage they shared with their brethren on the continent.

At no other time in American history did such pride among blacks manifest itself as it did in the sixties. Even without the victories in Africa, African Americans, galvanised by the civil rights movement, found a renewed sense of purpose in their lives as a distinct group proud of their identity and forcefully proclaimed their pride as black people. As Eldridge Cleaver, the minister of information of the militant Black Panther Party, said:

"They have seized on their blackness and rallied around it."

Stokely Carmichael, who later changed his name to Kwame Ture after he moved to Africa and probably the most prominent advocate of Black Power, had this to say:

"It is time to stop being ashamed of being black – time to stop trying to be white. When you see your daughter playing in the fields, with her nappy hair, her wide nose and her thick lips, tell her she is beautiful. *Tell your daughter she is beautiful.*" – Stokely Carmichael, *This Fabulous Century: 1960 – 1970*, New York: Time-Life Books, 1988, p. 32).

And as James Brown proudly said in one of his songs with the same title:

"I'm black and I'm proud."

It was a pride they shared with Africans in Africa. And it was a pride that went beyond slavery all the way back to Africa's ancient kingdoms and to the newly independent nations. It was also a pride that embraced African culture as a way of life and bond of unity between Africa and the African diaspora.

Many African Americans took African names and began to learn African languages, especially Kiswahili (popularly known as Swahili), which got its biggest boost in 1966 when Maulana Karenga, one of the most prominent black militants in the sixties, started the Kwanzaa festival based on Nguzo Saba (a Swahili term meaning Seven Principles) and encouraged other blacks to learn the language which transcends ethnic identity as a Pan-African language.

No single African ethnic group can claim Kiswahili as its own language like Yoruba, Zulu, Kikuyu or any of the other African languages. It evolved from many African languages and is older than modern English.

Not only did many black Americans – since 1988 known as African Americans – start to learn Kiswahili in the sixties; they adopted African life styles, wearing African clothes, eating African foods, dancing to African music and singing African songs. They also embraced African traditional beliefs and religions; and started buying, promoting and producing African art, and decorating their homes with African carvings, paintings and other items. And they proudly wore the Afro hair style and braids and called themselves Afro-Americans. They were no longer Negroes. As Malcolm X said in one of his speeches: "Where is Negroland?" He emphatically stated that black people in the United States were Africans: "You are nothing but Africans" born in America.

All that racial pride and identification with their ancestral motherland strengthened their ties to Africa.

The manifestation of black pride and admiration of the African heritage among black Americans was also expressed in another very significant way: demand for the establishment of Black or Afro-American studies departments in colleges and universities across the United States.

It was in the sixties, especially from the mid-sixties, that Afro-American and African studies became an integral part of the curriculum in institutions of higher learning across the nation. And the introduction of these studies, after persistent demands by black students and faculty members including some of their white supporters, had a profound impact in transforming education in the United States and in projecting a positive image of black

Americans and the continent of Africa and its people.

The transformation coincided with, and was partly reinforced by, the emergence of African countries from colonial rule as independent nations.

It was in the sixties when, for the first time, Africans emerged on the international scene not only as a free people but as a people who spoke for themselves, and defined themselves, and were no longer defined and dominated by the imperial powers who had exploited them and muzzled them for so long when they were colonial subjects.

Before the sixties, no black African countries were represented in international forums as independent nations except Liberia and Ethiopia.

Tragically, the sixties were also years of conflict. It was a period that witnessed some of the most violent conflicts in the history of Africa, most notably in Congo and Nigeria, two black nations which had the potential to be the best hope for Black Africa because of their wealth and size.

The Nigerian civil war from 1967 – 1970 was the bloodiest conflict in modern African history up to that time and remained one for decades until it was surpassed by the death toll in the Sudanese civil war and by the carnage in the Great Lakes region of east-central Africa where the death toll from the late nineties to the early part of the twentieth-first century reached 5 million.

Almost 1 million people, mostly Tutsi, were massacred in Rwanda during the 1994 genocide. More than 200,000 Hutus were killed – in eastern Congo where they had sought refuge – in retaliatory violence at the hands of the the Tutsi-dominated Rwandan Patriotic Army (RPA) to avenge the massacre of the Tutsi by Hutu extremists during the genocide. And about 4 million people perished since August 1998 in the Democratic Republic of Congo, mostly in the eastern part of the country.

At least 300,000 people, mostly Hutu, were killed in

the civil war in Burundi in 10 years since October 1993 when Melchior Ndadaye, the country's first democratically elected president in the country's history since independence in 1962, was assassinated by Tutsi soldiers after being in office only for about three months.

All these conflicts had their genesis in the turbulent sixties and in the flawed nature of the institutions of authority Africans inherited at independence which did not reflect or accommodate African realities.

The conflicts also had their origin in the way power was transferred to the new African rulers without taking into account conflicting ethnoregional interests and the asymmetrical relationship between different ethnic and regional groups in the allocation of power and distribution of resources; and in the way the colonial rulers themselves exacerbated tensions and helped ignite and fuel conflicts by transferring power to members of some ethnic groups and excluding others. For example, in Nigeria the Hausa-Fulani assumed power at the expense of the Yoruba, the Igbo and other ethnic groups. That was one of the main causes of the Nigerian civil war.

In Burundi the Tutsi, although a very small minority, assumed power at the expense of the Hutu who constitute the vast majority of the population in both Rwanda and Burundi, two states in the Great Lakes region which are almost a mirror image of each other in terms of ethnic composition and inequity of power between the two ethnic groups.

Besides all these conflicts, the sixties were also the years which witnessed the consolidation of the nation-states across the continent and the emergence of authoritarian rule which in many cases amounted to dictatorship and tyranny as many African leaders justified curtailment of freedom and suffocation of dissent on grounds of national unity; contending that if the people were allowed "too much freedom" – a relative term depending on the context in which it is used – and the right to form opposition parties, the countries would break up since those parties would most likely be formed on ethnic and regional basis, fueling ethnoregional rivalries leading to conflict. And there were cases in which this was a rational fear.

One of the most effective ways to avert such catastrophe, hence neutralise dissent, was by encouraging and sometimes forcing people to support or join the ruling party which usually was the party that led the struggle for independence. Thus, the emergence of authoritarian rule, therefore dictatorship – with the leaders invoking the spectre of national disintegration to mobilise the masses and rally support – led to the introduction and institutionalisation of one-party rule which became one of the most prominent features of the political landscape and national life in most countries across the continent for decades.

All that had its beginning in the sixties. But as African leaders assumed more power and worked hard to strengthen the one-party system, another phenomenon came to affect national life and profoundly changed the way African countries were governed. This new phenomenon was military coups which led to the introduction of military rule in many parts of the continent.

After the first military coup took place in Togo in January 1963, many others followed in different parts of the continent, including the one in Nigeria in January 1966, a seminal event which led to a series of catastrophes including the Nigerian civil war. Another major coup took place in Ghana with the help of the CIA and led to the ouster of Dr. Kwame Nkrumah in February 1966.

In addition to military intervention in government, a phenomenal event in those years and in the following decades, there were other important events and developments which took place in the sixties and changed the course of African history. One of those events was the founding of the Organisation of African Unity (OAU) in Addis Ababa, Ethiopia, in May 1963.

Although the OAU did not achieve many of its goals and became no more than a debating and social club for corrupt and despotic rulers – what Julius Nyerere called "a trade union of tyrants" – it did play a major role in supporting the liberation movements on the continent, especially in southern Africa and in the Portuguese colony of Guinea-Bissau in West Africa. That was undoubtedly its biggest achievement; and the OAU will always be remembered for that.

Another major event in the sixties was the unilateral declaration of independence by the white minority regime in Rhodesia under the leadership of Ian Smith in November 1965, two-and-a-half years after the OAU was formed.

It was an act of ultimate defiance by the white settlers and a major challenge to the black African majority in that country and the rest of Africa.

African countries were too weak to bring down the Smith regime, although Nkrumah wanted to send troops to topple Smith; one of the reasons Akwasi Afrifa in his book *The Ghana Coup* – as well as other Ghanaian army officers – gave to explain why they overthrew Nkrumah. Afrifa also stated that Nkrumah wanted to send Ghanaian soldiers to fight in a country that was so far away and a war they had nothing to do with; a sentiment that could be expressed only by someone who did not care about the freedom and wellbeing of fellow Africans and who did not see them as his brothers and sisters.

The unilateral declaration of independence – which came to be known as UDI – only helped to intensify the liberation struggle on the continent and was one of the main factors that led to the adoption of guerrilla tactics which became the main feature of the liberation wars not only in Rhodesia but throughout southern Africa.

In fact, the freedom fighters had already started waging

guerrilla warfare in some of the colonies even before the white settlers in Rhodesia declared independence. In Angola, the Popular Movement for the Liberation of Angola (MPLA) launched the armed struggle against the Portuguese colonial rulers in 1961. In Portuguese Guinea in West Africa, the independence struggle began even earlier, in 1959. And in Mozambique, another Portuguese colony, the Front for the Liberation of Mozambique (FRELIMO) started waging guerrilla warfare in 1964.

But the illegal seizure of power by the white minorities in Rhodesia gave impetus to all those struggles and in Rhodesia itself where guerilla warfare by the nationalist forces of the Zimbabwe African People's Union (ZAPU) and the Zimbabwe African National Union (ZANU) started a few years later in 1974; coincidentally, in the same year Guinea-Bissau won independence after waging an armed struggle for 15 years against the Portuguese colonial forces, becoming the first Portuguese African colony to win independence after more than 500 years of colonial rule.

While the liberation struggle was an African phenomenon, and an African initiative as well an indigenous military expression of political aspirations, it also entailed foreign involvement and became very much a part of the Cold War between the East and the West as the two ideological camps competed for control of the Third World of which Africa was an integral part and one of the main theatres of conflict.

Thus, as the liberation wars started in earnest, the Cold War also came to Africa in the sixties with a fury. It had a profound effect on the course of events in different countries and influenced the course of African history. As independent nations, Africans were no longer mere spectators as they once were during colonial rule. They became active participants in the international arena sometimes in a way that offended big powers even though they played only a peripheral role because of their weakness.

But it was precisely their weakness that was also their strength as world powers in the East and the West competed for ideological allies among these weak countries, hoping to turn them into what Dr.Nkrumah described as "client states." As Nyerere warned: "We are not going to allow our friends to choose our enemies for us."

Some of them became client states of Western or Eastern powers, as Africa got caught between the two ideological camps contending for hegemonic control of the Third World.

It was not until after the collapse of the Soviet Union and her satellites in the late 1980s and early 1990s that African countries escaped the scourge of the Cold War, but only to come under domination of the industrial West, the driving force behind globalisation in the post-Cold War era in this unipolar world dominated by the United States. All this has echoes from the sixties when the United States was also the world's undisputed industrial and economic giant enjoying enormous prosperity despite the challenge to its military might by the Soviet Union.

The United States also projected its image in Africa and other parts of the Third World in the sixties with the establishment of the Peace Corps. As John F. Kennedy stated in his inaugural address on 20 January 1960 when he again spoke about the need for the Peace Corps:

"To those people in the huts and villages of half the globe struggling to break the bonds of mass miscry, we pledge our best efforts to help them help themselves, for whatever period is required – not because the communists may be doing it, not because we seek their votes, but because it is right. If a free society cannot help the many who are poor, it cannot save the few who are rich."

The Peace Corps became a reality less than two months

later when President-elect Kennedy issued an executive order establishing it.

Under the peace Corps, many young American men and women, mostly fresh out of college, were sent to many parts of the Third World to help the people in developing countries meet their own needs. One of those areas was education, and many Peace Corp volunteers went to teach in African countries and elsewhere in the developing parts of the world.

When I was a teenager in Tanzania in the sixties, some of my teachers were American Peace Corps.

I remember very well what one of our first Peace Corp teachers said when he introduced himself to us in class at Mpuguso Middle School in Rungwe District in the Southern Highlands one morning in the early part of 1964 when I was in standard eight, what Americans call the eighth grade. He said: "My name is Leonard Levitt. I am a Jew from New York City."

I also remember that he followed the news very closely including the conflict in Congo and pronounced African names well. He had quite a way of saying "Antoine Gizenga," "Christophe Gbenye."

More than 40 years later, Gizenga, an enduring political phenomenon who also served as deputy prime minister of Congo under Lumumba, again emerged on the political scene when he ran for president in 2006. He won a respectable 13 per cent of the vote in the first round in August in a field of about 20 presidential candidates.

The leading contender, President Joseph Kabila won 45 per cent of the vote, and his most serious rival, Jean-Pierre Mbemba won 20 per cent. Nzanga Mobutu, the son of former president, Mobutu Sese Seko, won 5 per cent, and another candidate Oscar Kashala won 4 per cent.

Both Gizenga and Nzanga Mobutu later endorsed Kabila against Mbemba in order to keep the country united.

Probably many people in the 1960s did not think

Gizenga would still be on the political scene more than 40 years later. But there he was again, in 2006, as a serious contender for president. However, his political fortunes were greatest in the sixties when he was Lumumba's deputy and later one of the main leaders of the pro-Lumumbist nationalist forces fighting the Western-installed government in Leopoldville during those turbulent years.

The year 1964 when Leonard Levitt became our teacher was one of the worst in Congo's history. I remember the Simba rebellion and the battle for Stanleyville very well and Levitt liked to talk a lot about that and other events in Congo.

Our country was still called Tanganyika. Just a few months later, it united with Zanzibar on 26 April the same year to form Tanzania. The new country was simply known as the United Republic of Tanganyika and Zanzibar until October 29th when it was renamed Tanzania.

I was 14 years old in 1964 at that boarding school for boys and Leonard Levitt taught us math and English, together with another Peace Corp teacher whom we simply called Mr. Wayne from Colorado. Little did I know that I myself would end up in the United States only eight years later.

When Levitt returned to the United States in 1966, he wrote a book, *An African Season*, about his experiences at our school and in Tanganyika in general. He also wrote about his trips to Rhodesia and South Africa during those days. His book was one of the most well-read about the experiences of American Peace Corps around the world. He later became a news reporter. He worked for *Newsday* in Long Island, New York, and wrote for other newspapers including *The New York Times*.

After Mpuguso Middle School, I went to Songea Secondary School where I was also taught by some American Peace Corps. But most of our teachers were African and British.

The Peace Corps made a great contribution to education and in other fields not only in Africa but in other parts of the Third World. That is one of the most important legacies of the sixties and President Kennedy's policies.

It was a decade that changed the destiny of Africa. Africa has never been the same since then because of what happened in the sixties.

Probably more than anything else, the sixties was a decade of excitement as Africans celebrated the end of colonial rule in most countries across the continent.

The people had indeed regained their dignity and the right to rule themselves. And they were highly optimistic of the future, riding on a wave of excitement and high expectations for the fruits of independence although they did not see any tangible benefits right away.

The excitement did not last long. When they woke up the next day, things were the same. Little had changed. Even years later, nothing much had changed.

The only major change they witnessed, or were aware of, was the transfer of power from Europeans to Africans. And the most obvious difference was in the race and skin colour of the rulers. In most cases, white rulers relinquished power to blacks and in some cases to other non-whites as well. They were the people who led the struggle for independence and were an integral part of the indigenous elite that assumed the leadership of the newly independent countries.

But in terms of power and institutional arrangements, and the relationship between the leaders and the led, things remained almost the same as they were under colonial rule. The power structure instituted by the colonialists remained intact; only that this time it had new masters: the indigenous elite. To the new rulers, one of the most attractive features of the colonial power structure was centralisation or concentration of power in the hands of a few people at the centre under a unitary state.

In a very disturbing way, the departing colonial rulers

found many comfortable allies among the indigenous elite who admired European ways of life and institutions. It was clear where they got this influence. Almost all the new African leaders were educated in schools which had been established by the missionaries or by the colonial governments.

Like the colonial rulers, the missionaries themselves came from Western countries. The education they provided, as did the colonial authorities, was based on the Western intellectual tradition. And the values they instilled in their African students were also Western.

Many educated Africans became carbon copies of Europeans, although poor copies. They could never be the same as the original.

Yet, in spite of all that, they still and quite often tried to be more European than the Europeans themselves. Among them were dedicated "nationalists" who led the struggle for independence.

Some of the best examples of this abjectly servile and despicable imitation of the imperial masters were the leaders of Francophone Africa who after independence remained beholden to France and were unabashedly Francophile. There were only a few exceptions, notably Sekou Toure of Guinea and Modibo Keita of Mali.

Another good example of imperial devotion among African leaders was Dr. Hastings Kamuzu Banda of Malawi who was very British in his manners, values and attire. He even established a school in Malawi named after him, Kamuzu Academy, where he allowed only whites to teach in order to produce a generation of African Anglophiles who would follow in his steps to spread Western education and "civilization" in Malawi and, hopefully, in other African countries as well.

He also ended up being one of the most brutal dictators Africa has ever produced. Soon after independence, he turned against his colleagues such as Kanyama Chiume and Henry Chipembere, the very same people who had invited him to return to Nyasaland from Britain to lead the struggle for independence.

By the time he was invited, he had lived in the United States and Britain for 40 years, mostly in Britain. He also spent some time in Ghana after his friend Kwame Nkrumah became prime minister of that country, only to become a tyrant soon after he led Nyasaland to independence.

His former colleagues were forced to flee their homeland and sought refuge in neighbouring countries, especially Tanzania and Zambia.

Banda was just one among many African leaders who went on to establish authoritarian or despotic regimes soon after independence.

Therefore, while independence was supposed to have ushered in a new era of freedom, the people soon learned that the freedom they had been promised was more apparent than real. Yet, one of the most attractive slogans African leaders used in their campaign for independence was that they would establish democracy the people had been denied under colonial rule. But when independence came, it was an entirely different story.

In almost all African countries, the new African rulers had little respect for freedom. They justified curtailment of freedom on grounds of nation unity and security, contending that they could not afford the luxury of freedom which entails the establishment of opposition parties in pursuit of partisan interests to the detriment of national unity and wellbeing.

Therefore multiparty democracy was out of the question, not only for the sake of national unity but for other reasons as well: nation building and consolidation of independence could not be achieved without mass regimentation.

Freedom of speech was curtailed and opposition parties were strongly discouraged or banned, ushering in what became a new era of one-party rule and dictatorship on a continent where the people had been promised freedom during the struggle for independence.

There were only a few exceptions in countries such as Nigeria with its regionally entrenched parties dominated by the country's three main ethnic groups – the Hausa-Fulani in the north, the Yoruba in the west and the Igbo in the east; Botswana, Gambia, and Senegal; also Zambia but where the ruling party (UNIP – United National Independence Party) remained dominant at the expense of two opposition parties which, unfortunately, thrived on ethnoregional loyalties in the western and southern provinces.

Kenya is another example. The ruling party, KANU (Kenya African National Union), wanted a strong central government under a unitary state but virtually as an ethnocracy dominated by Kikuyu.

Soon after independence, Jomo Kenyatta and other KANU leaders neutralised KADU (Kenya African Democratic Unity), the opposition party in parliament which wanted a federal constitution under which there would be devolution of power to the regions to safeguard the interests of smaller ethnic groups which were afraid of being dominated by the country's main ones: the Kikuyu and the Luo.

The situation was the same in the other countries which had opposition parties. The parties were neutralised or simply withered soon after independence. In many cases, they were banned right away.

Even in countries such as Tanganyika where the opposition party, the African National Congress (ANC), was simply overwhelmed at the polls by the ruling party, TANU (Tanganyika African National Union), and thus died a natural death in the early sixties, laws were passed to give legal status to one-party rule leading to the establishment of the one-party system. Tanganyika became a *de jure* one-party state in 1965. That was only within five years after independence when it was a *de facto* one-party state like most were across the continent.

One-party states became the dominant feature of the African political landscape at the expense of freedom soon after independence. Tolerance of dissent was equated with weakness and abdication of responsibility by the leaders.

Some people still spoke up, but at their own risk. They knew that criticism of government was tantamount to treason. And the authorities left no doubt in any one's mind how they would respond. They were ruthless in their suppression of dissent.

Thus, paradoxically, the new era of freedom led to denial of freedom. If the new nations could not be built into cohesive units because the people had the freedom to disagree on how to build those nations, then freedom had to go.

Therefore in most African countries, freedom became the first casualty under the new African leaders who felt that it was only they who knew what was best for the people and not the people themselves. It was a betrayal of trust and the people became increasingly distrustful of their own leaders who not too long ago had led them to independence and promised them freedom.

But freedom was not the only casualty. Nation building, which the new leaders argued could not be achieved if opposition parties were allowed to exist and if criticism of government even by individuals was allowed as well, also suffered because the people were not given the opportunity to examine and challenge government decisions and policies.

Had they been allowed to do so, and had opposition parties which were truly national in character been allowed to exist, African countries would have had the chance to pursue alternative policies which in many cases would probably have been better than the policies pursued by the government.

But the people were not allowed to do that. They could not even freely discuss government policies and offer constructive criticism even among themselves without fear of being arrested. They were muzzled.

All that led to apathy with dire consequences for the new nations in terms of nation building and national development. For, without the people's involvement in decision making all the way down to the grassroots level, meaningful change including development is virtually impossible. It is the people themselves who know what is best for them. Yet the leaders turned a deaf ear to what they had to say except in a few cases. The result was formulation and implementation of wrong policies leading to stunted economic growth.

This was compounded by a lack of high-level manpower and necessary skills needed in many areas to implement development projects and provide efficient administration throughout the country.

At independence, almost all African countries lacked a critical mass of educated people and professionals as well as administrative skills not only in technical fields but in almost all the other areas as well. For example, when my home country, Tanganyika, won independence from Britain in December 1961, it had only two engineers and 12 doctors.

The situation was the same in most countries across the continent except in countries such as Ghana and Nigeria which had a significant number of educated people compared with other African countries.

Without trained workers and high skills, it was obvious the young African nations would not be able to develop. The only place they could turn to for help to meet their needs was foreign countries including their former colonial msters.

But foreign aid, which included financial and technical assistance, did not solve Africa's problems. In most cases, there were no trained people or well-established institutions to use aid effectively and on the right projects. In some cases, the wrong kind of aid was sought or provided, sadly demonstrated by rusted machinery which one could see in many countries on the continent. The equipment could not be used and was simply left out there to rust.

In other cases, when the equipment arrived, there were no skilled people to use it; or there were no spare parts or someone to fix it when it broke down. Sometimes it was the wrong kind of machinery that was sent; for example, snow ploughs, instead of tractors, sent to Guinea from the Soviet Union.

Also, because the new governments lacked accountability since there was no organised or formal opposition to act as a watchdog over those in power, mismanagement of resources including outright theft became a major problem in the early days of independence.

Ethnic loyalties was also a major factor in the allocation of power and resources and, most of the time, those in power usually came from one or only a handful of ethnic groups, thus accentuating ethnic cleavages in multiethnic societies. People sought power to help themselves and "their people," members of their own tribes, in many cases to the total exclusion of other ethnic groups.

Thus, while the leaders who led the struggle for independence also campaigned against tribalism and regionalism, contending that the colonial rulers had used divide-and-rule tactics by keeping tribes separate from each other and sometimes even turning some against others, they did exactly the same thing when they assumed power.

They used ethnic and regional loyalties to perpetuate themselves in power by keeping their opponents divided. They also outlawed opposition parties even if there were some prospects that some of those parties could have become truly national in character, transcending ethnic loyalties, regionalism and other forms of partisanship militating against national unity.

Yet, there were some leaders who made genuine attempts to achieve national unity on the basis of equality for all regardless of race, class, ethnicity, national origin or religious affiliation: Nkrumah, Nyerere, Sekou Toure, Obote, and Kaunda among others. They were also some of the most prominent Pan-Africanists and among the strongest advocates of African unity on a continental scale and on regional basis.

Nkrumah stood out alone among them as an opponent of regional federations or formation of any regional blocs which he described as "balkanization on a grand scale" and an obstacle to continental unification.

But in spite of genuine attempts by a number of African leaders to create a sense of national unity and identity among their citizens, ethnoregional loyalties remained strong and an intractable problem in most countries; it was also one of the most devastating. And it was only one among many problems the young nations faced in their early days of independence in spite of the optimism the leaders and the people had for the future free from colonial rule.

Therefore, in the initial euphoria after independence, even the leaders themselves did not realise the scope and magnitude of the task that lay ahead especially in terms of nation building. And in many cases, it is a task that has yet to be accomplished.

A large number of countries across the continent remain fractured along ethnic and regional lines. And most of them are still trapped in poverty 50 years after independence.

The struggle for power among different ethnic and regional groups, mainly because many of them have been excluded from the decision-making process and allocation of resources, is a perennial problem. And it has been one of the major causes of conflict on the continent since independence.

But that and other subjects are the focus of another study exclusively devoted to the post-colonial era since the sixties.

The sixties is indeed a decade to remember. For those of us who grew up in the sixties, and witnessed what happened in the sixties, we will always remember the sixties. Always.

Appendix I:

The Nigerian Civil War: Memories of Survivors

IT WAS the bloodiest conflict in the history of post-colonial Africa up to that time. It was also one of the deadliest in the continent's history and in modern times.

More than 1 million people died during the war. Some estimates say up to 2 million perished, mostly from starvation. Countless also died from bombing raids by the Nigerian federal forces backed by Britain and the Soviet Union.

Those who survived never forgot what they went through. They lived to tell what happened. Here are two of those survivors:

Before Port Harcourt Fell

Omekenyi Theresa Muotune

In 1968 Port Harcourt fell. The bomb started falling in the early morning. It kept on falling, and falling, and falling and when I woke up, fear has taken a hold of everybody.

My father came back from work around 9 p.m. and told us that we had to move because the country is falling. Soldiers we knew came to our house and told us to leave Port Harcourt.

Within some hours to come, we left Port Harcourt and went straight to my hometown Oguta. We trekked miles and miles, until we came to Ungbudi.

When we reached Ungbudi, it was nearer for us. Then we used canoes to cross the river to Oguta. When we reached Oguta, the town was quiet. There was no sign of war at all. Things were going normal.

When Ojukwu came to Oguta

We were there when Ojukwu came with his soldiers. Ojukwu addressed his soldiers and told them that if Oguta was not rescued, that it is finished and the vandals (the Nigerians) would have won the war. In Oguta, it is do or die. Many of the Oguta citizens were crying because they are homeless and fearful of the war.

I stayed near the tower because I wanted to see how they were going to fight. I was there when Ojukwu ordered the shooting. Nigerian troops that were on the sea on the Oguta lake was shelling and shelling the town.

So, Ojukwu climbed on top of the tank with his officers and began shelling Oguta, even shelling inside the water. The Biafran soldiers were shelling. I was there until the next morning. The Oguta lake completely sunk the ship that the Nigerian soldiers came with.

At that time, Ojukwu and his soldiers had shelled Oguta, killing the foreigners and the Nigerian soldiers that were aboard the ship.

At dawn, I was among the people that went to the waters because it was my town and I did not know where else to go. I went down to the lake.

When I got there, I saw corpses of white people, of

these white mercenaries. Their corpses were like sand. I also saw Nigerian soldiers that drowned in the Oguta lake and those that died in the ships.

But those white people that came out of the ship looked like they were trying to swim but was drowned because the waters of Oguta is a great deity.

We don't joke with the lake. The water is a big deity. The towns of Oguta do not use the water to joke. The lake killed the white mercenaries.

Each one that tried to swim drowned and their corpse lay there. The lake pushed the corpse to the shore because it does not carry any corpse. When the lake killed someone, it will push the person out. It does not touch it. So, the lake killed all the white people.

When you come in, and you look around, you will see a bags of rice, everything, beans, corned-beef were filled inside the ship.

So, some of the Oguta boys went inside and were bring out corned-beef, taking out bags of rice, bringing out beans. Whatever they were able to get, they took back to their homes.

But those that entered the ship were mostly men. The men were not afraid to enter the ship. You know that with men, fear did not stop them from entering the ship. The women were afraid to go because there were corpses lying in there.

When It All Started

Veronica Uwechia

My name is Veronica Uwechia. I am a Nigerian, and I was in Nigeria when the war broke out.

Before the declaration of our own section of Nigeria as Biafra, I was at Onitsha. I was living in my house all through. I was a widow, with children, 5 children. My occupation was business and when the war broke out, there was a lot of running up and down and trying to save our necks from their stray bullets.

In the morning, by the month of July in 19...ninety (When was Jideofo born), 19 ninety (airplane noise), 1968 (fades out). In 1967, there was a coup by the military and that was what sparked off the war. We the ordinary people then can't even understand what was going on but we know there was trouble between the states and we are the Eastern states and the whole trouble was more on our own state.

Everything got so heated that when they declared the state of Biafra, whoa, there was trouble everywhere, people started running and coming home from other states where they were living, we started seeing soldiers, moving around, hearing the booming of guns, no lights in the night, and we can't get certain things from the other states but we were trying to manage our life, it continued and by 1968, it got so heated that we couldn't even stay in our houses during the day.

We keep running away into the bush to hide under thick clustered groves or we will run from our own area when the bullets started coming across the Niger.

The other side of the Niger that is the western part, were coming into eastern states, we keep on running. We were running all the day.

There was no market any longer, people trade under shades of a tree, they bring what they can sell and you can buy. It started going like that and some people started going into the central part of the eastern states. Somebody like me didn't feel it right to keep running to other villages or towns because I have no relatives there and I can't manage five children outside Onitsha.

So we stayed in Onitsha hoping that it will be alright. We started killing our chickens for meat and share it. We have cassava, we had yams, we had rice, these...thing that at least will last at least six months to one year. We were not talking of eating bread because we cannot afford it. We don't talk of sugar because we can't afford it.

We started living on our own Nigerian food. I had a lot of plantain trees in my house, luckily about that time they were fruiting, when it got ripe we will go and cut it. We either roast it or boil it, no more frying because we cannot get oil so easily and we have our own native things like Egusi growing in my house. We can wash it, shell it, and use it to cook soup.

We have palm trees which we cut the nuts and make red oil and red soup out of it. We have cassava. We have different ways of eating cassava. There is one we soak, after it's soft, we wash it and make it into Akpu, we grind gari with a grater then we make abacha or Iwu Akpu. We dry that and soak it in the water, so at least we still have something to keep us going.

We didn't start running, and then what we heard is that the soldiers were advancing, and when the war started hitting was in 1968. Then people were moving out of Onitsha, evacuating the whole place because bullets have started to come into the town. We were hiding in our house, some of us slept in the wardrobe, some of us slept under the bed and when morning comes, we come out and do our daily job, until towards everyday.

The whole thing was coming up, everyday they were coming nearer and nearer and people started moving for their dear lives, abandoning their house, their goods.

We were still doing our routine, we didn't bother to run until on that eventful march a bomb fell in Onitsha and there was chaos.

Everybody was running, everybody was running, we hid in our house, later by the afternoon the whole town was so cool, no noise, no voice, we keep on hiding in our house, and we were using kerosene stove to cook our food.

Before I surrendered to Murtala Muhammad

We were in the house for five days and we don't hear voice. We don't hear people, we were hiding inside hoping for change, there was no change until that eventful Monday.

The only thing we have to know what is happening is a little transistor, instead of buying food, I will buy battery so that we could hear what is happening.

Then when you want to hear what is happening from other parts of Nigeria, you tune to radio Kaduna, it will tell you everything and the locations of where the army are and if you want to hear about Biafra, you tune to radio Biafra and it will tell you.

It's from this transistor that we heard from that Onitsha has fallen and that the soldiers have occupied parts of the town.

We didn't know what to do, we were just staying. But everyday when we looked out the window, one of the windows that is facing the major road – the Expressway, we saw army trucks moving towards from the left side and moving to the right side and the right side of it is where we call the Fegge area. We see them moving, every evening, so we knew that Onitsha has fallen but we didn't come out until after five days.

And what made us come out that eventful day was that the bombing was very near our house because of the grove near our house.

Then we were forced to run out and we surrendered ourselves, asking them what is their mission.

Did they come to rescue or did they come to exterminate all of us? They said no, what they want is peace, and when I was talking I didn't know that it was the man commanding the Nigerian soldiers, the late Murtala that I was talking to.

And we asked for help that if they could give us some soldiers so that we can get one or two things out. They told us no but that they will stay here and wait for us for one hour, if we don't come out, they would move on.

So we rushed back, my mother was with me and when we got home we told the children, okay, come out, come out, come out, everybody came out and then we started running towards them. And that is how they rescued us. We entered a van, all of us, and we were driven to this part of Onitsha called Fegge where we were stationed for the night.

And in the morning I was called out to face the press. I later knew that it was the World International Press that I was facing.

They asked me a lot of questions and I answered to my ability. And they asked me why I didn't run. Well, I said I did not feel like running because with my children I don't know what would happen to us. So I decided rather than leave Onitsha, let us die here.

Luckily for us, we were rescued by the General commanding the two division and that we were very lucky.

Appendix II:

Nyerere: Reflections

YOU WANTED me to reflect. I told you I had very little time to reflect. I am not an engineer (reference to the vice-chancellor of the University of Dar es Salaam who identified himself as an engineer in his introductory remarks) and therefore what I am going to say might sound messy, unstructured and possibly irrelevant to what you intend to do; but I thought that if by reflecting, you wanted me to go back and relive the political life that I have lived for the last 30, 40 years, that I cannot do.

And in any case, in spite of the fact that it's useful to go back in history, what you are talking about is what might be of use to Africa in the 21st century. History's important, obviously, but I think we should concentrate and see what might be of use to our continent in the coming century.

What I want to do is share with you some thoughts on two issues concerning Africa. One, an obvious one; when I speak, you will realise how obvious it is. Another one, less obvious, and I'll spend a little more time on the less obvious one, because I think this will put Africa in what is going to be Africa's context in the 21st century.

And the new leadership of Africa will have to concern itself with the situation in which it finds itself in the world tomorrow – in the world of the 21st century. And the Africa I'm going to be talking about, is Africa south of the Sahara, sub-Saharan Africa. I'll explain later the reason why I chose to concentrate on Africa south of the Sahara. It is because of the point I want to emphasise.

It appears today that in the world tomorrow, there are going to be three centres of power: some, political power; some, economic power, but three centres of real power in the world. One centre is the United States of America and Canada; what you call North America. That is going to be a huge economic power, and probably for a long time the only military power, but a huge economic power.

The other one is going to be Western Europe, another huge economic power. I think Europe is choosing deliberately not to be a military power. I think they deliberately want to leave that to the United States.

The other one is Japan. Japan is in a different category but it is better to say Japan, because the power of Japan is quite clear, the economic power of Japan is obvious.

The three powers are going to affect the countries near them.

I was speaking in South Africa recently and I referred to Mexico. A former president of Mexico, I think it must have been after the revolution in 1935, no, after the revolution; a former president of Mexico is reported to have complained about his country or lamented about his country. "Poor Mexico," said the president, "so far from God yet so near the United States."

He was complaining about the disadvantages of being a neighbour of a giant.

Today, Mexico has decided not simply to suffer the disadvantages of being so close to the United States. And the United States itself has realised the importance of trying to accommodate Mexico.

In the past there were huge attempts by the United States to prevent people from moving from Mexico *into* the United States; people seeking work, seeking jobs. So you had police, a border very well policed in order to prevent Mexicans who *seek*, who *look* for jobs, to *move* into the United States. The United States discovered that it was not working. It *can't* work.

There is a kind of economic osmosis where whatever you do, if you are rich, you are attractive to the poor. They will come, they'll even *risk* their own lives in order to come. So the United States tried very hard to prevent Mexicans going into the United States; they've given up, and the result was NAFTA. It is in the interest of the United States to try and create jobs in Mexico because, if you don't, the Mexicans will simply come, to the United States; so they're doing that.

Europe, Western Europe, is very wealthy. It has two Mexicos. One is Eastern Europe. If you want to prevent those Eastern Europeans to come to Western Europe, you jolly will have to create jobs in *Eastern* Europe, and Western Europe is actually *doing* that. They are *doing* that. They'll help Eastern Europe to develop. The whole of Western Europe will be doing it, the Germans are doing it.

The Germans basically started first of all with the East Germans but they are spending lots of money also helping the other countries of Eastern Europe to develop, including unfortunately, or *fortunately* for them, including Russia. Because they realise, Europeans realise including the Germans, if you don't help *Russia* to develop, one of these days you are going to be in trouble. So it is in the interest of Western Europe, to help Eastern Europe including Russia.

They are pouring a lot of money in that part of the world, in that part of Europe, to try and help it to develop.

I said Western Europe has two Mexicos. I have

mentioned one. I'll jump the other. I jump Europe's second Mexico. I'll go to Asia. I'll go to Japan. Japan – a wealthy island, *very* wealthy indeed, but an *island*. I don't think they're very keen on the unemployed of Asia to go to Japan. They'd rather help them where they are, and Japan is spending a lot of money in Asia, to help create jobs *in* Asia, prevent those Asians dreaming about going to Japan to look for jobs. In any case, Japan is too small, they can't find wealth there.

But apart from what Japan is doing, of course Asia *is* Asia; Asia has *China!* Asia has *India*, and the small countries of Asia are not very small. The population of Indonesia is twice the population of Nigeria, your biggest. So Asia is virtually in a category, of the Third World countries, of the Southern countries; Asia is almost in a category of its own. It is developing as a power, and Europe knows it, and the United States knows it. And in spite of the *huge* Atlantic, now they are talking about the Atlantic *Rim*. That is in recognition of the importance of Asia.

I go back to Europe. Europe has a second Mexico. And Europe's second Mexico is North Africa. North Africa is to Europe what Mexico is to the United States. North Africans who have no jobs will not go to Nigeria; they'll be thinking of Europe or the Middle East, because of the imperatives of geography and history and religion and language. North Africa is part of Europe and the Middle East.

Nasser was a great leader and a great *African* leader. I got on extremely well with him. Once he sent me a minister, and I had a long discussion with his minister at the State House here, and in the course of the discussion, the minister says to me, "Mr. President, this is my first visit to Africa."

North Africa, because of the pull of the Mediterranean, and I say, history and culture, and religion, North Africa is pulled towards the North. When North Africans look for jobs, they go to Western Europe and southern Western Europe, or they go to the Middle East. And Europe has a specific policy for North Africa, specific policy for North Africa. It's not only about development; it's also about security. Because of you don't do something about North Africa, they'll come.

Africa, south of the Sahara, is different; *totally* different. If you have no jobs here in Tanzania, where do you go? The Japanese have no fear that you people will flock to Japan. The North Americans have no fear that you people will flock to North America. Not even from West Africa. The Atlantic, the Atlantic as an ocean, like the Mediterranean, it has its own logic. But links North America and Western Europe, not North America and West Africa.

Africa south of the Sahara is isolated. That is the first point I want to make. South of the Sahara is totally isolated in terms of that configuration of developing power in the world in the 21st century – on its own. There is no centre of power in whose self-interest it's important to develop Africa, *no* centre. Not North America, not Japan, not Western Europe. There's no self-interest to bother about Africa south of the Sahara. Africa south of the Sahara is on its own. *Na sijambo baya*. Those of you who don't know Kiswahili, I just whispered, "Not necessarily bad."

That's the first thing I wanted to say about Africa south of the Sahara. African leadership, the coming African leadership, will have to bear that in mind.

You are on your own, Mr. Vice President. You mentioned, you know, in the past, there was some Cold War competition in Africa and some Africans may have exploited it. I never did. I never succeeded in exploiting the Cold War in Africa.

We suffered, we suffered through the Cold War. Look at Africa south of the Sahara. I'll be talking about it later. Southern Africa, I mean, look at southern Africa;

devastated because of the combination of the Cold War and apartheid. Devastated part of Africa. It could have been *very* different. But the Cold War is gone, thank God. But thank God the Cold War is gone, the chances of the Mobutus also is gone.

So that's the first thing I wanted to say about Africa south of the Sahara. Africa south of the Sahara in those terms is isolated. That is the point I said was not obvious and I had to explain it in terms in which I have tried to explain it. The other one, the second point I want to raise is completely obvious. Africa has 53 nation-states, most of them in Africa south of the Sahara. If numbers were power, Africa would be the most powerful continent on earth. It is the weakest; so it's obvious numbers are not power.

So the second point about Africa, and again I am talking about Africa south of the Sahara; it is fragmented, fragmented. From the very beginning of independence 40 years ago, we were against that idea, that the continent is so fragmented. We called it the Balkanisation of Africa. Today, I think the Balkans are talking about the Africanisation of Europe. Africa's states are too many, too small, some make no logic, whether political logic or ethnic logic or anything. They are non-viable. It is not a confession.

The OAU was founded in 1963. In 1964 we went to Cairo to hold, in a sense, our first summit after the inaugural summit. I was responsible for moving that resolution that Africa must accept the borders, which we inherited from colonialism; accept them as they are.

That resolution was passed by the organisation (OAU) with two reservations: one from Morocco, another from Somalia.

Let me say why I moved that resolution.

In 1960, just before this country became independent, I think I was then chief minister; I received a delegation of Masai elders from Kenya, led by an American missionary.

334

And they came to persuade me to let the Masai invoke something called the Anglo-Masai Agreement so that that section of the Masai in Kenya should become part of Tanganyika; so that when Tanganyika becomes independent, it includes part of Masai, from Kenya.

I suspected the American missionary was responsible for that idea. I don't remember that I was particularly polite to him. Kenyatta was then in detention, and here somebody comes to me, that we should break up Kenya and make part of Kenya part of Tanganyika. But why shouldn't Kenyatta demand that the Masai part of Tanganyika should become Masai of Kenya? It's the same logic. That was in 1960.

In 1961 we became independent. In 1962, early 1962, I resigned as prime minister and then a few weeks later I received Dr. Banda. *Mungu amuweke mahali pema* (May God rest his soul in peace). I received Dr. Banda. We had just, FRELIMO had just been established here and we were now in the process of starting the armed struggle.

So Banda comes to me with a big old book, with lots and lots of maps in it, and tells me, "Mwalimu, what is this, what is Mozambique? There is no such thing as Mozambique." I said, "What do you mean there is no such thing as Mozambique?" So he showed me this map, and he said: "That part is part of Nyasaland (before it was renamed Malawi in 1966). That part is part of Southern Rhodesia, that part is Swaziland, and this part, which is the northern part, Makonde part, that is *your* part."

So Banda disposed of Mozambique just like that. I ridiculed the idea, and Banda never liked anybody to ridicule his ideas. So he left and went to Lisbon to talk to Salazar about this wonderful idea. I don't know what Salazar told him. That was '62.

In '63 we go to Addis Ababa for the inauguration of the OAU, and Ethiopia and Somalia are at war over the Ogaden. We had to send a special delegation to bring the president of Somalia to attend that inaugural summit, because the two countries were at *war*. Why? Because Somalia wanted the Ogaden, a *whole* province of Ethiopia, saying, "That is part of Somalia." And Ethiopia was quietly, the Emperor quietly saying to us that "the whole of Somalia is part of Ethiopia."

So those three, the delegation of the Masai, led by the American missionary; Banda's old book of maps; and the Ogaden, caused me to move that resolution, in Cairo 1964. And I say, the resolution was accepted, two countries with reservations, and one was Somalia because Somalia wanted the Ogaden; Somalia wanted northern Kenya; Somalia wanted Djibouti.

Throw away all our ideas about socialism. Throw them away, give them to the Americans, give them to the Japanese, give them, so that they can, I don't know, they can do whatever they like with them. *Embrace* capitalism, fine! But you *have* to be self-reliant.

You here in Tanzania don't dream that if you privatise every blessed thing, including the prison, then foreign investors will come rushing. No! No! Your are dreaming! *Hawaji*! They won't come! (*hawaji!*). You just try it.

There is more to privatise in Eastern Europe than here. Norman Manley, the Prime Minister of Jamaica, in those days the vogue was nationalisation, not privatisation. In those days the vogue was *nationalisation*. So Norman Manley was asked as Jamaica was moving towards independence: "Mr. Prime Minister, are you going to nationalise the economy?" His answer was: "You can't nationalise *nothing*."

You people here are busy privatising not *nothing*, we did *build* something, we built *something* to privatise. But quite frankly, for the appetite of Europe, and the appetite of North America, this is privatising nothing. The people with a really good appetite will go to Eastern Europe, they'll go to Russia, they'll not come rushing to Tanzania! Your blessed National Bank of Commerce, it's a branch of some major bank somewhere, and in Tanzania you say,

"It's so big we must divide it into pieces," which is *nonsense*.

Africa south of the Sahara is isolated. Therefore, to develop, it will have to depend upon its own resources basically. Internal resources, nationally; and Africa will have to depend upon Africa. The leadership of the future will have to devise, try to carry out policies of *maximum* national self-reliance and *maximum* collective self-reliance. They have no other choice. *Hamna*! (You don't have it!)

And this, this need to organise collective self-reliance is what moves me to the second part.

The small countries in Africa must move towards either unity or co-operation, unity of Africa. The leadership of the future, of the 21st century, should have less respect, less respect for this thing called "national sovereignty." I'm not saying take up arms and destroy the state, no! This idea that we must *preserve* the Tanganyika, then *preserve* the Kenya as they *are*, is nonsensical! The nation-states we in Africa, have inherited from Europe. They are the builders of the nation-states par excellence. For centuries they fought wars!

The history of Europe, the history of the *building* of Europe is a history of war. And sometimes their wars when they get hotter although they're European wars, they call them *world wars*. And we all get involved. We fight even in Tanganyika here, we *fought* here, one world war.

These Europeans, powerful, where little Belgium is more powerful than the whole of Africa south of the Sahara put together; these *powerful* European states are moving towards unity, and you people are talking about the atavism of the tribe, this is nonsense! I am telling *you* people. How can anybody think of the tribe as the unity of the future? *Hakuna!* (There's nothing!).

Europe now, you can take it almost as God-given, Europe is not going to fight with Europe anymore. The Europeans are not going to take up arms against

337

Europeans.

They are moving towards unity – even the little, the little countries of the Balkans which are breaking up, Yugoslavia breaking up, but they are breaking up at the same time the building up is taking place. They break up and say we want to come into the *bigger* unity. So there's a *building* movement, there's a *building* of Europe. These countries which have old, old sovereignties, countries of hundreds of years old; they are forgetting this, they are *moving* towards unity. And you people, you think Tanzania is sacred? What is Tanzania!

You *have* to move towards unity. If these powerful countries see that they have no future in the nation-states – *ninyi mnafikiri mna future katika nini*? (what future do you think you have?).

So, if we can't *move*, if our leadership, our future leadership cannot move us to bigger nation-states, which I *hope* they are going to try; we tried and failed. I tried and failed. One of my biggest failures was actually that. I tried in East Africa and failed. But don't give up because we, the first leadership, failed, no! *Unajaribu tena*! (You try again!). We failed, but the idea is a good idea. That these countries should come together.

Don't leave Rwanda and Burundi on their own. *Hawawezi kusurvive* (They cannot survive). They can't. They're locked up into a form of prejudice. If we can't move towards bigger nation-states, at least let's move towards greater co-operation. This is beginning to happen. And the new leadership in Africa should encourage it.

I want to say only one or two things about what is happening in southern Africa. Please accept the logic of coming together. South Africa, small; South Africa is very small. Their per capita income now is, I think $2,000 a year or something around that. Compared with Tanzanians, of course, it is very big, but it's poor.

If South Africa begins to tackle the problems of the legacy of apartheid, they have no money! But compared with the rest of us, they are rich. And so, in southern Africa, there, there is also a kind of osmosis, also an economic osmosis. South Africa's neighbours send their job seekers *into* South Africa. And South Africa will simply have to accept the logic of that, that they are big, they are attractive. They attract the unemployed from Mozambique, and from Lesotho and from the rest. They have to accept that fact of life. It's a problem, but they have to accept it.

South Africa, and I am talking about post-apartheid South Africa. Post-apartheid South Africa has the most developed and the most dynamic private sector on the continent. It is white, so what? So forget it is white. It is South African, dynamic, highly developed. If the investors of South Africa begin a new form of trekking, you *have* to accept it.

It will be ridiculous, absolutely ridiculous, for Africans to go out seeking investment from North America, from Japan, from Europe, from Russia, and then, when these investors come from South Africa to invest in your own country, you say, "a! a! These fellows now want to take over our economy" - this is nonsense. You can't have it both ways. You want foreign investors or you don't want foreign investors. Now, the most available foreign investors for you are those from South Africa.

And let me tell you, when Europe think in terms of investing, they *might* go to South Africa. When North America think in terms of investing, they *might* go to South Africa. Even Asia, if they want to invest, the first country they may think of in Africa *may* be South Africa. So, if *your* South Africa is going to be *your* engine of development, accept the reality, accept the reality.

Don't accept this sovereignty, South Africa will reduce your sovereignty. What sovereignty do you have? Many of these debt-ridden countries in Africa now have no sovereignty, they've lost it. *Imekwenda* (It's gone). *Iko mikononi mwa IMF na World Bank* (It's in the hands of

339

the IMF and the World Bank). *Unafikiri kuna sovereignty gani*? (What kind of sovereignty do you think there is?).

So, southern Africa has an opportunity, southern Africa, the SADC group, *because* of South Africa.

Because South Africa now is no longer a destabiliser of the region, but a partner in development, southern Africa has a tremendous opportunity. But you need leadership, because if you get proper leadership there, within the next 10, 15 years, that region is going to be the ASEAN (Association of South-East Asian Nations) of Africa. And it is possible. But forget the protection of your sovereignties. I believe the South Africans will be sensitive enough to know that if they are not careful, there is going to be this resentment of big brother, but that big brother, frankly, is not very big.

West Africa. Another bloc is developing there, but that depends very much upon Nigeria my brother (looking at the Nigerian High Commissioner – Ambassador), very much so.

Without Nigeria, the future of West Africa is a problem. West Africa is more balkanised than Eastern Africa. More balkanised, tiny little states. The leadership will have to come from Nigeria. It came from Nigeria in Liberia; it has come from Nigeria in the case of Sierra Leone; it will have to come from Nigeria in galvanising ECOWAS. But the military in Nigeria must allow the Nigerians to exercise that vitality in freedom. And it is my hope that they will do it.

I told you I was going to ramble and it was going to be messy, but thank you very much.

Source:
Mwalimu Nyerere Memorial Site: Written Speeches, South Centre, Geneva, Switzerland, 2001.
This is an abridged version of Nyerere's speech at an international conference at the University of Dar es Salaam, Tanzania, December 15, 1997. The transcription

of the non-written speech came from Mrs. Magombe of the Nyerere Foundation, Dar es Salaam.

Translation of Kiswahili words, phrases and sentences in Nyerere's speech into English in the preceding text, done by the author, Godfrey Mwakikagile.

www.ingramcontent.com/pod-product-compliance
Lightning Source LLC
Chambersburg PA
CBHW071220290326
41931CB00037B/1505